Hitler's Coo reakers

German Signals Intelligence in World War 2

Edited by
John Jackson

BookTower
PUBLISHING

First published by BookTowerPublishing 2012
Redditch, Worcestershire
www.booktowerpublishing.co.uk

2

A catalogue record for this book is available from the
British Library

BookTower Publishing
ISBN 978-0-9557164-4-7

Printed and bound by CreateSpace

Set in Georgia font 10 pt

PREFACE

The wartime story of codebreaking has almost exclusively centred around Allied successes, particularly that of Bletchley Park. Anglo-American Sigint successes played a major part in the winning of the war, and undoubtedly were far more successful than the main Axis powers of Germany, Italy and Japan.

However, the Germans in particular were extremely active in codebreaking and had their successes. But it was not until after the war that the extent or otherwise of their triumphs could be gauged. With the war in Europe at an end, in April-May 1945 British and American codebreaking teams hunted for their German counterparts to find out just how good they had been. There were lessons to be learned for the post-war period for Western intelligence.

Furthermore, just how far had the Germans moved in the field of technological innovation? They did not develop the Bletchley Park equivalent of the bombe – which broke messages enciphered on the Enigma machine – or Colossus and Tunny – which broke messages enciphered on the Lorenz cipher attachment machine, which were transmitted by teleprinter and contained the secret traffic of the German High Command and Hitler personally.

This publication is based on European Axis Signal Intelligence in World War II as revealed by 'TICOM' Investigations and by other Prisoner of War Interrogations and Captured Material, Principally German and completed in May 1946. This is available on the NSA website. TICOM – Target Intelligence Committee – was a shadowy Anglo-American organisation set up in October 1944 whose cover name disguised its real purpose – the seeking out in the immediate aftermath of the war of German Sigint staff for interrogation.

This fascinating insight into German cryptography shows how they understood that the Enigma cipher machine had its weaknesses, and that they had various ingenious machines either manufactured or under development to strengthen their security as the war drew to a close.

Lack of resources – and running out of time – put paid to any major operational deployment of this machinery, but underlines the fact that German ingenuity came close to a situation where they could have made Bletchley Park's task almost impossible.

To assist the reader both an index and a glossary have been added as well as a National Archives document (HW40/158) which details the interrogation of five leading Nazis including Goering and Ribbentrop on their views about Signals Intelligence.

The nine TICOM volumes on the National Security Agency web site (www.nsa.gov) have the following reference numbers, each preceded by ID DOC:

Volume 1: Synopsis (3560861)
Volume 2: Notes on German High Level Cryptography and Cryptanalysis (3560816)
Volume 3: Signal Intelligence Agency of the Supreme Command, Armed Forces (3560827)
Volume 4: Signal Intelligence Service of the Army High Command (3486746)
Volume 5: The German Air Force Signal Intelligence Service (3560829)
Volume 6: The Foreign Office Cryptanalytic Section (3486663)
Volume 7: Goering's Research Bureau (3486670)
Volume 8: Miscellaneous (3560798)
Volume 9: German Traffic Analysis of Russian Communications (3633965)

CONTENTS

Chapter 1

General Overview

TICOM origins

TICOM – Target Intelligence Committee – was the cover name given to a special Anglo-US intelligence body, established in October 1944, and aimed at the investigation and possible exploitation of German cryptologic organisations, operations, installations and personnel, as soon as possible after the war. TICOM originally planned airborne operations even before the end of the war to seize key German signals intelligence targets. There were four objectives:

- To learn the extent of the German cryptanalytic efforts against the Allies;
- To prevent the results of such German cryptanalysis from falling into unauthorised hands;
- To exploit German cryptologic techniques and inventions before they could be destroyed by the Germans; and
- To uncover items of signal intelligence value in prosecuting the war against Japan – a conflict that did not end until August 1945.

The airborne policy was abandoned in spring 1945 because known German signal intelligence agencies were dispersing or retreating in great disorder and pinpointing of locations was not possible. It would not be possible to seize German personnel and material and hold them through the confusion of major battles. So, in March 1945, TICOM setup six Anglo-US target teams to take over and exploit known or newly discovered targets of signal intelligence interest and to search for other signal intelligence targets and personnel. The first team was sent in April 1945 to the Neumünster-Flensburg area in northern Germany and other teams were rapidly dispatched to other areas as soon as they were overrun. As a result of these efforts, 4,000 documents weighing five tons were captured along with many cryptographic devices and machines. There were 196 reports issued by TICOM based on the interrogation of German signals intelligence personnel as well as miscellaneous reports and translations.

TICOM prisoner-of-war interrogations and captured documents, plus interrogations conducted by other Anglo-US agencies, in particular CSDIC – the Combined Services Detailed Interrogation Centre – gave investigators a 'reasonably complete picture of German signal intelligence.'

Successes against Allied signals

Successes against British medium and low-grade military and naval communications systems were 'considerable' and their cryptanalytic successes against the Russians exceeded that of their efforts against the United States. Successes against the diplomatic communications of Italy, Japan, France, Turkey, Bulgaria, Greece, Portugal, Spain, Switzerland and other smaller nations also achieved important results.

Signal intelligence organisations

Germany possessed six main cryptologic organisations with a total strength of around 30,000 people. The total of European Axis Sigint (signals intelligence) personnel was around 36,000. This compared with a total Allied Sigint staffing level of around 60,000 people. Of the six main German organisations, four were military and two civilian.

The four military organisations were:

- Army High Command (OKH/GdNA): Handled Allied Army traffic;
- Naval High Command (OKM/4SKL III): Handled Allied Naval traffic;
- Air Force High Command (OKL/LN Abt 30): Handled Allied Air traffic;
- Armed Forces Supreme Command (OKW/Chi): Handled Allied, neutral or friendly diplomatic traffic, commercial traffic and news broadcasts.

The two civilian organisations were:

- Foreign Office Cryptanalytic Section (Pers Z B): Also handled diplomatic traffic whether Allied, neutral or friendly;
- Goering's Research Bureau (FA): A Nazi Party agency which also handled diplomatic traffic, news releases, broadcast and telephone monitoring and other types of communications intelligence, Allied, neutral or friendly.

Army High Command: Oberkommando des Heeres, General der Nachrichten Aufklärung (OKH/GdNA)

Located at Jüterbog, about 60 miles south-west of Berlin, it comprised about 12,000 people, and was the main unit of the German Army signal intelligence unit in 1945. Other units were:

- Two intercept stations operating directly under the Signal Intelligence Agency (SIA), and supplying it with intercepts of Allied high-level traffic;
- Nine field signal intelligence regiments assigned to various Army Groups for interception, traffic analysis, cryptanalysis and evaluation of Allied Army low-level tactical traffic in the Army Group areas. These regiments were independent of the Central SIA, but supplied the latter with intercepts and reports.
- A small signals intelligence section, assigned to the Army C-in-C West, which co-ordinated the two Signal Intelligence Regiments on the Western Front.

This Army High Command Sigint organisation had a number of successes, going back to pre-war days. Before 1939 it had established the Order of Battle of Britain, France and Holland, achieved by cryptanalysis of French codes and Dutch Army double-transposition ciphers, and direction finding and traffic analysis directed against British Army communications systems. It also established the Russian Order of Battle and location of strategic reserves from early in the war through 1943. This was achieved using traffic analysis and cryptanalysis of Russian two, three, four and five-figure codes, both Army and Soviet Secret Police (NKVD). It also provided Field Marshal Rommel with intelligence of 'great operational value' during the fighting around Tobruk, made possible by solving the super-encipherment of an (unidentified) British code.

Tactical information was also found about Allied bombing and artillery targets, weather reports, and reports on the size and location of Allied units passing military police control points in France, by reading Slidex, a British hand cipher, for protecting operational and low-level traffic. Slidex was used by both British and US forces, and various versions of it were solved, usually in from one to three hours.

The OKH Sigint organisation also solved traffic passed on the Hungarian internal networks in 1941, which provided evidence that the transportation of German troops over Hungarian railroads could be carried out in safety. Successful codebreaking also took place against Yugoslav and Greek partisans, Czech and Russian agents and the Polish resistance movement. Each of the nine Signal Intelligence Regiments supplied information directly to Army Group, Army and Corps levels, looking to them for primary directives on missions and priorities. They co-operated closely with the local Luftwaffe signals regiments.

The Signal Security Agency of the Army High Command (Inspektion 7/IV, abbreviated to 7/IV), issued Army codes and ciphers until 1944, when this task was taken over by the SIA of the Supreme Command of the Armed Forces.

Luftwaffe High Command: Oberkommando der Luftwaffe, Luftnachrichten Abteilung 350 (OKL/LN Abt 350, formerly Chi Stelle OBdL)

This was the principal Luftwaffe Sigint service. It had eight field units: three autonomous Sigint regiments comprising eight battalions and five autonomous signal intelligence battalions, in total employing 13,000 individuals. TICOM describes the codebreaking efforts of these units against the RAF and the USAAF as 'outstanding' and providing a 'comprehensive and continuous picture of the battle order and deployment of USAAF and RAF units in the UK, in the Mediterranean theatre and, after D-Day, on the Continent.' The information came mainly from traffic analysis, radio-telephone monitoring and monitoring of airborne radar devices. The solution of RAF four-figure codes from March 1940 until 1 November 1942 gave basic data which was enlarged upon until the end of the war.

TICOM says that OKL Sigint gave 'prompt and accurate warning' of RAF and USAAF bomber missions resulting from advanced traffic analysis methods and radio-telephone and radar monitoring, as well as immediate warning of tactical operations by Allied ground support aircraft. As well as solving the Allied bomber code, OKL codebreakers broke into Slidex, Syko and Rekoh manual systems, used by the RAF and for a short time by the USAAF, both by capture and cryptanalysis to obtain important information throughout the war.

They also had great successes against the Russian Air Force, and read their two, three and four-figure administrative and operational codes – and some five-figure codes – providing a complete Order of Battle for the Russian Air Forces from 1937 until the end of the war. A study of air networks also produced results. From partial decipherment of air-ground traffic, plane-to-ground radio-telephone monitoring and radio direction finding of bombers when airborne, OKL Sigint 'was able to give accurate warnings of all Russian long-range strategic bombing raids.' From cryptanalysis of each Russian Air Army's two, three and four-figure traffic, from traffic analysis, plane-to-plane radio-telephone monitoring and radio direction finding of planes in flight, advance information was obtained of impending operations by fighters and fighter-bombers.

Navy High Command: Oberkommando der Kriegsmarine, 4 Seekriegsleitung III (OKM/4 SKL/III)

Navy Sigint was responsible for traffic analysis, cryptanalysis and evaluation of British, American, Russian, French and Swedish naval traffic. It had a staff of around 1,000 and had operational control of a field organisation of about 2,500 individuals. The field units were:

- Four detachments in Flanders, Brittany, Wilhelmshaven and Pomerania engaged in cryptanalysis of low-level systems, interception and direction finding. Each detachment had a complement of about 200 men including 100 intercept operators and ten cryptanalysts.
- Eighteen primary direction finding stations whose main duties were interception rather than direction finding. Each station had a strength of 100, including 650 intercept operators and five cryptanalysts.
- Twenty-five secondary direction finding stations whose duties were direction finding and traffic analysis. Each station had 26 personnel.

Small detachments were occasionally set up for special missions.

The main successes of OKM Sigint were that in 1939 they were able to establish the war-time organisation and disposition of the Royal Navy by the solution of Royal Navy Code No. 2. In spring 1940 they obtained complete information concerning the proposed British and French Norway expedition – Operation Stratford – by solving Royal Navy Cypher No. 4. This was followed by the immediate invasion of Norway. During the Norwegian campaign information from this cipher gave detailed information on Allied counter-measures such as proposed British landing fields, transport arrival schedules and the disposition of British and French land forces. Throughout 1942 and part of 1943 it provided important intelligence on Allied convoys by a current – and nearly 100 percent – solution of Combined Cypher No. 3, used by both Britain and the US. The average monthly Allied shipping losses during this period were about six times the average monthly losses in later periods. Minor successes included solving the British Inter-departmental cipher, solving in 1943 a RAF torpedo-bomber transposition cipher used for practice exercises in the English Channel, and solving various other smaller Royal Navy and Merchant Navy codes and ciphers.

Detachment Flanders, at Bruges, helped in the February 1942 escape of the battle cruisers *Scharnhorst* and *Gneisenau* during their famous 'dash' up the English Channel from Brest to Kiel. This same unit read Royal Naval traffic during the Dieppe raid.

Armed Forces Supreme Command: Oberkommando der Wehrmacht, Chiffrierabteilung (OKW/Chi)

OKW/Chi employed around 800 people except intercept and had three main functions: first, it intercepted, studied and evaluated diplomatic, military attaché and 'agent' traffic. Second, it monitored and evaluated commercial radio traffic and news broadcasts, and third, it made security studies of the codes and ciphers used by the OKW, the three armed Services and government departments, vetoing – after 1944 – the use of those it deemed insecure. OKW/Chi operated at least thirteen radio intercept stations of its own and received radio traffic from other agencies, notably Goering's Research Bureau (FA). With the exception of military attaché systems, it did not work on Allied Service traffic.

The most important cryptanalytic achievements of OKW/Chi from 1939-1944 seem to have been achieved with French systems. The Hagelin B-211, adopted by the French, was solved, and limited success was also achieved in the French Hagelin BC-38, while an important military attaché code, ASA trigraph FVD, was solved at the beginning of the war. After 1940, all Vichy French systems were automatically compromised when filed with the German Armistice Commission in Wiesbaden. At least four Japanese diplomatic codes, including those designated by ASA trigraphs JAE, JAH and JBA, were solved. In 1938 and 1939 OKW/Chi collaborated with the German Foreign Office cryptanalytic section (Pers ZS) in a current solution of daily keys for the Japanese Foreign Office 'Red' machine, used for diplomatic traffic. Croatian Enigma traffic was solved through compromised machine wirings.

Polish, Turkish, Greek and Latin American systems were solved extensively, and prior to 1943, appreciable success was achieved in the solution of Italian diplomatic codes. In the first half of 1944 codes designated as VN codes (Verlässliche Nachrichten) were 3,000 a month. One of OKW/Chi's most important responsibilities by the end of the war was evaluating the cryptographic systems of other Services, including cipher teleprinters, Enigma machines, specially designed Hagelin machines and small cipher devices and hand systems. It was OKW/Chi that rejected two important recommendations which would have rendered the Enigma and Lorenz SZ-42 machines secure. This was that the SZ-42 be replaced by the cipher teleprinter T-52d and that Enigma be fitted with pluggable reflector wheels.

German Foreign Office

This department had two cryptologic sections – the cryptanalytic section, Personal Z Sonderdienst des Auswärtigen Amtes (Pers ZS) and the cryptographic section, Personal Z Chiffrierdienst des Auswärtigen Amtes (Pers Z Chi), of which the former was the senior agency, and had been organised in 1919 or before, and had a staff of about 200. It was involved in the solving of foreign diplomatic codes and ciphers, and had one small intercept station at Dahlem. The rest of its intercept services were provided by OKW/Chi, Goering's FA and the German Post Office. The cryptanalytic section was successful against diplomatic codes and from 1935 until 1942 had practically a 100 percent success against Italian diplomatic codes. It also solved the British 'R' codes and the British Government Telegraph codes as well as the US State Department Grey, Brown and A1 codes. In 1940 it was solving around 75 percent of French diplomatic codes, and a number of Japanese codes were also read. The section also solved two machine ciphers – the Japanese Red machine in 1938 was read currently until February 1939 and in 1941, after a partial solution by Goering's FA, Swiss diplomatic Enigma traffic was solved.

Pers Z Chi was responsible for the preparation, compilation, distribution and security of Foreign Office codes and ciphers, and is believed to have been responsible for the code systems known as the Deutsches Satzbuch, enciphered by 'Floradora' and one-time pad, all of which were read by Anglo-American cryptanalysts.

Goering's Research Bureau: Reichsluftfahrtministerium Forschungsamt (FA)

The FA was formed in 1933 and, in addition to non-military cryptanalysis, it monitored telephone conversations in Germany and later in Austria,

Denmark and 'German' Poland. It had access to all messages sent over German commercial teletype and telegraph facilities, and had investigators in all main postal censorship offices. During the war it liaised closely with the Abwehr – military intelligence – and later Himmler's Reich Security Head Office (RSHA), and served the latter body as a cryptanalytic agency for Russian agent messages. It also monitored worldwide broadcasting organisations, particularly the BBC. It operated six wireless intercept stations, one for intercepting foreign diplomatic and commercial traffic. The FA was not primarily concerned with cryptanalysis. However, in 1941 Pers ZS solved the Swiss Enigma and in 1938 decodes of French traffic revealed that, lacking British support, the French government would not oppose the Anschluss with Austria with force. In 1938, during the Munich Conference between Germany, Italy, Britain and France, the FA is said to have solved the British system which carried Prime Minister Neville Chamberlain's messages to London. TICOM states: 'Hitler once delayed a conference with Chamberlain for several hours in order to get such decodes.' Solution of Russian internal wireless messages revealed bottlenecks in the Russian military supply system. The FA had more than 2,000 personnel and TICOM says it apprehended less than one percent of these for interrogation.

Cryptographic collaboration

The Germans never developed an inter-Service single codebreaking organisation such as Britain's Government Code and Cypher School (GC&CS), based at Bletchley Park during the war. However, prior to 1943, there was some sort of collaboration between the various branches of the German armed forces in cryptographic matters. TICOM reveals that there was reference in its material to a passing 1942 reference to 'the big executive committee' – a group which apparently had some responsibility for cryptographic changes and improvements in a cipher-type teleprinter. An order in October 1943 from Field Marshal Keitel, Chief-of-Staff to the High Command, made the introduction of new ciphers for branches of the armed forces contingent upon the agreement of the OKW, and probably of OKW/Chi.

In 1944, General Praun, who was both High Command Chief Signal Officer and Army Chief Signal Officer, made the OKW/Chi SIA a central clearing house for all German cipher development and security scrutiny work. On 5 September 1944, General Praun ordered that the cryptographic development and testing functions of the Army be turned over to the OKW/Chi SIA. Personnel from the Army Security Agency (In 7/IV) and Inspectorate 7/VI who were engaged in cryptographic work were transferred into this body. While the production of keys remained an Army responsibility, the OKW/Chi SIA devised the cipher systems and provided the material for Army key production.

With the Navy and Air Force, they continued their cryptographic development work and retained the right to say which of their systems was to be used in which place – so long as the SIA of OKW/Chi concurred on security grounds in the original introduction of the systems. However, with Waffen SS ciphers, the OKW/Chi SIA had consultative powers only, and was never allowed to know the details of Foreign Office ciphers, although they used both cipher teleprinters and Enigma machines.

Cryptanalytic collaboration

TICOM says that, in general, co-operation between the FA and OKW/Chi SIA 'were not overly cordial' and that the Navy High Command 'maintained a traditional navy reserve in dealing with other agencies. There was no high-level Sigint co-ordination, and there was frequent overlapping and duplication of effort between the agencies dealing with diplomatic cryptanalysis'. However, there seems to have been as much liaison and co-operation as was necessary, particularly with military field organisations.

Relationships between Pers ZS), FA and OKW/Chi SIA

Pers ZS enjoyed 'reasonably good working relationships' with the other two organisations, and co-operative attacks on difficult problems were not uncommon. However, relations between the latter two bodies, as stated above, were not cordial. Pers ZS received most of its intercepts from the other two bodies, and received numerous keys and compromised codebooks from both agencies. Regarding Japanese 'Red' messages, Pers ZS tackled messages on even days, and OKW/Chi SIA on odd days – precisely as was the case between the US Army and Navy prior to Pearl Harbour. Results were exchanged. Pers ZS and FA co-operated on Swiss Enigma and exchanges were frequent between additives and enciphering keys, especially on British, Italian and Vatican systems. Pers ZS and OKW/Chi SIA also exchanged personnel.

The FA was formed from a small group of cryptanalysts who left the cipher department of the Reich Defence Ministry, the predecessor of OKW/Chi, a defection that may account for the bad feeling between the two agencies. There are no known examples of direct cryptanalytic exchanges between them, nor were there personnel exchanges. The FA did not have access to the special cryptanalytic machinery of the OKW/Chi SIA, although it was available to other organisations. Relationships might have improved but for the attempt by Goering's FA to take over OKW/Chi SIA. But there was complete exchange of traffic, and about one-third of the OKW/Chi SIA intercepts came from the FA, who in turn, always received their intercepts.

Chapter 2

Inter-Organisation Relationships

Military agency cryptanalytic relationships

Relationships between the Army signal intelligence agencies and OKW/Chi SIA were excellent. However the OKW agency's commitment was diplomatic and military attaché traffic, so no broad basis for cryptanalytic liaison existed. Army and Air Force SIAs maintained permanent liaison on Royal Navy and RAF systems. Army-Navy-Air Force field collaboration was usually excellent. Eastern Front Luftwaffe Signal Regiment 353 (LN Regt 353), the Army Signal Intelligence Regiment (KONA) 1 and naval units dealing with Russian Black Sea fleet traffic worked closely with the Luftwaffe signal intelligence organisations in the West, at Paris and Noisy. During 1940-1942, the Navy and Air Force SIAs, the FA and OKW/Chi SIA, all worked together on the British inter-departmental cipher, and FA-Navy co-operation on the British Government Telegraph Code (South Africa) and Bentley's Code. The Army Agency Inspectorate 7/VI worked on Turkish diplomatic traffic by agreement with FA, and had Army SIA (KONA) 4 intercept this traffic for them, probably duplicating the efforts of the OKW/Chi SIA.

Military agency exchange of personnel

In 1942, a number of cryptanalysts were transferred to Intercept Control Station East (HLS), a predecessor of the Army High Command SIA to work on the Russian army five-figure code. On one occasion Air signal personnel from LN Regt 353 went aboard the cruiser *Prinz Eugen* to monitor traffic from the Russian Baltic fleet air arm, while a naval commander in the Aegean put his radar intercept personnel and equipment under the command of Air Signal LN Regt 352. In spring 1942, the Naval High Command SIA exchanged personnel with the Army and Luftwaffe in order to train IBM operators.

Military agency co-operation on IBM (Hollerith) and rapid analytic machinery

It was the Army SIA In 7/IV who pioneered the use of IBM (Hollerith) machinery when its installations were set up in the winter of 1939 and

1940, later transferred to In 7/VI, a predecessor of Army High Command SIA. In March 1942, the FA and the SIAs of C-in-C Air Force and the Navy High Command visited the Army installations and obtained valuable information as to the possible use of IBM machinery in cryptanalysis. OKW/Chi SIA never owned its own IBM machinery and used the Army facilities. In 1944, OKW/Chi SIA developed a number of decoding devices, some of which were handed over to the Army, Navy and Foreign Office. The Digraph Weight Recorder was handed over to the German Weather Service (WENEUB).

Military agency co-operation on interception

The FA occasionally gave Chi Stelle OBdL intercepted traffic and passed some traffic of naval interest to Navy High Command, while the Navy passed its weather intercept to the Luftwaffe, who had some inter-Service responsibility for solving weather traffic. On operational fronts, when Army search receivers found Air Force frequencies, the information was supplied to the appropriate Luftwaffe intercept units. OKW/Chi SIA controlled a naval direction finding station in Spain.

Military and civilian co-operation on agents' systems

There was extensive German effort against agent-partisan systems. The organisations involved were the SIAs of OKW/Chi, Army Inspectorate 7/VI, perhaps the FA and a small organisation which did little or no cryptanalysis – the Radio Defence Corps of the Supreme Command, Armed Forces (OKW/WNV/FU III), with collaboration in both intercept and cryptanalysis. At the beginning of the war responsibility for monitoring clandestine transmission in Germany and the occupied territories was carried out by the Radio Defence Corps. A request by this body to have its own cryptanalytic section was rejected, and accordingly, a cryptanalysis section on agent transmissions was established in Army Inspectorate 7/VI and was known from the name of its chief as 'Referat Vauck'.

Originally located in Berlin, Referat Vauck moved to Dorf Zinna, near Jüterbog in autumn 1943 along with the Radio Defence Corps. In Autumn 1944 it was transferred to the newly formed Army High Command SIA, being transferred yet again early in 1945 to the Signal Intelligence Agency of the Supreme Command, Armed Forces (OKW/Chi/Gr. IV). These changes were administrative, the section remaining with the Radio Defence Corps at Jüterbog. Most of the work of Referat

Vauck and the Radio Defence Corps was concentrated on western agent networks – France and Belgium. In the East and Balkans, other agencies handled the bulk of agent interception and cryptanalysis as follows:

- Russian Partisan: Referat Vauck's work covered mid-1942 to mid-1943 and was taken over by KONA 6 and later the Army High Command on NKVD-partisan networks.
- Yugoslavia: Most interception and cryptanalysis was conducted by a special detachment of Army Signal Intelligence Regiment (KONA 4), based in Belgrade. Cryptanalytic work on more difficult Balkan systems was conducted in Berlin by Balkan Section Referat Bailovic of Army Inspectorate 7/VI, thus complementing the activities of Referat Vauck.
- Polish Resistance: In 1943 Referat Vauck solved the principal system used by the Polish government in exile in London for communicating with the Resistance in Warsaw. Because of its importance, eight members of Referat Vauck's section were transferred to the Supreme Command, Armed Forces Signal Intelligence Agency Polish Section. The intercept work of the Radio Defence Corps was augmented by the OKW/Chi SIA intercept station at Lauf and IBM assistance was provided by Army Inspectorate 7/VI. There is some evidence that the FA was also involved in resistance movement systems.

Other European Axis cryptanalytic agencies

Italy: Until their surrender in September 1943, there were four Italian cryptographic agencies, the two most important being for the Army and the Navy, each of which had both cryptanalytic and cryptographic functions. The Foreign Affairs Ministry had a small cryptographic office to compile diplomatic codes and ciphers, while the Inspector-General of Political Police in the Ministry of the Interior also maintained a cryptanalytic section to handle communist and foreign agent codes and ciphers. The Italian Air Force Intelligence Service had its own intercept organisation but no cryptanalytic personnel, the Navy Intelligence cryptanalytic section acting for the Air Force.

The Army Intelligence Agency Service (SIM) cryptanalytic section maintained four fixed intercept stations in Italy. The Navy Intelligence Service cryptanalytic section (SIS) had seven fixed intercept stations in Italy and its possessions, and also controlled intercept groups on naval command flagships. TICOM says that Italian cryptanalytic successes 'seem to have been limited'. Army cryptanalytic section worked on diplomatic, military attaché, commercial and army systems, while the Navy concentrated on the Royal Navy and RAF operational codes. Both sections were small and trained cryptanalysts were at a premium. The Army apparently read a British five-figure code, an unenciphered four-figure, two-part British diplomatic code – possibly the Foreign Office 'R' code used for diplomatic traffic – and French, Turkish and Rumanian systems. Naval Section read Royal Navy tactical codes, the daily-changing Air code enciphering tables and an unidentified Anglo-American naval code. A four-figure Royal Navy code was read from 1941 until the North African landings in Operation Torch in November 1942. TICOM reports: 'The Germans had a low opinion of Italian cryptanalytic capabilities, and considered their cryptographic procedures to be highly insecure. As a result, good co-operation was never achieved.'

Hungary: The Hungarian Cryptanalytic Bureau (General Staff, Section X) was subordinated to the Ministry of Defence and had a staff of about 50. Its main work was on Turkish codes and ciphers as well as Italian, Polish and Russian systems. TICOM recovered about 90 code books from this agency covering work on codes from 16 countries. It was said to have had an excellent relationship with OKW/Chi and the Finnish cryptanalytic organisation.

Austria: A small Austrian bureau had been in existence some years prior to 1934 and had at least five cryptanalysts working mainly on British, US, Italian, French, Swiss, Yugoslav and Spanish systems. Before 1934, and during the critical period prior to annexation its personnel made a regular 'black market' exchange of cryptanalytic results with the German War Ministry SIA. After the Anschluss its cryptanalysts worked for various German signal intelligence agencies.

Finland: Finnish signal intelligence was part of the General Staff and was of about battalion strength, divided into intercept, cryptanalytic and evaluation units. It was highly regarded by German cryptanalysts, with whom it worked closely, and handled military, naval and diplomatic traffic. Priority was Russia, followed by Poland, Sweden and US traffic. They solved the five-figure Russian military code used during the first Russo-Finnish war.

Bulgaria: TICOM has only one reference to Bulgaria, when in 1944 OKW/Chi SIA gave a training course to some Bulgarian cryptanalysts.

Liaison between German Sigint and other Axis cryptanalytic agencies

The four German military cryptanalytic agencies had active liaison with other similar Axis agencies. TICOM did not discover any foreign liaison by the FA or Pers ZS. OKW/Chi SIA seemed to have primacy, especially in relations with Japan. Naval High Command SIA tried to give the Japanese data on Royal Navy Cypher No. 3 (the convoy cipher), receiving in return some strips and settings for the US Strip Cipher 'DUPYH'. There was a formal liaison between OKW/Chi SIA and the Japanese military attaché in Berlin. In January 1945, a German inter-Service cryptanalytic delegation was to be sent to Japan by submarine, but the plan did not materialise.

There was little practical cryptanalytic collaboration with the Italians, but code book groups were exchanged. The Germans had no confidence in the security of Italian cryptographic systems. Liaison with Hungary had existed since the 1920s. In Spring 1944 one-eighth of intercepts used by OKW/Chi SIA came from Hungary. From April 1944 until January 1945, a Hungarian intercept company was attached to III/Air Signals Regiment 353. The Hungarians also sent Italian, Rumanian and Polish traffic to OKW/Chi, who returned solution methods on this traffic back to them. Liaison with the Finns on Russia 'seems to have been the most satisfactory co-operation undertaken by the Germans' according to TICOM. Luftwaffe signals intelligence personnel worked with the Finns at Mikkeli, in eastern Finland and the wartime HQ of the Finnish armed forces and Sortavala, now in the Republic of Karelia, Russia. There were permanently assigned liaison officers both Finns and Germans at the Finnish agency and the Army SIA East (HLS/Ost). Co-operation included exchange of intercepted traffic, work on keys and systems and equipment exchanges. There is some evidence that the Finns did not provide the Germans with all the cryptanalytic material available. Cryptanalytic liaison between Spain and Bulgaria appeared to be unimportant.

Chapter 3

High-Level Cryptographic Systems

Insecure but brilliantly conceived

German high-level cryptographic systems were insecure, but brilliantly conceived. The Luftwaffe lost the Battle of Britain in 1940 because it entrusted bomber-target information to the insecure Enigma, and the German Army suffered terrific casualties and losses of materiel in North Africa because of the insecurity of both Enigma and the teleprinter cipher attachment Lorenz SZ-42. The German Navy lost a staggering number of U-boats for a similar reason – the insecurity of the Enigma naval version. The German Foreign Office used three main systems, all insecure. Two of them – the Deutsches Satzbuch – both enciphered and unenciphered, were read by the Allies, while a third system, a one-time pad, was only read in the last six months of the war, but provided information of much military value against the Japanese.

Secure devices under development

While German high-level cryptography was a practical failure, they had many secure devices under various stages of development. For example, a variable-notch rotor, called Lückenfüllerwalze – would probably have prevented the reading of Enigma after 1942 if it had been produced in quantity and installed. As U-boat commander and later naval supremo Grand Admiral Karl Dönitz said at the Nuremburg trials: 'The Battle of the Atlantic was nearly won prior to July 1942 when German losses were within reasonable limits. But they jumped 300 percent when Allied aircraft, aided by radar, which came like an epileptic stroke, were used in the fight.'

Another security improvement under development was an irregular-drive Enigma, Cipher Device 39 (Schlüsselgerät 39 or SG-39), that would have defied all known methods of solution at the time. An improved cipher-teleprinter, T-52e (Schlüsselfernschreibmaschine T52e or SFM T52e) had been built, installed on several circuits and used, which prevented easy reading of teleprinter messages in depth. Even if reading in depth was accomplished, the machine remained secure against known methods of attack as far as all other messages enciphered by it were concerned. Apparatus was being developed to encipher a radio teleprinter circuit – i.e., applying a basic cryptographic process even before any intelligence was superimposed on the emissions. Known as Cipher Attachment 42c (Schlüsselzusatz 42c – SZ-42c) it was to have been used with a continuously operating, crystal-controlled, synchronised teleprinter.

Another invention was a mechanical, portable, keyboard-operated cipher machine, Cipher Device 41 (Schlüsselgerät 41 – SG-41), employing an interacting wheel-motion principle applied to Hagelin-type wheels, which had been developed, built and partially distributed, which would have been completely secure against reconstruction even if messages were read in depth. Among other devices in varying stages of development were the Cipher Box (Schlüsselkasten) and the Cipher Disk (Schlüsselscheibe), two miniature enciphering devices intended for use by secret agents and by the Army.

Internal security studies

The Germans failed to realise that Enigma and their teleprinter cryptographic apparatus were insecure because they were unable, in their security studies, to put forth the costly practical effort required to solve them. Their security studies were only theoretical because actual traffic was never obtained for such studies. According to TICOM: 'They were completely without practical knowledge of how successfully a careful and determined attempt at traffic analysis can provide daily "cribs" and other data for cryptanalytic attack.'

They had not advanced sufficiently in applied cryptanalysis to realise that determined engineering staff could produce items like the Enigma-breaking bombe or the Lorenz-busting Colossus machines. Flashes of intuition and inspiration that come from doing, as well as theorising, were denied them. A report on naval ciphers of 10 July 1944 stated that solution of the Navy Enigma was conceivable based on the assumption of extraordinary mechanical outlay on the part of the enemy for cryptographic activities.

Navy Sigint took the view that while they could conceive of a machine for such work, they had none available or even under consideration, as it did not, in their view, justify undertaking 'such a difficult special constructional problem'.

Interrogation of Allied POWs

The TICOM report revealed that the Germans never became aware of the Allied solution of their high-grade systems, and not even a hint of this fact came to them through their agents, their interrogation of prisoners-of-war, or cryptanalysis. However, the secret of the Polish Enigma-breaking bomba was almost revealed in 1939 when three deciphered German messages were found by them in Poland. The Germans became alarmed and conducted many interrogations and the case was reopened in 1942 and 1943, but at no time did the Germans discover the Polish success. The Germans became convinced that probably the Enigma indicator system was at fault – as it partly had been – but since it was changed in 1940, they were no longer concerned with the suspected solutions. Fears by intelligence officers over Enigma security was based on inference and not on direct proof.

In November 1942, at the time of the North African landings in Operation Torch, a Luftwaffe High Command intelligence officer expressed suspicions to the Air Chief Signal Officer, General Martini, which caused him to reduce his belief in 100 percent security to eighty percent. Moreover Anglo-US security regulations on the use of ULTRA – the intelligence derived from codebreaking – were so closely adhered to that knowledge of the Allied successes were kept secret from the enemy. The interrogation of an Allied POW in North Africa revealed that the Allies operated a very large joint IBM machine operation, but this interrogation was never followed up.

Enigma insecurity

The Germans were aware that the 'commercial' Enigma, with no plugboard, was insecure. Because of its insecurity, every message enciphered by it was supposed to be re-enciphered at a second setting, which would have made messages secure, but it is doubtful whether this procedure was carried out because of the difficulties involved. The 'counter' Enigma, so-called because it had a letter counter in its mechanism, had multiple-notch rotors, but could be solved by short cribs. Regulations were issued that messages on this machine should also be double-enciphered. There were about 100 of these machines manufactured and were issued to military attachés, withdrawn in 1943 and issued to military intelligence (Abwehr). Some were also sold to the Dutch government. The standard plugboard Enigma was believed to be secure if used properly. It was believed that if the maximum length of messages was followed, then 'everything would be all right'. However, even when used properly, Allied codebreakers managed to overcome it.

TICOM says that 'it is an astonishing fact' that although the Germans knew at least as early as 1943 that it was possible to solve the Enigma with a crib 'they seemed little concerned about this possibility and failed to realise that a practical solution might be based on it.' One naval Sigint officer suggested an IBM method of solving Enigma using a twenty-five letter crib, based on a hand method. According to a Lieutenant Frowein of the Navy High Command SIA, IBM machinery would be used with a three-wheel Enigma and only 70,000 cards would be required. He added: 'The enemy could have produced the 70,000 cards at the beginning of the war and this catalogue would have been valid throughout the life of the three-wheel Enigma.

The first IBM card-sorting process would take 200 machine-hours, the second only eight machine-hours, and so on.' Therefore, about 200 IBM machines could test a crib, or put another way, ten sorters could test one crib in a day. TICOM says that neither the High Command nor Army cryptographers worried about the results of this officer's theory. However, naval cryptographers did take the idea seriously. Lieutenant Frowein comments: 'The official reaction to the findings of the investigation was the immediate decision [by the Navy] that only rotors with two turnovers should be allowed to be used in the right-hand (fast) position. This was introduced at the beginning of December 1944.' He added: 'The view of the German Army was that their Enigma was theoretically solvable. The four-rotor [naval] Enigma was not considered theoretically solvable and the Army were astonished at the Navy's view based on this investigation.' Lieutenant Frowein was awarded the War Merit Cross for his work, although the action taken by the Navy in answer to the problem he had indicated was ineffective.

Enigma weakness understood

Although the cryptographers discovered every weakness that Enigma had, their theoretical studies and conclusions did not impress them. According to one senior naval cryptographer, there were five weaknesses of the standard three-rotor Enigma:

- Rotor I – the fast rotor – moved uniformly;
- Rotors II and III moved too seldom;

- The machine needed more than three rotors to be inserted – the 26 x 26 x 26 combination (17,576 positions in total) was too small;
- The machine needed to be issued with more than the standard five rotors. The combination of 60 wheel orders with five wheels was too small; and
- The reflector was not pluggable, and the Allies could set up the 60x26x26x26 alphabets of the machine in its unplugged form, possibly proceeding to a position from there.

As TICOM commented: 'Improvement in any one of the foregoing particulars could easily have pushed the plugboard Enigma beyond the reach of already-straining Anglo-American cryptanalytic fingers, and possibly altered the course of the war. If the multiple turnover rotors of the 'counter' machine had been inserted in the plugboard Enigma, if ten rotors had been issued instead of five, if five rotors simultaneously could have been used in the machine instead of three, if the rotors already in it had been kept more active by suitable motions, or if a pluggable reflector had been universally adopted, regular, day-by-day solution would hardly have been possible.' Allied cryptologists recall with horror the introduction by the Luftwaffe of the pluggable Reflector D in January 1944, making the bombes obsolete. One German cryptanalyst is quoted by TICOM as stating that the need for additional security was not considered important by the Supreme Command as the plugboard 'was the real safeguard'. The Army said the pluggable Reflector D was 'too much trouble.'

Variable-notch rotor security

Daily solution of the standard plugboard Enigma would probably have been prevented had the variable-notch rotor (Lückenfüllerwalze) been introduced in 1943 as planned. This rotor was to hold the security line until Cipher Device 39, designed in 1939, was introduced. The variable-notch rotor would have made impossible the foretelling of exact successive rotor settings, when preparing to 'bombe' a crib. Assumptions would have to be made as to the presence or absence of turnovers of the middle and left-hand rotors at each successive element of text. This would have multiplied the number of trials necessary to test cribs.

Cipher Device 39 security (SG-39)

This device, said TICOM, was to have been 'the epitome of Enigma perfection'. It was to have everything: end-plate plugboard, pluggable reflector, four variable-notch rotors, three added Hagelin-type irregular drive wheels and a simple interacting motion. It would have a keyboard and print both plain and cipher texts at 85 words a minute. The plan was to put the machine into large-scale production by the end of 1944. In February 1942, discussion took place about the development of a Machine 42, to be an Army plugboard Enigma with three extra rotors inserted between the plugboard and lampboard. The first of these three extra rotors was to step each time a letter was enciphered and the second and third were to be stepped by notches in the customary Enigma manner. Such traffic could not have been solved by normal bombe methods, and for practical purposes Machine 42 would have been secure. However, it never passed the theoretical development stage because of engineering and procurement difficulties.

Chapter 4

Cryptographic Teleprinters

Teleprinter cryptographic types

There were two main types of cryptographic teleprinters – cipher attachments which could be associated with or attached to any teleprinter, and cipher teleprinters, in which the cryptographic mechanisms were integral parts of the teleprinter. Of these cipher attachments (Schlüsselzusätze), SZ-40 (later discarded), SZ-42a and SZ-42b were insecure. SZ-42c, designed to encrypt the radio circuit as a whole, would probably have been completely secure. Of the cipher teleprinters (Schlüsselfernschreibmaschinen) models T-52a, T-52b and T-52c first and second models, were insecure and were discarded by the Germans following their own security studies. Models T-52d and T-52e could not have been solved by any of the known methods of attack. The T-43 was a one-time tape cipher teleprinter and secure if proper tapes were inserted, and if certain electrical elements in the apparatus were properly adjusted.

A number of these models carried high-level communications and practically all of them were used at some time by the Army down through division. Landlines carried most of the traffic, avoiding interception. Radio links were beamed transmission and difficult to intercept, yet important Army links using such transmissions were intercepted. They included, among others, circuits between Berlin and Athens, Salonika, Rome, Bucharest, Belgrade, French ports, Paris, Rotterdam and Oslo. They also included Wehrkreis (Greater Germany military districts) circuits. British cryptanalysts gave the cover name 'Fish' to teleprinter cryptographic traffic, 'Tunny' to cipher attachments and 'Sturgeon' to cipher teleprinters.

Cipher attachments were insecure

Teleprinter cipher attachments – Tunny machines – were important to Allied codebreakers in showing them what not to do. All of the actually built models of these machines were insecure. One German cryptographer told TICOM that their security 'was good for about two years', but he allowed the SZ-42a and SZ-42b to be used past the two-year mark.

In the opinion of this same cryptologist, referring to the original SZ-40 model, which had ten wheels, he said it could be solved with single messages of 1,000 characters, so it was decided to introduce a machine with an irregular element in the wheel motion, which was the regular SZ-40 machine with 12 wheels with changeable patterns. Allied cryptographers solved messages sent on this machine by statistical recovery of the wheel patterns of the regularly-stepping wheels and the removal of their effects from the cipher texts. This was followed by recovery of the pin patterns of the irregularly-stepping wheels and the removal of their effects. The German cryptographer believed that solution could be obtained by attacking the motion of the five irregular wheels first and suggested the SZ-42a, which gave an additional irregular control to these irregular wheels. Then the SZ-42b was developed with a third element contributing to the irregularity, namely, a control of the second regular wheel. None of these additional security measures were able to defeat Allied cryptanalysis since the attack was to ignore temporarily the irregular-moving wheels, and to remove the effects of the regularly-moving wheels first. This made attack on the irregular-moving wheels possible. The Germans had evolved elaborate protection for the wrong end of their machine

Proposed SZ-42c with synchronisation This machine was being developed to encipher a whole radio teleprinter circuit. They were to operate at all times transmitting a stream of characters forming an entirely unintelligible message whenever bonafide enciphered messages were not being sent. An interceptor would be unable to distinguish any signals representing real messages from those corresponding to unintelligible or random sequences of characters. Therefore the number, length, precedence, classification and timing of messages would not be known to Allied intercept, and the circuit would be secure against traffic analysis. The Germans were also developing a crystal-controlled synchronising apparatus (gleichlauf) to keep the teleprinter synchronised regardless of radio fading and interference.

The nonsense to be transmitted on air whenever messages were not being sent would be 'pure key' generated by the SZ-42c, and Allied cryptographers would have a great advantage in trying to cryptanalyse the machine. However, the machine appeared to be secure for normal operation. The SZ-42c was to have ten wheels which moved constantly unless interrupted. Interruption of the motion of wheels 1-5 – which moved in unison – was accomplished by the action of wheels 9 and 10. Interruption of wheel 6 was accomplished by wheels 8 and 2, or 7 by 9 and 3, of 8 by 10 and 4, of 9 by 6 and 5 and of 10 by 7 and 1. If all wheels became stationary – resulting in monoalphabetic encipherment – the machine counted to three and then wheels 1-5 stepped automatically. Lorenz, who were developing the SZ-42c, were using electromagnetic drive rather than mechanical, and called the machine SZ-44. Lorenz also planned an SZ-45 which was to have been identical to SZ-44 except for an eleventh wheel, which was to step the machine past 'dead spots' so that the counting device used in SZ-42c for that purpose would not be needed.

Secure cipher teleprinters

The Germans developed five main types of cipher teleprinters: T-52a/b, T-52c (first model), T-52c (regular), T-52d and T-52e. The T-52d (probably) and the T-52e (certainly) were secure against known methods of attack, but were not much use on radio circuits. All five machines were important because they introduced a new principle into teleprinter cryptography – that of transitionally transposing, as a form of super-encipherment, the five separate 'bauds' constituting the set corresponding to each cipher character after the normal or basic encipherment had been accomplished. Inspectorate 7/VI discovered that the T-52c was breakable in 1942 and suggested alterations that led to the T-52d. Single messages might have been partially read by a crib-matching method, also suggested by Inspectorate 7/VI. Model T-52e had wheel motion identical to the T-52d but its order of transposition switches was not changeable, but each of the transposition switches and the key-text switches was operated by the combined pattern of a set of four wheels chosen for it from the ten wheels. The T-52e was therefore also probably secure.

T-43 used one-time tape

The T-43 used a one-time key tape to supply the sequence of keying characters instead of mechanical cipher wheels as in the other T-series models. This meant the T-43 was just as secure against cryptanalysis, since the key tapes employed consisted of random characters. The key tape was generated by running a 50 metre-long loop of random tape over and over through a T-52d machine, with the T-52d punching out the key tape as long as desired. The key tape was not random in a true sense, but it was unpredictable for practical purposes, and secure. A serious electrical defect with the T-43 was discovered by radio engineers and corrected as it had rendered the machine insecure. It resulted because at the instant of encipherment the keying character was electrically slightly out of phase with the plain-text character. Therefore, minute inspection of the cipher characters on an oscilloscope permitted separation of the composite cipher characters into their plain-text and key-text elements, resulting in a solution without cryptanalysis.

Conclusion

Although Bletchley Park was able to read teleprinter traffic because of the insecurity of the SZ-42a/b cipher attachments and the willingness to build Colossus to break these machines, the T-series were completely secure. The T-series were designed along different lines from those taken by the Allied development of teleprinter cryptographic apparatus. Their main features were:

- Irregular and interacting wheel motions; and
- Use of baud transposition as an additional protection, superimposing this on the basic substitution process.

The attempted development of a cipher attachment (SZ-42c) for enciphering a radio circuit, thus protecting it against traffic analysis as well as cryptanalysis, indicated that the Germans were giving serious thought to all phases of the cryptographic problem.

Chapter 5

Other Cipher Devices

Cipher Device SG-41

Cipher Device 41 (Schlüsselgerät (SG) 41) was a Hagelin-type mechanical cipher and was originally intended for use forward of division. The Army, Air Force, Weather Bureau and others had ordered around 11,000 machines but only a small, but unknown, quantity were manufactured and put in use. Cipher Device was remarkable for two reasons: First, although it required no electric power, being operated by a hand crank, it was compact, portable, printed both plain and cipher tapes, and had a typewriter keyboard. Second, the daily wheel settings and pin patterns were protected against reconstruction by cryptanalysis even when 'pure key' was available. This was because even though the plain texts of identical-keyed messages could readily be obtained by well-established procedures and the corresponding portion of the keying sequence reconstructed, nevertheless this reconstructed sequence (pure key) did not provide data whereby the wheel settings and pin patterns could also be reconstructed, so no other messages on the same day could be read. This is not usually the case in other Hagelin-type machines.

Security of Cipher Device SG-41

The machine's security came from the interacting and irregular movements of its cipher wheels. The enciphering principles were as follows: it had six mechanical Hagelin-type pin wheels, prime to each other, the first five of which had 'kicks' of 1, 2, 4, 8 and 10 respectively. Wheel 6 made these 'kicks' positive or negative. The enciphering cycle (one turn of the hand crank) consisted of three elements:

Element 1: This element of the cycle took place if – and only if – when 6 had an active peg, then all the following events occurred: Wheel 1 moved one step and each of the remaining four wheels moved one step unless the wheel to its left had an active pin in its 'motion index position', in which case each such wheel moved two steps.

Element 2: A key 'kick' was generated, which was the sum of all the kicks of wheels which had active pegs in the 'kick index positions'. This was so unless wheel 6 had an inactive peg in the 'kick index position', in which case the key kick which resulted was equal to '25 minus the sum of the kicks' of the wheels with active pegs. This key kick was, in effect, the 'key text' or 'key character' which was 'added' to the plain text character in encipherment – encipherment took place at this point.

Element 3: This element of the cycle was identical in principle to Element 1, except that it occurred whether or not wheel 6 had an active peg in the 'motion index position'. The purpose of this element was to ensure some change in the wheel positions before the encipherment of the next letter of text, if any.

In 1945 Britain intercepted certain traffic enciphered by German agents with Cipher Device 41. Several messages were read because of improper mechanical working of one of the machines. The machine itself, however, was not solved thereby, and remained a mystery until capture revealed its construction. Investigators believed its design was poor but that its faults could probably be corrected by improved engineering. Mechanical problems probably prevented its wider and earlier use. Cipher Device 41Z was a modification of the standard model 41 and was designed to encipher ten figures instead of twenty-five letters, for use by the Weather Bureau. A model of Cipher Device 41 which would be more compact and eliminate the typewriter keyboard was also under consideration, for use by frontline troops.

Cipher Box to replace Enigma

A mechanical device, made of aluminium and weighing one and three-quarter pounds, was being developed, which involved cryptographic principles entirely new to German cryptography. The device was to have replaced Enigma in the Army above Division level. Called the Cipher Box (Schlüsselkasten), it made use of the cryptographic principles of sliding strips. A senior Sigint officer reported that field tests had been 'so successful and had brought out the handiness and speed of operation of the machine so clearly, that its introduction into the field army was ordered.' The main security organisation, the RSHA, had got in ahead of the army with an order for 70,000 items and mass production was introduced. It was scheduled to produce 1,000 devices by October 1945 and to reach 10,000 a month by January 1946.

TICOM says that no Cipher Box was ever captured but in the interrogation of one senior Sigint official it consisted of a small box, in the top of which was inserted a slide rule which consisted of two mixed alphabets which were written in by pencil with each key change. Half of the first mixed alphabet was written on the upper base part of the slide rule, the remaining half of the alphabet on the upper slide part of the slide rule. Half of the second mixed alphabet was written on the lower base part of the slide rule, the remaining half of the alphabet on the lower slide part of the slide rule. The two alphabets were so written in, that when the halves of the first (upper) alphabet were in phase with each other, the halves of the second (lower) alphabet were out of phase, and vice-versa.

Encipherment of a letter was accomplished by reading off the letter opposite it on the slide rule and was chosen from whichever alphabet was 'in phase' at the time of encipherment. There were twenty-six possible reciprocal encipherment alphabets. Any sliding-strip device is secure if the successive settings of the sliding strip are unpredictable, so security of the Cipher Box rested primarily in the manner of successfully setting the slide. The Cipher Box was an improvement over another device, the M-40, which employed three Hagelin-type wheels for alphabet selection. It was considered reasonably secure but was never adopted.

One German Sigint officer told TICOM that the security of the machine was 'very high and was considered superior to that of the Enigma'. The safety margin for the daily cipher was calculated at around 40,000 to 50,000 letters, whereas with Enigma the safety margin was 20,000 letters.

Cipher Disk

The Cipher Disk (Schlüsselscheibe) was to be a simplification of the Cipher Box, and was one of two miniature cipher devices. In a TICOM interrogation, a Sigint specialist said 'the machine was not to exceed in size a shoe polish can.' The encoding principle was similar to the Cipher Box. It consisted of a rotatable inner disk and stationary frame, both of which were provided with scrambled alphabets similar to the Cipher Box. The inner disk rotated against the frame, and thereby in a manner similar to the Cipher Box, put a spring under tension. By a pressure and blocking notch the disk is returned in various step lengths back towards its original position. In contrast to the Cipher Box, in this machine only control wheels with fixed notches were to be used. Three control wheels to be set from the outside were to be included. The number of notches was to be determined once and for all for each pair of devices – one for the agent and one for central office. For this, a hand punch was thought of for punching the notches. Security investigations were so successful that it was decided to use the disk for forward army units and forward of regiment HQ. The requirement was for 10,000 Cipher Disks and 20,000 sets each of three pin disk blanks.

German Foreign Office Number Printer

The Foreign Office Number Printer (Numerierwerk) printed one-time pads used to encipher the Diplomatic Code Book (Deutsches Satzbuch). Cryptanalysts believe one-time pads are secure if made up on random additive or key. The emphasis must be on the 'random' as well as the 'one-time'. The German Foreign Office cryptographic section overlooked the 'random' in using the Number Printer, which looked like a large printing 'job press'. The type bed carried 240 small wheels, similar to those on a rubber date stamp. Each wheel carried a sequence of ten digits around its periphery. The wheels were individually removable and interchangeable, as well as interchangeable in groups. Each time the press operated it printed a sheet of paper with 240 numbers on it – eight lines of six groups of five digits. The press could be adjusted to print up to thirty sheets of paper identically, but was usually adjusted for two sheets identically, one of which became a page in a one-time 'send' pad, the duplicate being a page in the corresponding one-time 'receive' pad.

Before printing the next set of two sheets the machine turned all 240 wheels up one notch except such wheels as were at the moment kept from turning by special mechanical means. The laws governing which wheels paused in their movements, when and how often, were very simple, and were accomplished by non-turnover notches. The result was that while each page contained numbers that were random so far as that page alone was concerned, any given position on such a page was related to the same position on all the succeeding pages, and this non-random property permitted reconstructing sequences involved on the printing wheels. Shuffling of the sheets before binding into pad forms added to the difficulties of cryptanalysis, but did not prevent almost total reading of messages.

Captured German Foreign Office files showed that Number Printer apparatus was purchased from private sources as far back as 1925. Indeed, similar Number Printer apparatus was offered to Britain by an

English firm on 14 June 1932. The British were told that the apparatus was for printing given numbers of copies of cipher telegrams, although it was apparent to the British that its real purpose was to generate pages of random additives. The company told the British Government that the German Government had printed two million pages without a breakdown and kept an extra set of 250 spare wheels from which to choose. Britain eventually lost interest in the project.

Chapter 6

Enciphered Speech Apparatus

Enciphered speech apparatus unsuccessful

German experiments on speech encipherment – ciphony – were unsuccessful, and no satisfactory method was developed at any time. Speech encipherment experiments were conducted by seven German firms between 1937 and 1940. In 1943 only Telefunken and Dr. Vierling at the Laboratorium Feuerstein (Firestone Laboratory) at Ebermannstadt worked on speech encipherment. Dr. Vierling's laboratory was captured almost intact as he had been ordered not to destroy the expensive equipment. Ciphony and other varied electronic researches were in progress at the surrender. Six ciphony methods had been developed:

- Frequency inversion
- Noise superimposition
- Time scrambling
- Little building block
- Big building block
- Triple wobbling

Frequency inversion insecure

Frequency inversion usually required speech frequencies from 250 cycles per second to 2,750 cycles be beat against a 'carrier' frequency of about 3,000 cycles. The resultant frequencies are the differences in frequencies and these differences are transmitted. Thus, a low speech frequency of 300 cycles would be transmitted as a high frequency of 2,700 cycles, or 3,000 cycles minus 300 cycles, whereas a high speech frequency would be sent as a low one. The German inversion apparatus was large – the size of a field telephone installation. With an ordinary receiver it was possible to re-establish the impulses normally and was withdrawn in 1942. At the time, the system was considered insecure by most engineers everywhere.

Bad quality of noise superimposition

This system requires that the superimposed noise frequencies cover the speech frequency bandwidth so that the noise can mask out the speech. At the receiving end, a noise is applied exactly equal to that at the sending end, but 180 degrees out of phase so that the noise component is cancelled out and clear speech remains. Experiments by the Lorenz company between 1937 and 1939 found that frequency distortion over transmission lines was too great as being faulty, and that noise cancellation gave poor speech quality. From 1939 to 1943, experiments by Telefunken showed it was impossible to cancel the noise correctly, and that speech quality would never be acceptable. However, an ultra-high frequency radio link between Athens, Crete and Derna continued noise superimposition tests, which were also disappointing.

Time scrambling insecurity

Time scrambling devices (Tigerstedt – after a Swedish inventor of that name) required that the speech at the sending end should be recorded immediately – usually magnetically on a steel tape – as a means of storing it for encipherment. Encipherment results from breaking up the stored speech into small elements of 60 milliseconds duration in the case of the German devices and transposing them. The transposed elements are then transmitted by radio or wire to the receiving station which stores them, transposes them and puts them into the receiving telephone as speech. Siemens attempted to divide the speech into three frequency bands and scramble each band separately. But despite the large size of this equipment – each station weighed about 100-150kg, this process did not deliver completely unintelligible speech but the device was never manufactured. Time-scrambling possibilities re-emerged in late 1944 when a US Mustang aeroplane was shot down and found to have in its equipment a time-scrambling radio-telephone apparatus, known by the Americans as SIGJIP. German technical experts believed that with the availability of necessary equipment, the apparatus could be solved in ten minutes. Traffic was picked up on a sound track, photographed and, through the regular division of the track, it was possible for an expert to read the conversation.

There was controversy over the development of a German version of the Mustang apparatus as forward units believed it was impossible to carry out any tactical interception of such traffic since they would require a large quantity of special equipment. There is no indication in TICOM interrogations that these devices were ever adopted and used by the Germans.

Big Building Block control difficulties

Since too much time would be required to develop secure ciphony apparatus, plans were developed for an independent construction of a machine to be built quickly as a stop-gap. The first attempts resulted in Building Block (Baustein), later renamed the Big Building Block (Der Grosse Baustein), after it was discovered that a second and still simpler device – the Little Building Block – would be needed. The Big Building Block used the principle of 'ring wobbling', the name given to a process by which the voice frequencies were shifted up and down the frequency scale. When shifted up, frequencies at the top were electrically taken out of the spectrum and put back in at the bottom of the scale. When shifted down, frequencies at the bottom were electrically taken out of the spectrum and put back in at the top of the scale. This process was called 'ring' because what went off at the top came back around to the bottom and vice versa. It was called 'wobbling' because the frequencies wobbled or shifted by being modulated on a 'wobble frequency' carrier.

Little Building Block for land-line use

The Little Building Block (Der Kleine Baustein) was intended to be a low-security speech scrambler for land-line use only and was to be secure against the human ear only. It combined noise superimposition and frequency inversion. Speech frequencies from 300 cycles per second to 1,300 cycles were accepted by the filter system. These were inverted alternately by a 1,700 cycles per second carrier resulting in a frequency band from 2,400 cycles to 1,400 cycles. The alternations in choice of carrier for inversion occurred about three to six times per second, depending on the speech volume level. Into whichever of the frequency bands the speech was not inverted, noise was superimposed. Thus, if inverted, speech occurred in the 400-1,400 cycle band, noise occurred in the 1,400-2,400 cycle band and vice versa. This apparatus was under test at the end of the war, but only a single-way circuit had been constructed for the tests. The apparatus was not complete when captured.

Triple wobbling hopes

German engineers recognised as early as 1939 that synthetic speech might prove easier to encipher than actual speech. Apparatus called 'Anna' was developed which divided actual speech into eight separate frequency bands by means of filter networks, producing eight carrier frequencies to correspond to the eight speech bands. When the energy level of the speech band varied, the amplitude of the corresponding carrier frequency varied in proportion. These carrier frequencies, plus two more carriers, each of which represented variations in the pitch of the speech fundamental and whether the speech was 'voiced' or 'whispered', formed the set of ten carriers which was then to be enciphered. Triple wobbling was the method proposed for the encipherment. By this process, the composite set of carriers – ranging in frequency from 450 to 2,110 cycles per second – was passed through a single stage of ring wobbling much as in the Big Building Block. The output from this wobbling stage was split by filters into halves, and each was separately ring-wobbled. These two outputs were combined and passed through a third stage of ring wobbling. The signal was then passed through a fixed carrier modulator which restored the scrambled signal to a transmittable frequency range. Wobbling was to have been done by three separate times, was to have been controlled by a specially built cipher machine and not by an autokey system as in the Big Building Block. German hopes of successful ciphony apparently centred on synthetic speech enciphered by 'triple wobbling'.

Conclusion

Germany had no usable ciphony machines and probably would not have had any usable machines even if the war had gone on several more years.

Chapter 7

IBM and Rapid Analytic Machinery

German use of IBM equipment

Electric accounting machines using punch cards, called Hollerith in Britain and Europe and IBM in the United States – after International Business Machines Corporation – was a primary yardstick at the time of cryptanalytic progress. The table below lists the total estimated number of IBM machines used by the German non-naval bureau. Four key punches, two sorters, one collator, two reproducers, one multiplier and one tabulator was the total of captured IBM equipment belonging to the German signal intelligence organisations. They belonged to the Foreign Office cryptanalytic section (Pers ZS). Their wires were all ripped out and the plugboards were missing. After a brief study by a TICOM team, they were destroyed by dynamite. In TICOM interrogation reports, the extent of the use of IBM machines was discussed 'but scantily'. However, scattered remarks indicated the use to which these machines were put by the Germans, and under what conditions.

ESTIMATED NUMBER OF GERMAN HOLLERITH MACHINES					
	Navy	Foreign Office	Research Bureau	Supreme Command	Luftwaffe
	Crytanalysis/ Cryptology	Crytanalysis/ Cryptology?	Cryptanalysis	Crytanalysis/ Cryptology	Cryptanalysis
Punches, verifiers	30	20	10*	40	20
Reproducers	6	2	1	8*	2*
Sorters	7	10	4	30*	5
Collators	1	2	0	4*	?
Multipliers	3	1	0	0	?
Interpreters	0	0	0	0	?
Tabulators, all types	7	6	3	2	3*
Special Equipment	2 tape to card readers	1 comparator counter, 1 selective	?	?	tape to card readers?
Personnel	80	45*	15*	150*	50*

*estimate

According to one German Army High Command Sigint official, some of the larger machines were always being provided with new wirings for special cryptanalytic purposes, as for non-carrying addition and subtraction in code work. Most tasks consisted of the usual statistics – digraphs, trigraphs, 'chain' statistics, 'column' statistics and simple figure calculations, e.g., in work on Hagelin machines. He added: 'But, as a rule, no tasks were undertaken which could not have been carried out by hand by perhaps 100 people in a reasonable time'. At Bletchley Park, the basis was 20-25 persons. Evidently, Army code problems – usually finding messages in depth – were less thereafter were turned directly over to the IBM section. An interrogation reported stated that a new Russian code came in October 1941, and depths were less thereafter. The mathematicians were withdrawn from this work in November 1941, and the problem was largely handed over to the IBM section.

However there were some problems with the IBM machines as another interrogation revealed. This revealed that the breaking of cipher texts – without a crib – was possible when the pin arrangement of the pin wheels could be discovered from column statistics of the cipher text. The calculation was carried out with an IBM machine provided with special wiring. As mistakes were frequent and the time required was considerable 'the construction of special calculating machines for this purpose was proposed'. The Americans had found out that IBM machines were not well adapted to solution of the Hagelin machine. They discovered that the number of operations required furnishing all necessary statistics by the IBM method 'allows for too many handling errors'.

A further reference to German Army use of IBM machines was made regarding a double transposition used by the Allies in February 1945. Such messages included time of origin in their plain text, with such times of origin first enciphered by digraphs involving infrequent letters – these enciphering alphabets never changed. The whole messages were then subjected to the double transposition encipherments. The times of origin were seldom more than half an hour before the times of sending, so the Germans had information they could 'crib into' the cipher text once they had broken the digraphic substitution. These cribs were at least four letters long, and in short messages could almost always be placed accurately, so a four-letter entry could be obtained. Such a combination would be run through all the possible IBM machine widths. The time required to break these messages was one to five days, depending on the number of men and machines available.

Some of the Army IBM machines were evidently not working too well. One interrogation showed that with regard to the making up by the Army of some of its own keys and tables, daily changing trigraphic substitution tables were introduced. They were made at first by IBM, then the section moved to Weimar later in the war, and there the machines were so old and out of repair that they made too many mistakes in the tables. As a result, the tables were handset by a printer, which proved more efficient. A Luftwaffe interrogation revealed that the breaking of strip traffic was subject to time lags of two months before the receipt of IBM machines, but only two to four weeks afterwards.

IBM machines were also used in 'brute-forcing' – the discovery of depths by double repeats. This method was used against a Royal Navy cipher to find double repeats at intervals of up to ten. The machines also provided a catalogue of differences, repeats and double repeats and the reciphering of captured subtractor groups – the latter meaning that captured additive was applied to high frequency unenciphered code groups to obtain a catalogue of likely enciphered code groups against which messages could be tested. A 'baby brute force' – an index of single hits between messages known to be from approximately the same part of the additive tables – was also carried out by IBM in connection with British codes. Five percent of IBM capacity was devoted to producing the German cipher systems. They constructed reciphering tables, substitution tables and the Signal Tafeln – reciprocal two-letter tables and three and four-digit figure tables. The number of cards needed for each substitution table was one set, for two-letter tables was 26x26 and for the three and four-figure tables, was 1,000 and 10,000 respectively.

Rapid analytic machines built on simple lines

German cryptanalysts felt that in special cases they needed a more rapid means of searching, comparing and otherwise statistically treating code and cipher texts than hand and IBM methods, and developed a series of teleprinter tape devices – employing photocell readers – which accompanied these tasks speedily, inexpensively and very practically. Such machines could be termed 'rapid analytic machinery' and, in general, employed teleprinter tapes rather than celluloid film. However, the first German film device was in process of construction at the end of the war, with an estimated search speed of 10,000 letters per second. Their research was conducted almost entirely by a special section of OKW/Chi.

The following special machines were developed:
- Digraph 'weight' recorder
- Polygraphic coincidence counter
- Statistical 'depth increaser'
- Differencing calculator (non-recording)
- Differencing calculator (recording)
- Likely additive selector
- Simple counting apparatus
- Proposed repeat finder

Digraph 'weight' recorder

The 'Bigramm Suchgerät' was a device for making frequency evaluations of digraphs and recording the evaluations, and was used to solve Japanese two-letter transposed code (J19 or 'Fuji'), could find the solution in less than two hours and do the work of twenty people. It was once used for work on a British meteorological cipher, figure traffic employing a stencil. The machine consisted of two teleprinter tape 'reading heads', a relay-bank interpreter circuit, a plugboard 'weight' assignor and a recording pen and drum. Each head read its tape photo-electrically at 75 positions a second. As a result, the line traced by the pen was a cylindrical spiral. The interpreter took the two impulses from the reading heads at any given moment, and translated them from two separate letter impulses into one digraphic impulse, which it sent to the plugboard, which contained 676 jacks on its left side, representing digraphs. These could be wired at will to any jack in any one of five different sets of jacks on the right side of the plugboard, these sets representing 'weights'. Thus, on the plugboard, any digraph could be assigned any integral weight from one to five by simply plugging the digraph to the weight. Unplugged digraphs had the value 'zero'. The recording device was, in effect, an undulator. It consisted of a paper drum revolving at an even rate under a pen, which in turn moved on a spindle across the drum. As a result, the line traced by the pen was a cylindrical spiral. Undulations occurred in this spiral wherever a digraph occurred with a weight other than zero. The heights of the undulations varied directly with the weights assigned the corresponding digraphs.

The device was said to have made solution of a single transposition easy. Such a message must, in effect, be broken into likely columns and these matched against each other, with the resulting digraphs being examined for their 'goodness' to determine whether or not such matches are probable. If, for instance, the message is broken into sixteen columns, there are 1,307,674368,000 (factorial 15) possible matches, but these are attacked by successive steps: one column is tried against each of the other fourteen and the most probable combination selected before proceeding further.

With this pair as a basis, another of the remaining thirteen columns is selected to add to the left or right of the initial pair, and so on. In solving single transposition problems, two duplicate teleprinter tapes were punched, corresponding to the message to be solved, each tape then being formed into a loop and one loop being made one space (or more) longer than the other, so that as they revolved through the tape reading heads, they would 'slide' relative to each other. Digraphic weights, probably logarithmic in nature, were then plugged up on the plugboard and the machine started. The result would be an undulatory graph indicating, digraph by digraph, for every possible juxtaposition of the whole message against itself, the probability of a good match at each point along its length. Careful investigation of this graph would thus show visually – by dense areas of tall undulations – those positions where good matches occurred, and the limits in length of each good match, e.g., the length of the columns involved.

The machine could also be used to locate coincidences between messages. The digraphs aa, bb, cc .. zz could be plugged up to the value 1 and all other digraphs left unplugged. Then when two message tapes would be run against each other, coincidences would be shown by the undulator. This could be especially valuable in revealing interrupted repetitions.

Polygraph coincidence counter

The 'Sägebock' or 'Sawbuck' recorded the frequency of polygraphs occurring within one message, or for counting polygraphic coincidences between messages, and was especially useful for work on periodic substitutions. Polygraphs could be of any size up to and including decagraphs. The apparatus consisted of two teleprinter-tape read heads, a calculator and ten different recorders. Each head read its tape photo-electrically at 75 positions per second. Each recorder comprised a pen which recorded dashes on a paper strip twenty inches wide, making a short dash whenever the recorder received an impulse from the calculator. The short dashes combined to form dashes of varying lengths. One recorder was assigned to count single letters, another digraphs, yet another trigraphs, and so on up to ten. To record the number of polygraphic coincidences occurring within one message, two duplicate tapes corresponding to the message were prepared as described above in conjunction with the digraph weight recorder, the looped tapes then being inserted in the two reading heads and the machine started.

During the first revolution of the loops, each recorder would make a short vertical stroke every time a coincidence of the length assigned to that recorder occurred between the tapes. Thus, if there were ten digraphic coincidences between the tapes during the first revolution, then recorder number two made ten small strokes, each above the other, so that a line ten units high resulted. If there were four trigraphic coincidences, then recorder number three made four strokes, and so on. All the recording pens then returned to zero, and the paper in all the recorders moved along one step automatically, to be set for the next revolution of the tapes, wherein the tapes were at a different juxtaposition. To record the number of polygraphic coincidence between two different messages, a tape would be punched for each message, and similar procedure followed with these two different rather than duplicate tapes, as in the first case.

A senior Sigint official told TICOM that the problem was to determine the periods in short periodic substitutions by finding the distances between repeats in a message. The counter could also be used to find two Enigma messages in depth. This machine was one of a class called 'Fasen Suchgerät (Perioden)' or 'Phase Search Apparatus (Periods)'.

Statistical depth-increaser

The 'Turmuhr' or 'Tower Clock', so named because it ticked after each set of calculations, was used to test a sequence of thirty consecutive cipher letters statistically against a given 'depth' of their sequences to determine whether the former belonged to the given depth. It was used primarily for use against the US strip cipher when cribbing was impossible. The apparatus consisted of a single teleprinter tape reading head with a speed of one and a half symbols per second; a storage means, by which any of five different scores could be assigned, on a frequency basis, to each of the letters in the thirty separate monoalphabets that resulted from the thirty columns of depth; a distributor that rotated in synchronism with the tape stepping, and selected which set of thirty scores was to be used as a basis for evaluating the successive cipher letters; and a pen recording device.

To use the machine, first, several sections of cipher text, believed from statistical study to be enciphered with the same set of strips and on the same generatrix – a geometric element that generates a geometric figure, especially a straight line that generates a surface by moving in a specified fashion – were superimposed properly. As a result, the letters within columns fell into successive and separate monoalphabets with characteristic frequencies. A new section of thirty letters of cipher text would have to match these alphabets, e.g., show a greater than random number of coincidences with them before it could be added to this depth. The machine was used to test the accuracy of such a match.

Weights were assigned each letter in each of the basic thirty alphabets, depending on the frequency therein, and these weights were stored in the machine. A message under study was punched on tape, which was run through the machine, which read the cipher text in sequence of thirty. For each sequence it applied the proper weights to each of the letters by choosing the weights from the thirty alphabets in succession. It recorded the total weight for each sequence by strokes of the recording pen. A long resultant stroke meant a great total weight, while a sequence giving a long resultant stroke probably therefore belonged to the basic set of superimposed sequences.

Differencing calculator (non-recording) and additive tester

This was a manually-operated device – German name unknown – designed to assist additive recovery in super-enciphered code problems by speeding the differencing of depths of super-enciphered code groups and the trial of likely additives thereon. It had a capacity of thirty five-figure groups and consisted of five small metal rods arranged vertically and side by side. Down each rod were 31 small metal rollers, each carrying on its periphery the sequence of figures 0, 1, 2, 3 ... 9. The top roller of each rod was fastened permanently to its rod and each of the lower thirty rollers was rotatable independently on its rod so that it would be set at will to any of its ten possible positions. Each of the five rods revolved at will, carrying all of its thirty-one rollers around with it simultaneously. It had a lid which, when closed, revealed only the one figure at the centre of each roller.

Differencing a depth of five-figure enciphered code groups was simple. The five rods were locked into position with the top (fixed) row of rollers reading '00000'. Then the first enciphered code group in the depth was set up on the next row of rollers, then the second group was set up on row two, the third on row three, etc., until all the enciphered code groups were set up. Then the five rods were unlocked. To subtract the first group (in row 1) from all the others, all one had to do was rotate each of the five rods until the rollers in row one read '00000'. The numbers appearing in all the lower rows now represented 'differencing'.

These differences could now be looked up in 'difference tables', and the most probable unenciphered pairs of code groups they represented would be noted down for trial. To try one of these likely unenciphered groups with the aid of the machine, it was necessary to rotate the five rods until it appeared in the window instead of the enciphered code group supposed to be representing it. Immediately all other rows represented the consequences of the assumption, and the very top row – above the row marked '1' – represented the enciphering additive. This device could be operated by a cryptanalyst at a desk.

Differencing calculator (recording)

Probably called the Differenzen Rechengerät or Difference Calculating Apparatus, this machine was designed to compute a 'flag of difference' for a set of enciphered code groups. It consisted of two teleprinter tape photo-electric reading heads, a set of calculating relays and a recording electric typewriter. Its speed was limited to seven symbols a second by the typewriter speed, with time out for carriage return and line feed. It worked as follows: the figure groups between which differences were to be made were punched onto a tape. A duplicate of the tape was made, with one additional blank group. The two tapes were formed into loops and placed into the reading heads, so that the first group of the duplicate tape and the second group of the original tape were ready to be read at the same time. The machine was then started. The calculating relays computed the difference (modulo 10) between the two groups and the typewriter recorded it. The two tapes then stepped simultaneously, and the difference between the second and third was computed and stored, then between the third and fourth, etc. Second time round, since the duplicate was one group longer than the original, the 'offset' was automatically changed so that the first group was now differenced with the third group, the second with the fourth, etc. Thus every group was eventually differenced with all other groups. The 'flag' came out as a triangle rather than as a square, i.e., the difference between the first group and the second was recorded, as also was the difference between the second and first – a complementary difference. Thus all minor differences could be ignored and only major ones considered.

A second version of this machine was built, in which one tape was left in strip form and one tape used as a loop. The strip tape moved through the reading head for one group only and this group was read and stored in the computor. The loop tape revolved, the computor subtracted the stored group from each group in turn of the revolving tape. When the revolving tape made one complete revolution, the strip tape moved up to its second group, which was stored in the computor and subtracted from every group of the revolving tape etc., until each group had been subtracted from every other one.

Likely-additive selector

The Brainbox or 'Witzkiste' was an exceptionally simple device for removing additive from a column of super-enciphered code groups arranged in depth, and could be used with any four-digit (or smaller) enciphered code, the frequency of whose unenciphered code groups had been discovered from previous removal of additives. Five-digit codes had to rely on the differencing calculators described above. As an example, suppose a four-digit code was under study and that the following three unenciphered code groups were known to be high frequency groups from the removal of additive from previous depths: 0032, 0033 and 6748. Then, if enciphered code group 0000 appeared in a new depth, it very likely resulted from additive 0078, 0077 or 4362. Similarly, if enciphered code group 0001 appeared in the same depth, it very likely resulted from additive 0079, 0078 or 4363 – note that additive 0078 has been indicated twice. Any other enciphered code group in the depth would also have a set of three likely additives associated with it. A tally of these additives would show highest frequency for the most likely additive for that depth. The device tallied such likely additives photographically.

In essence, the machine consisted of a lattice-frame, with each cell representing one of the different possible additives from 0000 to 9999; a black-enamelled glass plate which fitted under the lattice-frame and was removable. There was a light source behind both and a camera in front. Whenever enciphered code group 0000 appeared in depth, the glass plate would be placed between the lattice and the light source, and the lattice photographed. Only additive positions 0078, 0077 and 4362 would be photographed because only in those spots would light appear. In case enciphered code group 0001 appeared, in the depth, the same glass plate would be placed between the lattice and the light source, but moved one position over, and the lattice would be photographed on the same piece of film. Only additive positions 0079, 0078 and 4363 would be photographed this time. But since 0078 would now have been photographed twice, it would appear darker when the film was developed. Thus the one glass plate could be slid around and made to tally likely additive for any one of the 10,000 possible enciphered code groups that might be encountered in a depth – and the additive whose position was darkest, after development of the film, was the most probable one, i.e., statistically, it was likely to be correct.

The Witzkiste was complicated slightly because additive-encipherment addition is non-carrying (modulo 10). To make the same glass plate and lattice do for all enciphered code groups, in view of the non-carrying addition, the glass plate had to be sixteen times as large as it would have been with normal addition – each additive scratch having to be entered in 2x2x2x2 different positions instead of one – and the lattice frame had to be four times as large. Final photographs could be printed out on print paper or projected onto a screen for study.

Simple counting apparatus

By this means it was possible quickly to work statistics when there were not more than 100 different elements. There were 100 counting machines (Post Office counters) put side by side. The text for which statistics were to be worked out were punched on a tape, the perforated strip read and the symbol in each case put on the corresponding counter, which were read off and their positions photographically recorded. In practice this apparatus was used with success within the scope of the investigations into the security of the German systems.

Proposed 'repeat-finder'

This ultra-high-speed machine was planned and in production but not finished by the end of the war and was designed to study from twenty to twenty-five messages for repetitions of five or more characters. Each message could be 500 letters or figures in length. Thus study of approximately 10,000 letters of cipher text could be undertaken at any one time. The 10,000 letters were recorded one after another as five-unit alphabetical symbols onto an ordinary film and a duplicate was made. Both strips were passed at high speed in front of a reader working without inertia – i.e., a photocall reader. In the event of the two strips being completely identical for at least five letters, this passage would be likewise registered without inertia. The strips were passed before the reading device at 10,000 symbols per second. Nearly three hours would be needed to work through 10,000 letters (10,000 x 10,000 = 100,000 comparisons).

Rapid analytic machinery experiments

There were ill-fated attempts by German High Command cryptologists in Inspectorate 7/VI to build rapid analytic machinery. The limited width of IBM card was soon found to be inconvenient, particularly in counting out of repeats for lining up two cipher texts. The solution seemed to be to work with perforated strips and five-unit alphabet. Orders were given to construct such a machine. However, Section VI had a completely inadequate workshop and was unable to get any more tools, so agreement was made with the IBM firm that a few rooms, and workshop machines, tools, etc., in buildings at Lichterfelde Ost should be placed at their disposal. The repeat counting machine was ready in the autumn of 1943 or winter of 1943-1944. It worked on a mechanical-engineering principle, the speed not very high – about 40 pairs of letters per second – and there was an idling period which was very inconvenient.

When this apparatus was completed, a Sigint official told TICOM, 'none of the specialist department doing practical cryptanalysis had any use for it, so that the question was justifiably raised why such an apparatus had been built at all. I do not think it was ever used for practical tasks.'

In the winter of 1943-1944, the workshop became engaged on the construction of various mechanical aids, but they cannot be described as cryptanalytic machines. For example, a machine was made which automatically punched on IBM cards the Russian teleprinter traffic taken on perforated strips with five-unit alphabet. Plans were also made in the spring of 1944 for machines to perform certain calculation tasks such as those which arose during work on Hagelin machines. However, these were not cryptanalytic machines either, but special calculating machines.

Apparently the situation was better at OKW/Chi, where there was no IBM department and so felt the necessity of developing and constructing special devices, and these machines were very satisfactory. At the Foreign

Office Cryptanalytic Section (Pers ZS) the 'automaton' was successfully developed for mass deciphering of American strip cipher messages. This was not properly a rapid analytic machine – although it used a statistical principle – but was a rapid deciphering machine. The total material – American State Department messages sent in strip cipher O-2 – could not be deciphered by hand because of its immense size, and the number of qualified English-speakers was too small. Deciphering through moving the strips by hand required six to seven minutes on average, so that the work would have taken a year, provided that four collaborators had worked eight hours a day! It was therefore vital that the automaton was available to decipher the material at the time when all the keys had been worked out. The decipherment consisted of two operations:

- Arranging the strips so that the cipher text letters were made to line in a row;
- Selecting the line containing the true reading out of 25 parallel lines.

The adjustment of the strips that move up and down, so that the true reading can be read horizontally, is accomplished by the machine automatically, as the ciphertext is touched by hand on the keyboard of a typewriter, or taken by means of a sensing device from the IBM cards that had already been punched. Finding the true reading is simplified because the most frequent letters in the English language – about 80 percent of true reading – are printed in a heavy tone, the others in a light tone. A line consisting of fifteen letters chosen at random would contain six bold ones on average, while the true reading line of fifteen letters with twelve bold ones on average stands out distinctly. The thirty strips necessary for the decipherment of a double line are arranged side by side in two groups of fifteen each for the line if the left-hand group is in the first movement, the right-hand one is in the second movement and vice versa. During the time when the clerk copies the true reading from the indicated line on the typewriter, the machine automatically prepares the adjustment of strips for the next line, and performs it at the touch of a key. In this way, the decipherment of a double line requires barely half a minute on average. By means of this machine, the total material could be deciphered within a month.

Chapter 8

German Cryptanalytic Methods

Cryptanalysis generally against medium-grade systems

German cryptanalytic successes were against medium security systems which consisted, for the most part, of codes – either enciphered or unenciphered – the solving of some of which required perseverance, intelligence and linguistic ability, but very little 'higher cryptanalysis'. In their solution of these relatively easier systems, they developed no important cryptanalytic methods already used by the Allies. In higher cryptanalysis, especially high-grade machine ciphers, the record of what the German cryptanalysts did not accomplish is a long one. Although successful with the Japanese Red (diplomatic) machine, they did not solve its successor, the Purple machine. They failed against both British and US machine systems including the Anglo-US Combined Cipher Machine (CCM). It is very doubtful that they were even aware of the Anglo-US high security ciphony system (SIGSALY) as no reference to it can be found in any TICOM document. They failed to solve the British Typex machine or the Russian B-211 or the French modified B-211. In their security studies they certainly did not develop and probably were not aware of practical methods of solving the plugboard Enigma or their teleprinter cipher attachments. It cannot be said that this failing was necessarily due to inability or ignorance. Perhaps, Japan being Germany's ally, Germany felt it was not worth expending the great energy necessary to solve the difficult Japanese Purple machine.

The cryptanalytic failure in the case of Purple and that this failure probably led higher authority to conclude that it was secure against cryptanalysis, had immeasurably disastrous consequences on the German war effort. Since Purple was regarded as secure, very important information was constantly being given Japanese representatives in Europe without reservation, which was promptly forwarded to Tokyo using the machine. Thus, from about February 1941, when the US gave Britain the solution to the Purple system, until the end of the war in both hemispheres, Anglo-American intelligence had the benefit of *authentic*, *accurate* and *timely* information about conditions within Germany and the occupied countries, German intentions, results of bombing, war potential etc. This was the central fact in the reluctance of the US High Command to have any public investigation and disclosure of the secret facts and events preceding the Japanese attack on Pearl Harbour. Perhaps German inability to read Anglo-American high-grade systems should be credited to the Allied successful cryptography rather than to German cryptanalytic incompetence, because security studies showed these systems to be secure.

But, in order to make valid studies of cryptographic security there must be cryptanalytic competence, and had the Germans been competent in this respect they would have realised the extent and significance of their cryptographic insecurity. It must be added that as regard the German security studies on the plugboard Enigma, which revealed to them no practical method of solving it, who can say that either British or US cryptanalysts would have thought of the bombe as a practical answer, if Polish cryptanalysts had not invented or devised the first crude apparatus from which the final bombe was developed? The German cryptanalytic methods had no very bright highlights. Their ciphony breaking was not advanced, enciphered teleprinter messages were solved only by finding 'depths' and processing them by long known procedures. Only the easiest, commercial-type Enigma was solved in actual attempts to solve Allied traffic. Solutions of messages enciphered by Hagelin machines of the US M-209 type were accomplished only where messages in depth were found as a precondition. German cryptanalytic highlights, such as they were, are discussed below.

Washington-London commercial radio-telephone networks

Conversations over the commercial radio-telephone circuits between London and Washington were monitored, solved and recorded by the German Post Office Research Laboratories at Eindhoven in Holland, and by the press monitoring group (Gruppe VI) of the OKW/Chi SIA, located at Ludwigsfelde, about 25 miles south of Berlin. Some of the participants in these conversations were:

- Winston Churchill
- Anthony Eden, when in Washington
- The British Minister of War Transport and his representative
- The same minister and the British Shipping Minister
- The British Foreign Office and the British Embassy

- Dutch government representatives in London and Washington
- Russian embassies
- The US embassy and the State Department

These radio-telephone circuits were enciphered by a frequency scrambling principle. The speech frequencies 450 cycles wide and the small blocks were rearranged in positions within the speech frequency spectrum to give the finally enciphered speech. Simple frequency scrambling of speech can usually be solved by examining the spectrographic records of the enciphered speech, cutting out the 'blocks' of frequencies with scissors, rearranging them by sight into proper order and pasting them back together to reveal the 'pattern' or key. Simpler yet, if the scrambling pattern has a sufficiently long duration, the rearranging can be done electrically, with the ear for a guide. On the Washington-London commercial radio-telephone circuit, scrambling and recombining of frequencies was by a pattern that remained fixed for twenty seconds, and then changed into another such pattern. There were only thirty-six such patterns in all, and then the whole procedure repeated. Thus the grand cycle was twelve minutes.

The German Post Office had no apparent difficulty in solving this system. They built a five-bank rotary switch with thirty-six positions, drove it with a synchronous motor so as to step every twenty seconds, repeating every twelve minutes, and controlled this operation accurately over twenty-four hour periods with a quartz crystal-controlled oscillator. Once the German engineer wired this switch correctly to match the patterns, they were able to monitor transmission 100 per cent and receive the speech instantaneously in the clear, so that they could record the speech traffic magnetically on steel tapes. The pattern cycle was rearranged by the US Telephone and Telegraph Company – e.g., the enciphering keys changed – only several times between April 1942 and April 1945.

After each change it took German Post Office engineers 'only a few hours' to reconstruct the new patterns and their sequence. Oscillographs, spectrographs, magnetophone recorders and quartz crystal oscillators for time control were available for this work, but well-trained ears were said to have played the most important role in the solution. While this commercial ciphony system was known by the Allies to be insecure, and therefore secret matters were normally kept in other channels, it is nevertheless important to Allied cryptographers and engineers alike to know that the Germans did solve it.

Early Russian ciphony solved by spectrogram analysis

Radio-telephone conversations between Moscow, Leningrad, Irkutsk, Alma Ata and Tscheljabinsk, involving the Russian Army and People's Commisariats were, until 1943, enciphered by two simple methods said to be easily solvable by German engineers at the Army Ordnance, Development and Testing Group, Signal Branch (Wa Prüf 7). These two methods of Russian enciphering were:

- Inversion, employing superimposed modulation of several audio frequencies; and
- Distortion, by artificial raising of amplitudes of speech harmonics

German scientists solved these two simple enciphering methods by recording the enciphered speech, making spectrograms from the recordings, and analyse them. Evidently the voice engineers could see the results of the inversion and distortion, on careful inspection, and could readily identify the frequencies and methods used for encipherment. It was tried only a few times, but was 'successful at will'. At the beginning of 1944, however, simple enciphering methods were dropped by the Russians, radio-telephone traffic networks themselves were changed, and no further entry was gained by the Germans.

One interrogated OKW/Chi Sigint official studied spectrograms of the later unsolved Moscow-Madrid radiophone traffic at Wa Prüf 7, where he became convinced that Russian ciphony then involved time-scrambling, with the length of the individual time segments being 10 milliseconds each, and a synchronising pulse occurring every 0.6 seconds. The number of 'pick-up heads' used by the Russians to obtain this time-scrambling was reported in one interrogation to be three, and in another, to be four. German engineers were unable to learn more than this from the spectrograms. German engineers believed that some form of one-time strip might have been used to key the time transposition, as no period whatever in the encipherments could be found.

Some Anglo-American teleprinter messages read

While the amount of Allied teleprinter traffic read is unclear from TICOM reports, it is doubtful if they ever solved any teleprinter enciphering machines themselves. One interrogation, from an official of the Army High Command SIA spoke of a section which 'undertook preliminary evaluation of British and American wireless teleprinter and automatic Morse traffic' and another section, charged with cryptanalysis of Russian secret teleprinters also 'worked on British and United States (non-Morse) systems'. But there was no reference to any reconstruction of British or US teleprinter cryptographic systems.

Russian teleprinter cryptographic apparatus may have been solved by Goering's Research Bureau in 1943, but traffic was supposed to have stopped soon after and the machine evidently went out of use. The Army did some work on a Russian teleprinter cryptographic machine, read a few depths, obtained about 1,400 letters of pure key, but went no further. Russian enciphered teleprinter messages, when sent in depth, were read by anagramming, and the corresponding keying characters recovered, but the machine itself was not solved. Reading of depths indicated that messages contained operational and reconnaissance information. Examination of the sections of key obtained from readings in depth led to the conclusion that the Russian enciphering device was similar in construction to the German teleprinter cipher attachment Lorenz SZ-42, with a 'motor' wheel or 'motor' wheels arranged somehow to give a cycle of forty-three. None of these surmises was investigated to ascertain its validity, it being claimed that the traffic was too scanty to effect a solution.

Swiss Enigma rotor wirings solved by cribs: other Enigmas compromised

Swiss diplomatic Enigma (K-type) was read regularly. The Swiss changed their Enigma rotor wirings every three months, but the changes were not effected on the Berne-Washington link at the time they were made on the Berne-London link. As a result, duplicate messages sent by the Swiss to Washington and to London during the periods of changeover provided the 'break' necessary to learn the new wirings. The Croat Enigma, used for both diplomatic and military traffic, was read regularly. This was no credit to the cryptanalysts involved as their problem was particularly easy:

- The rotor wirings were obtained from Konski & Krueger (Berlin), who made the rotors;
- There was no end-plate plugging involved;
- Rotor orders were not changed by the Croats;
- The ringstellung (devices enabling the notches and alignment indicator letters to be 'slid' in relation to the rotors) remained fixed;
- There were only 100 initial rotor alignments used by the Croats each month.

An excellent treatise on the Enigma-K machine solution was found in the files of the Foreign Office Cryptanalytic Section (Pers ZS). It involved obtaining many messages in depth, reading them by solving the successive (monoalphabetic) columns of superimposed text, and then applying the resultant cribs to recover the wirings of the rotors. British Typex was studied by OKW/Chi and discovered it to be an Enigma-type machine by statistical study of 10,000 letters of cipher text, but was unable to go further and no German cryptanalytic agency was able to solve it.

Converter M-209 traffic only solved by depths

The US Army Converter M-209, used by field forces, including the USAAF and Navy, was studied more or less constantly by OKW/Chi, and by the three Services High Command SIAs. Many theories were developed for statistical solution of the M-209 messages, although none was successful. Solutions depended entirely on reading messages in depth, recovery of the key, then obtaining absolute settings and reading the remaining messages in the same day's traffic. M-209 depths were found by using 'Fasensuchgerät' – a rapid analytic machine – probably the digraphic weight recorder described in the previous chapter. There was a statistical formula used with IBM machines for aiding in finding M-209 pin patterns. This consisted of writing the cipher text out 'on the width' of one of the wheels and applying a form of 'phi' test to the resulting alphabets, and alphabets having distributions which showed the least randomness were supposed to be indicative of inactive pins.

The US Army Security Agency had long experience with similar tests and stated that 'this particular one certainly would not have worked'. Another German cryptographer developed a statistical theory for solving US naval Converter M-209 based on the frequent use of 'Z' as a word separator, but this never worked on actual traffic. Another theory to attack the naval machine was how to guess plain text from a statistical study of the cipher text, but this was never made to work.

B-211 machines solved only in theory

German successes with the French (modified) B-211 Hagelin and the Russian B-211 were practically non-existent. A French version was captured and it was believed that an eight to ten-letter crib could solve the wheel settings, pin settings and plugs if the cipher wheel wirings were known.

A Russian version was also captured, and theoretical solution devised, but since no traffic was received this solution was never tested in practice.

Additive super-enciphered codes solved in 'usual' way

No great new cryptanalytic methods were developed by German cryptanalysts to assist in solving additive super-enciphered codes. They were solved as such codes usually are by superimposing identically-keyed texts – by virtue of identical indicators and by means of repetitions – removing the additive from the depths and reconstructing, from the resultant relative code values, the basic code – unless the code book is already known. One example of the foregoing type of solution by the Germans is their cryptanalysis of the British War Office Cypher, a four-figure super-enciphered code used between Army, Corps and Division, which was read during the 1940 North African campaign. The Turkish four-figure diplomatic code enciphered by repeating additives was solved without regard to indicators simply by superimposing sections of messages at the period of the additive – in this case a period of twenty – thereby obtaining enough depth to eliminate the additives and reconstruct the code.

The German Navy's solutions of Royal Navy codes – including British Naval Cypher No. 3 – are perhaps the most completely described solutions of the foregoing type in TICOM publications. These solutions extended from before 1939 to the end of the war.

Before 20 August 1941, when the indicator groups were not super-enciphered, messages were lined up in depth by indicators, and additives were eliminated by the use of 'differences tables' or by guessing stereotyped texts. Some of the codes themselves were solved by cryptanalytic reconstruction and some were captured. When, in 1942, the Merchant Marine code indicator systems became difficult, messages were lined up in depth by other methods, one such method being colloquially called 'brute force', e.g., pairs of messages were sort wherein at least two code groups in one message, separated by a definite interval, coincided with at least two code groups in the other message, separated by the same interval. Such messages were likely to have been enciphered with the same sections of additive, especially if the interval was not over ten, according to the Germans. However, they considered 'brute force' unreliable and used it as little as possible.

Whenever sections of additive were already known, messages were set against these sections by a technique of applying all of the individual additive groups of a known section to fifteen or twenty of the usually most frequently occurring unenciphered groups, thus obtaining a set of enciphered code groups most likely to occur in messages enciphered with the known additive section. If two or more such likely enciphered code groups occurred in a message, at an interval matching the interval between the groups of additive from which they were derived, then it was very likely that the rest of the message could be deciphered from that point on in the section of known additive.

The ordinary cryptanalytic aids such as difference tables – made by German cryptanalysts usually from the 300 highest-frequency code groups – known and frequently-used addresses, spelling groups, figure groups and place names, as well as stereotyped texts, aided them in aligning messages and eliminating additives. By such means, depths of two were often read – in fact, if the two messages were routine reports 'they were read without exception'.

Royal Navy 'SS Frame'

When the Royal Navy introduced the 'SS Frame' in December 1943, German cryptanalysts were able to analyse correctly the new cryptographic system being employed, and were able to read messages super-enciphered in this new system for one month. The Germans were able to superimpose a few messages in depth, which permitted them to recover several sequences of additive. They discovered that parts of one sequence of additive at times overlapped parts of other sequences, albeit out-of-phase and very irregularly, but by using this knowledge to test new assumptions, and after much trial and error, they were able to recover and reconstruct a complete set of number tables. They also solved the weak December 1943 indicator system which relied only on random co-ordinates to indicate the stencil position. As a result of these activities they obtained a fair understanding of the Royal Navy SS Frame.

According to the Royal Navy: 'We discovered that we had formerly had on the long subtractor system 1,500 starting points over a ten-day period, whereas we now had 10,000 different starting points on one daily table.'

On 1 January 1944 the Royal Navy changed their basic codes as well, and soon after began to use doubly enciphered indicators for the SS Frame. The Germans, with almost no depths possible, and with the basic code book unknown to them, could no longer read the traffic. A Naval High Command cryptographer explained:

'We came to the conclusion that we could not recover a system of this kind within six months without having the basic book. However, it was clear to us that if we were to capture the book, we should then be to break this system in a very short time. We provided our own proof for this. ... We constructed synthetic messages of our own on the pattern of the British originals. We began the first trial with 200 messages a day and broke all of them within three weeks. ... We then carried out a second trial with 100 messages. The staff was much more practiced and succeeded with a smaller number of messages in a shorter time.'

So far as is known, the Germans did not capture the book or continue solving the system.

Polish government in London

The Polish government in London used an additive super-enciphered code for military attaché messages, which was read regularly by OKW/Chi until about 1943, when the Poles changed their methods of obtaining the additives. The Poles had introduced their version of the 'SS Frame' at the suggestion of the British government – their stencils had from twenty-eight to forty randomly-placed apertures rather than 100 as in the British version. The Germans, having the Polish code book from their previous solutions, were able with it, and with depths obtained by IBM searches for repeats, to reconstruct additives, discover the irregular positions of the stencil apertures, to reconstruct the stencils and read the messages.

Mihajlovic double transpositions solved by anagramming

Yugoslav double-transposition Draza Mihajlovic traffic was solved in one to three days. In each message, the same key was used for the two transposition matrices, and these matrices were usually incompletely filled. The width of the transposition matrices were assumed each time 'with some degree of accuracy' based on previous experience with messages of the same length and on the same networks. This was a great advantage since it permitted a marking off in the cipher text of the approximate columns of the second transposition matrix. The words 'GENERAL DRAZA MIHAJLOVIC' which nearly always appeared as a signature, made an excellent crib because several of the letters were infrequent, and because these words could be written in as the final rows of the first transposition matrix. With the dimensions of the matrices chosen by good guessing, and with both the complete columns of the second transposition matrix and the final rows of the first transposition matrix delineated, an attempt was then made to match elements of the cipher text with elements of the crib, and by anagramming, recover plain text and the key.

Solutions of US strip ciphers by statistical analysis

Cryptanalytic success against US strip ciphers was obtained by at least three German agencies. The Foreign Office (Pers ZS) team of six cryptanalysts solved the US State Department strip cipher (O-2) in 1943 without any previous knowledge concerning the general system, required over a year for solution, the solving of which began in November 1942. This cipher did not employ strip elimination, but did make use of the principle of 'split generatrices' – e.g., thirty strips were chosen out of a possible fifty each day and arranged in a channel board according to the daily key. Messages were then enciphered by successively setting up thirty letters of plain text across one line of the strips, each time reading off fifteen letters of resultant cipher text from the first half of another line, chosen at random, and the remaining fifteen letters of cipher text from the last half of a third line, chosen at random. Messages were punched on IBM cards, repeats were found which indicated that intervals of fifteen and thirty were significant, the material was sorted into 'families' – a collection of homogeneous cipher material based on use of the same generatrix in the enciphering process – and the larger 'families' were solved, as similarly-keyed polyalphabetic cipher sequences, by analysing the material column by column. The alphabets recovered permitted reconstruction of many of the strips, and with their aid the remaining 'families' and strips were solved.

In 1941 Pers ZS received photographic copies from OKW/Chi of a set of instructions for an earlier US strip cipher (O-1) and 'four series of strips by means of which a number of messages could be deciphered.' Pers ZS files captured in 1945 also contained photographs of two Tables of Numerical Keys for the same earlier US State Department strip cipher O-1. OKW/Chi worked on US diplomatic strip systems, and they were not aided by captures, relying on cryptanalysis. OKW/Chi regarded US strip ciphers of sufficient importance to build a special rapid analytic machine (the statistical depth-increaser) for facilitating statistical solutions. The Air Force High Command SIA broke a USAAF strip cipher of the South Atlantic Ferry Command before 1943. The system was read as long as it was used. The Army High Command SIA also solved an American strip cipher which contained mixed military and diplomatic information, enciphered on US Army device M-94. An Army cryptologist broke a US Army cipher (M-94) carrying Iceland and Caribbean area traffic. Cribs were used with the aid of synoptic tables to determine the 'strip' (disk) orders – the aluminium disks of the M-94 could be considered to be strips from a cryptanalytic point of view – and IBM methods were later used to eliminate impossible keys.

Army cryptologists eventually recognised that the main cipher procedure used by the Americans was the strip method whereby twenty-five variously arranged alphabets were vertically laid out one alongside the other. Mechanical aids were constructed with the help of the IBM Section and by noting the addresses and signatures, the various alphabets were repeated. In summary, German cryptologists of both the strip cipher and the M-94 apparently developed no exceptional methods, although it did result in the construction of two special rapid analytic machines, the statistical depth-increaser and the automaton, referred to in the previous chapter.

Conclusion

German cryptanalysts were very successful on low-grade systems, not only because they were very sufficiently skilled to take advantage of the presence of low security traffic, but also because of the failure by Allied commanders to realise the extent to which the Germans were able to go in taking advantage of insecure practices. Medium-grade cryptanalysis was extensive and worthwhile, but no outstandingly different or unusual cryptanalytic methods were developed by the Germans in their medium-grade solutions. German cryptanalysis was not outstandingly successful against systems of high-security, and may have been not only because Allied high-security systems were actually of high security, and were to some extent insolvable to Anglo-American cryptanalysts as well, but also because the German cryptanalysts never became technically proficient enough to undertake even the solution of the less difficult of the high-security systems.

Chapter 9

Supreme Command Sigint

Background

Before the TICOM teams began their investigations in Germany, it was known that the Supreme Command of the Armed Forces (Oberkommando der Wehrmacht – OKW) contained a signal intelligence section (Chiffrierabateilung or 'Chi' – hence OKW/Chi). As such, it was given top priority among the TICOM targets. By the time TICOM began its operations, OKW/Chi had left Berlin in March 1945 and had separated into a northern and southern group. Most of their documents were subsequently disposed of and most of the personnel swallowed up in prison camps. They were then released into civilian life. There was, therefore, no question of capturing OKW/Chi as a group, but a number of individual prisoners were taken. Within OKW, the Signal Intelligence section was subordinated to the Armed Forces Group (Amtsgruppe Wehrmachtnachtrichtenverbinddungen, or Ag. WNV), which was in turn under the Armed Forces Operations Staff (Wehrmachtführungsstab, or WFSt). The general term OKW/Chi will suffice.

The three most important officials interrogated were Colonel Hugo Kettler, OKW/Chi chief from late summer 1943 until the unit left Berlin in March 1945 and a regular signal officer. Lieutenant-Colonel Mettig, another regular signal officer, was OKW/Chi second-in-command from December 1943 until immediately before the end of the war. Among his tasks he had been head of intercept and later the cryptographic division. Specialist Dr Erich Hüttenhain was the OKW/Chi chief cryptanalyst and had been with the organisation since 1937, and had built up the section which he headed – the cryptanalytic research section. This organisation tackled the more difficult enemy and neutral systems and investigated the security of German systems and made suggestions to cryptographers. He was an academic mathematician whose interest in the problem of Mayan chronology led to an interest in cryptography and to OKW/Chi. Technician (Lieutenant Grade) Dr Walther Fricke was a mathematician of some distinction who was drafted into the Signal Corps and assigned to the Signal Intelligence Service of the Army, and came to specialise in the development of German Army ciphers. He later assisted in the work of revising security.

The great bulk of the Supreme Command, Armed Forces Signal Intelligence Unit (OKW/Chi) documents, the archives of the unit, which consisted principally of broken messages and reports based on broadcast interception were moved from Berlin to Lauf near Nuremberg in spring 1945. From there, they were brought to the Schliersee, south of Munich, and when it became evident that high-level signal intelligence work was no longer possible, they were boxed and dumped into the lake. A waterproof box with some of these documents was recovered in July 1945 by accident and eventually taken over by TICOM. It contained a number of translations of decoded messages and some miscellaneous material, among which the most important was a file of correspondence between OKW/Chi and its intercept stations covering the years 1939 to 1945. Other boxes were recovered in September 1945 by American divers operating under the direction of TICOM, but the material there was not of such nature as to expand Allied understanding of the workings of OKW/Chi. From the material available, a fairly clear general outline was extracted of the charter organisation, and major cryptanalytic and cryptographic operations of OKW/Chi during the war, and particularly during the last two years of the war.

OKW/Chi pre-war

The 'germ' of what became OKW/Chi is to be found in a section of the old German Defence Ministry (Reichswehrministerium), formed in 1920 and staffed by World War One cryptographic personnel, and was originally part of Military Intelligence (Abwehr). With the formation of the Armed Forces Communications Group (Ag/WNV) within OKW, the section was taken from the Abwehr and transferred to Ag/WNV. OKW/Chi's early mission was primarily to attack the cryptographic systems of foreign nations. The 40 cryptanalysts working in OKW/Chi in 1937 were mainly linguists and known as 'Referat G', equivalent to a 'desk' and organised into language desks and getting along without the assistance of professional mathematicians. Between 1937 and 1939 systems of the following countries were under attack: Britain, United States, France, Holland, Belgium, Switzerland, Russia, Rumania, Bulgaria, Italy, Poland, Czechoslovakia and Yugoslavia. OKW/Chi's charter is said to have been originally confined to the Armed Forces systems of foreign countries, while the Foreign Office Pers ZS section handled diplomatic traffic. OKW/Chi later took on diplomatic systems, thus duplicating the work of the Foreign Office. A Principal Specialist Fenner emerges as a key OKW/Chi figure, and in the 1920s he assisted a Willi Korn in developing the Enigma cipher machine.

OKW/Chi took over diplomatic systems also, thus duplicating the work of the Foreign Office. Having taken these systems over, OKW/Chi refused to abandon them. Just when this extension of OKW/Chi's charter took place is unknown – it was definitely committed to diplomatic material by 1937. In 1939 the intercept stations at Lauf and Treuenbrietzen were given the task of' intercepting diplomatic traffic exclusively and were subordinated directly to OKW/Chi. At the beginning of the war it seems to have comprised a group of linguists with some cryptanalytic experience and a group of mathematicians who had been spending the past year familiarising themselves with cryptologic problems. In 1939 the mathematicians were given a status apart from the linguists and put to tasks such as stripping encipherments from codes.

Organisation 1939-summer 1944

OKW/Chi's mission was to intercept and interpret two classes of traffic:

- International wireless traffic of enemy and neutral states (enciphered and unenciphered telegraphic communications of diplomats, military attachés, government authorities, economic authorities, etc.); and
- Radio-telephone transmissions of enemy and neutral states; enemy and neutral commercial wireless transmissions of the major wireless stations and of the wireless news service.

The first part of the mission was high-level signal intelligence work, while the second part was essentially the work of a broadcast or news monitoring service. The main work of the service was divided among four sections. Chi I controlled the intercept of Class 1 traffic, and was principally one of liaison. The section head was briefed by the head of OKW/Chi who was aware of intelligence requirements. He was also in contact with the cryptanalysts, who knew what they could break. On the basis of this information he gave instructions to the intercept stations. The raw material from Chi I's intercept stations was passed on to Chi IV for breaking and translation, and the most important section of the service from an operational point of view. The bulk of the section personnel were linguists engaged on code-breaking, removal of simple encipherments and translation, and were organised into small groups or desks. The total number of desks increased to 22. During the war they were never all occupied simultaneously.

Organisation from summer 1944-March 1945

Events in the summer of 1944 resulted in a fundamental change in the official interpretation of OKW/Chi's mission and a corresponding change in the organisational structure, and centred around the bomb plot on Hitler's life on 20 July 1944. General Erich Fellgiebel, Armed Forces Chief Signal Officer, was heavily involved in the plot, was arrested and later executed. His deputy, General Thiele, was also arrested. The new Armed Forces Chief Signals Officer was Major General Albert Praun. Some leading Abwehr figures were also involved and the Abwehr was transferred to the RSHA, where it became a Military Department (Mil Amt) under SS Brigadeführer (Major-General) Walter Schellenberg, who was already head of the Foreign Security Service (SD Ausland), which was RSHA Department VI.

OKW/Chi became a prize for various leading Nazis, notably Goering's Research Bureau – whose activities duplicated almost completely those of OKW/Chi – which attempted to absorb its rival. The development of OKW/Chi was now away from intelligence and towards cipher security. Concerning cryptanalysis there was little change. Army, Navy and Air Force were to attack enemy systems as before, which left diplomatic and military attaché traffic as the cryptanalytic sphere of OKW/Chi. In addition, OKW/Chi became the clearing house for cryptanalytic information provided by the armed forces.

By 1 November 1944 there was a wholly new structure. The new emphasis on cryptography was evident in the separation of the main work of OKW/Chi into two divisions (Hauptgruppen). Division A was devoted to cryptography and Division B to cryptanalysis. In general, the work of OKW/Chi seems to have been much better articulated in the new organisation.

The history of the charter and organization of OKW/Chi during the war illustrates the development of the German idea of the purpose of a signal intelligence organisation at the highest command level. OKW/Chi began the war as a purely intelligence organisation, born within the Military Intelligence Department and incorporating news and broadcast monitoring as important parts of its operations. It ended as a high level security organisation where even the cryptanalysis of enemy traffic was intended primarily to assist in assuring German security among all branches of the Armed Forces and government agencies. This change was accelerated by changes in command caused by events wholly unrelated to signal intelligence.

OKW/Chi's two intercept systems

The dual character of OKW/Chi's operations, reflected particularly in the earlier organisation, is also apparent in the intercept structure. One intercept system concentrated on diplomatic Morse networks of enemy and neutral countries. Secondary commitments were nets of other government agencies (military attachés, economic authorities, etc.). This system consequently took mostly encrypted traffic. The material picked up was passed on to the breaking sections of OKW/Chi. The second system concentrated on monitoring foreign broadcasts, principally news broadcasts. A second important task was monitoring the reports of news agency correspondents. In addition, the second system seems to have had the mission of taking material requiring special apparatus, such as multiple Morse and commercial radio telephone. Some traffic of agents was apparently also covered, but most of the traffic picked up by the second system was in clear. The core of the first intercept system was constituted by two large intercept stations, one at Treuenbrietzen, near Berlin and the other at Lauf near Nuremberg. Treuenbrietzen was one of the old intercept stations It was apparently already in existence by 1933 and is said to have specialised in intercepting diplomatic traffic. It was definitely subordinated to OKW/Chi for the interception of diplomatic traffic in 1939.

Lauf was developed after the army was ordered to expand its intercept system in 1933. The original location was at Hersbruck and was intended primarily to operate against Czech traffic. By 1939, the necessity for intercepting Czech traffic had passed and the station was turned over to OKW/Chi for diplomatic traffic. Lauf had three small intercept stations subordinate to it. The one at Loerrach, near the Swiss border, picked up traffic from Switzerland on the ground wave, but could be heard at Lauf only with difficulty. Loerrach had eight or nine sets. While Lauf was being completed there had been a temporary station at Tennenlohe, which had four or five sets and was retained for emergencies. Finally, there was a subsidiary station at Libourne, near Bordeaux in France. This operated eight or nine sets from autumn 1943 until the spring of 1944, and was used principally for the interception of Swedish and Turkish traffic. The total establishment at Lauf, including the outstations, was 200-250 persons. After January 1944 about eighty of these were women. The operators were mostly soldiers organised in a military unit. The total number of sets, including those in the outstations, was eighty to ninety. Up to the beginning of 1943 the station attempted to cover all diplomatic traffic and that of the Polish underground. After this, Berlin assumed closer control and sent priority directives, as a result of which the total intercept dropped from 25,000 to 10,000 messages per month. The station carried on no cryptanalytic work, but had some experts in traffic identification.

Intercept stations in foreign countries had a special status. They were not large or elaborate enough to be called Fixed Intercept Stations, but unlike the smaller stations at home (and in occupied territory) they were subordinated directly to Group I of OKW/Chi rather than to a larger station. They were administered by Military Intelligence (Abwehr) through its organisation in foreign countries. Two such special outstations are known to have existed, one in Spain and one in Sofia. Of the latter, little is known beyond the fact that it existed and specialised in intercepting short-wave traffic from Britain.

However, considerable information is available about the intercept system in Spain. The OKW conducted a small network there which in 1941 employed about fifty men. It was established in 1940 to intercept Mediterranean traffic and also short-wave traffic from Sweden. The original plan seems to have been to supervise the Spanish stations of the other branches of the Armed Forces.

Communication between stations and to Berlin was by courier and wireless, for which the unit had a powerful transmitter. There were also teleprinter communications to Berlin. All intercepts were sent back to Berlin – no cryptanalytic work was carried on by the unit. The controlling station was in Madrid, originally situated in the German consulate. Because of interference from the nearby broadcasting station EFE, and perhaps for security reasons, the outfit was moved to the north-east section of the city. After 1942, perhaps as a result of expansion, the unit took over the Florida, a large night club in the vicinity. The largest outstation was on a German-owned cattle ranch north of Seville. Apparently, on the same site but under separate naval control, was a naval

D/F station. Previous to 1944, there had been some wireless operators, probably intercept people, in Tangiers. Whether they were subordinate to the Madrid unit is not entirely clear. On the Canary Islands, there was one intercept operator, who was in contact with Madrid by wireless.

The air intercept station at Barcelona came under exclusive Air Force control in 1942.There was also a sub-station in the Balearic Islands and a large one at Bordeaux (at first at Arcachon), almost certainly under Army control. The Spanish network was apparently conducted without the official approval of the Spanish government. Very elaborate security precautions were taken to keep the work secret, and personnel were encouraged to keep to themselves in small groups and to avoid contact even with other Germans. Married men might not be accompanied by their wives, and single men were strictly forbidden to marry Spanish women. In January 1944, the Seville station was betrayed to the Spanish police and had to be closed to avoid being raided. About the same time, the intercept operators in Tangiers were expelled. The personnel of the Madrid unit were believed to have been interned in April 1945.

A clandestine relationship did, however, exist with certain individual Spaniards, some of them highly placed in the Spanish Army. It was the job of two Military Intelligence (Abwehr) officials to contact such Spaniards as well as to take care of the economic side of the unit, doubtless as representatives of the War Organisation (Kriegsorganisation). The only known case of Spanish military co-operation with the Madrid intercept unit did not turn out happily for the Germans. Contact was made with the Spanish General Staff regarding the equipment of the naval D/F station at Seville which had been closed in January 1944. Colonel Sarmiento, Chief Signal Officer of the Spanish Army, was persuaded to agree to let the equipment be set up by Spaniards on Spanish military ground. Some of it was then to be operated by Germans for German purposes, while the rest was to become Spanish property. The equipment was delivered to the Spaniards, but was never set up and never operated. Apparently, it remained in Spanish hands, tactfully expropriated.

It is likely that around 1940 there was a plan to set up a number of inter-service networks in neutral and Allied countries under the control of OKW/Chi, which was at this time interested in establishing stations in Bulgaria for the Army, Navy and Air Force, but the Navy refused to come in on the project. At Varna in Bulgaria (cover name Kommando Nordland), the Air Force had already taken over the station, although it was part of the OKW complex. The station consisted of 22 men, who wore civilian clothes, and there were five receivers. They covered air force traffic in Syria, Greece, Rumania and some ferry flights in the Mediterranean. Plain language was dealt with on the spot, but cipher messages were sent back to Berlin.

It is clear from documents that the firm and permanent part of OKW's intercept structure consisted of the Treuenbrietzen station, the Lauf station with its subsidiary stations, Sofia and the Spanish network. A persistent difficulty was created by the heads of the language sections, who demanded that only traffic being currently solved should be intercepted, 'in order that the results of their work could appear more effective. Before that they seem to have had more choice of what they were to cover.

Various outside organisations contributed traffic to the OKW/Chi cryptanalysts. Of these the most closely related to OKW/Chi from an organisational point of view was the German Radio Defence Corps (Funküberwachung – Fu), which was also part of the OKW and was subordinated, like OKW/Chi, to the Armed Forces Communications Group (Ag.WNV). In conjunction with the Reichspost, OKM/Fu gave permission for transmission, distributed frequencies and call signs to Army and government agencies and industries, and was responsible for the distribution of codes.

There was a special unit attached to Fu III for cryptanalysis of agents' traffic, but some of the traffic picked up found its way into OKW/Chi. Military Intelligence (Abwehr) organisations in foreign countries conducted line-tapping operations in Bordeaux, Lisbon, Sofia and Ankara. The heads of OKW/Chi's special outstations in Madrid and Sofia had some liaison with the Abwehr on the matter, but actual operations were entirely in the hands of the Abwehr. Line intercepts formed about one-third of OKW/Chi's work. According to a German Sigint report, there was a monthly average of 36,480 wireless messages (both plain and enciphered) and 12,330 line messages were taken from January to June 1944. Of the other signals intelligence agencies, Goering's Research Bureau seems to have made the largest contribution to OKW/Chi's raw traffic – responsible for just over one-third between January and June 1944 – was intercepted and handed over by the Research Bureau. No mention is made of any other German signal intelligence service. In a list of sources of traffic dated 28 April 1943, however, mentions the Foreign

Office and Research Bureau. Budapest contributed about one-eighth of the traffic. Spanish material was handled by the Abwehr, the suggested source of which was said to be the Spanish Signal Intelligence Service, the head of which, Rafael Sarmiento, a leading Abwehr contact.

There was a second intercept system with its main station at Ludwigsfelde and the branch stations to the Fehrbellinerplatz in Berlin. At Ludwigsfelde there were eighty receivers but the site was completely destroyed by air attack on 2 January 1944 and was out of action until the autumn. Despite this setback, a report of June 1944 stated that the broadcast intercept system kept up a monthly average of 7,280 press reports and 7,340 radio-telephone transmissions – average duration twenty minutes – from January-June 1944. It seems, therefore, that the bulk of the OPW/Chi intercepts was either ordinary Morse or ordinary radio-telephone.

OKW/Chi had, apparently, no facilities for intercepting Baudot – teleprinter five-channel tape traffic, but some traffic had come from the Staats intercept station, run by the Reserve Army. Staats also picked up Multiplex, Duplex and Verdun transmissions and passed them to OKW/Chi. The only elaborate attempts to develop intercept facilities for special kinds of transmission were made late in the war, but were not directed by OKW/Chi, which had no particular interest in them. One military officer who had been engaged in signals intelligence on the Western Front in 1940 proposed a centrally-controlled intercept organisation with at least 3,000 technicians and between 1940 and 1942 pursued his idea, but he never had a chance to put his ideas into operation. In August 1944 this officer was made responsible for wireless questions in connection with rockets, including Allied transmissions which might be control beams or signals for rockets. Because this unit was involved in work along all wave lengths, it was tasked with covering all gaps in the German intercept scheme, particularly centimetre and decimetre wave lengths, which had been completely ignored by all German intercept organisations. To assist the unit there were three intercept stations. At Husum – midway between Schobüll and Husum town – there was an intercept receiver coupled to a sound film recorder (Tonschreiber) which picked up a considerable volume of traffic ranging between 30kcs and 60kcs. Radar impulses were also picked up which, it was thought, would be useful in developing radar counter-measures. Kahle Asten – on a hill near Winterberg overlooking the Ruhr – specialised in attempts to pick up Allied decimetre traffic, while another station was situated at Feldberg in the Black Forest.

Operations

Practical cryptanalysis

In a sense, the linguists were the core of OKW/Chi and seem to have represented the original German idea of a high-level intelligence organisation. Its guiding principle was to supply a steady stream of intelligence by breaking codes and ciphers which did not offer a very high degree of resistance to cryptanalysis, and by furnishing translations of clear texts so obtained and of signals originally sent in the clear text. Innovations such as the introduction of a mathematical research section and the late attempt to reorient the whole organisation towards cryptographic security rather than intelligence seem to have had little effect on this group. The final product of the linguistic section was the translation of decoded traffic called 'VNs' or 'Verlässliche Nachrichten' – 'reliable reports'. These VN codes were typed on form sheets headed by a large VN and classified 'Geheime Kommandosache' – 'Top Secret'. Missing groups and garbles were indicated by dots and doubtful groups by dots underneath the translation. Dubious translations were enclosed in parentheses and marked with question marks, and free translations were sometimes accompanied by a literal translation in brackets if necessary. The date of the message and of the publication was indicated. No evaluation was done by the sections and no reports were written.

The completed product was passed to the evaluation section, where material judged to be of no importance was put aside and the rest routed to authorised recipients. One copy went to the language section which had produced the VNs, where it was used in compiling lists of cribs and for similar purposes. Captured VNs recovered by TICOM represented the traffic of twenty-nine countries, and were mostly from the Foreign Ministry of the country in question to its representatives abroad and vice versa. The content of the captured VNs can be roughly classified as follows:

- Diplomatic household affairs such as personnel moves, exchange of stranded personnel through neutral countries, requests for jobs, moves of embassies into new quarters;
- Requests for passports and visas;
- Press reports
- Non-press reports; and
- Commercial and shipping arrangements.

From the point of view of the cryptanalysts, liaison was not very satisfactory and neither the Abwehr nor the heads of OKW/Chi seemed to have an adequate idea of the difficulties faced by the cryptanalysts. As a result, directives always came too late. When Lieutenant-Colonel Mettig, second-in-command of OKW/Chi was asked by his interrogators 'point blank' what was the OKW/Chi's greatest cryptanalytic achievement, TICOM recalls that 'he hesitated. It became apparent that OKW/Chi had not achieved any outstanding cryptanalytic success'. However there had been some minor successes, and between January and June 1944 around a monthly average of 3,000 VNs was produced by the linguists. During the same period, the number of completed diplomatic messages averaged 3,700 a month. However, OKW/Chi had been bombed out of its offices in the Tirpitzufer section of Berlin in November 1943 and during the first six months of 1944 worked in temporary quarters which were unheated, and in many cases without doors and windows. In 1944 there were about 320 crypto-linguists. Mettig mentioned the Turkish section as making perhaps the most important contribution. The information on the various countries is as follows:

Turkey: OKW/Chi Turkish desk consisted of about ten people and had particular success with Turkish military systems.

Poland: One of the largest language desks with about twenty people. Main success was against an enciphered four-figure code used by the London government in exile, and was solved towards the end of 1942 or beginning of 1943. By 1945, twelve different stencils and a large number of enciphering tables had been recovered. It was against this system that the special cryptanalytic device the Brainbox was specially developed along with the use of IBM machines. The most important Polish breaking was between the Polish underground and the government in exile in London. TICOM states that 'This traffic was said to have been particularly valuable during the period immediately preceding the Normandy invasion.' All wireless traffic from Britain was banned, but the traffic of Polish agents to Britain continued and was read. Most of this traffic seems to have been in a five-figure system and was originally broken not by OKW/Chi but Inspectorate 7/VI. The traffic proved so valuable in autumn 1943 that a group from the agents' section of 7/VI was transferred to the OKW/Chi Polish desk. The traffic was intercepted at Lauf.

Britain/USA: Success against US traffic was greater than against British messages, and there is 'no evidence for high-level success against

British systems'. TICOM says that a British Typex cipher machine was captured at Dunkirk and was on display at OKW/Chi, but was without rotors and that 'no rotors were ever obtained'. TICOM adds: 'The OKW/Chi prisoners could give a reasonably accurate description of the machine but they were not sure how many rotors were actually used. Carefully questioned on the subject, they were emphatic in their statements that it had never been solved, either by OKW/Chi or any other German cryptanalytic agency. There is a footnote to the TICOM report to the interrogation of Dr Eric Hüttenhain, OKW/Chi chief cryptanalyst and his deputy, Lieutenant-Colonel Mettig about whether the Germans had broken Typex: 'An unsuccessful effort was made to trap Hüttenhain and Mettig on this point. At the conclusion of the interrogation, even the most skeptical of the interrogators was convinced that they were telling the truth.' However, the British Interdepartmental Cipher was captured at Bergen in Norway and OKW/Chi collaborated with the Navy and Air Force in solving the encipherment and reading the traffic. There was no success against British diplomatic traffic although it was attempted. Hüttenhain told interrogators that no British systems had been read since 1943.

OKW/Chi had no success against US machine ciphers and the unit did not concern itself with American diplomatic traffic, and the main success here was from the Foreign Office Pers ZS section, who read the US strip cipher O2, as OKW/Chi did not work on US enciphered teleprinter messages. In addition, a US unenciphered code of about 100,000 groups in use since 1926 was read, as well as a code encipherment system using twenty-letter alphabets.

France: French high-level military traffic was read up to the end of October 1939, made possible by reconstructing French books.

Russia: During the war the Russian section was small and achieved nothing.

Japan: The Japanese desk was about fifteen strong and a number of systems were read but no Japanese military attaché systems were read.

Italy: This section, comprising between thirty-five and forty people, had considerable success. Between 19935 and 1942, Foreign Office Pers ZS 'read everything' in Italian. OKW/Chi read the AR22 diplomatic system and the Impero code.

Bulgaria, Rumania, Hungary and Finland: There are no details of success against Germany's smaller allies.

Scandinavia: Only Swedish unenciphered codes for which the books had been captured, were read. No Swedish Hagelin traffic was read.

Switzerland: Swiss Enigma traffic was read regularly. The wiring was changed on Enigma every three months, but the changes at Washington were not made at the same time as in London. Cribs provided by the Washington traffic made it possible to solve the London wirings.

Vatican and Greece: At the time of the Austrian Anschluss a Vatican book was broken, and one or more Greek books were broken.

Spain, Portugal and Latin America: It is not known what was accomplished against these countries.

Agents' traffic: Codes and ciphers of Allied and neutral agents were not a regular OKW/Chi commitment, but handled by a special section of 7/VI and known as 'Vauck's Section' after the name of its head. Located at Dorf Zinna, near Jüterbog, the group acted more or less independently. One particularly interesting episode is the handing over by Vauck to OKW/Chi of signals from the Rote 3 (Red 3) network of Russian agents operating from Switzerland. Ten of these messages were solved, then Vauck discovered that the encipherment was based on a book. However, this was not enough to solve all the traffic passed by the network. The 7/VI unit was later subordinated to OKW/Chi.

Cryptanalytic research, security and development

One of the outstanding achievements of the OKW/Chi cryptanalytic section was the development of various types of cryptanalytic machinery. There was a relay mechanism for changing teleprinter letters to digits, thus producing an additive for naval use. The machinery was extensively used in the security of German cipher systems. Cryptanalytic machinery was first introduced into German signals intelligence work with the adoption of machinery by the Army in 1941. OKW/Chi did not have any IBM machinery and may have used the Army's equipment for this purpose. IBM machinery could only be used for processes which can be reduced to sorting, and for processes which could not be so reduced, it was necessary to develop special apparatus. The aim was to build reading and recording apparatus in all conceivable forms in order to put together suitable equipment as soon as a practical problem arose.

An increasing amount of the available expert manpower of the research section was spent on security research and on the resulting problems in the development of cipher devices. Throughout most of the war there was considerable duplication of effort. With regard to Enigma, the simplest form of this machine – the non-plugboard commercial version – was known by the research section to be solvable:

- with a depth of twenty to twenty-five messages;
- with a short crib;
- without a crib by running the cipher text against a catalogue of the results obtained by enciphering the letter E, the most common German letter, in all possible positions of the machine (the so-called E-strip).

Commercial Enigma was used by the railways and instructions were given which required the double encipherment of every message.

A second form of Enigma – the 'counter' machine – had three wheels with an irregular motion and a moveable reflector, and was used by military attachés until the middle of 1943, and was known to be breakable on a ten-letter crib. As such they were withdrawn from military attachés and the military version used. The 'counter' Enigmas were used by the Abwehr. The most common Enigma machine had the plugboard, the keystone of the German cipher security structure during most of the war.

In October 1939, a captured Polish officer named Ruzek said that the Enigma 'had been worked on in conjunction with the French. This incident became known as 'Fall Wicher' or the Wicher Case, because the Polish Cipher Bureau was located at Wicher. Ruzek did not say the Enigma had been read'. In the remnants of the Polish cryptanalytic bureau files, the plaintexts of three German messages known to have been transmitted from a German cruiser in Spanish waters during the Spanish Civil War were found. It is said that there were many interrogations at the time, but the interrogators 'drew a blank' and they did not find out whether the messages were obtained by cryptanalysis or physical compromise. At the interrogations in Warsaw in 1942, one of the Poles interrogated was a Lieutenant-Colonel [*Gwido Langer*], the head of the Polish cryptanalytic bureau. A second series of interrogations was held in Berlin later in 1942. In 1943 the case was reopened and the prisoners interrogated again but 'no information was obtained'. OKW/Chi deputy head Lieutenant-Colonel Mettig attributed this failure to 'the stupidity of the Abwehr, which left the prisoners together before the interrogations so that they had an opportunity to agree on a consistent story'.

In the West, the Germans had no better luck. They discovered nothing in Belgium that threw any light on the vulnerability of their cryptographic systems, and when Paris was captured, the French cryptanalytic agency, the Deuxième Bureau, had moved to Vichy, but when Vichy was occupied no search was made. TICOM adds: 'From interrogations and visits to the cryptanalytic agencies of conquered countries, therefore, the Germans got no conclusive evidence that the Enigma was being broken, but enough was found to arouse their suspicions.' The doubts raised about German security led to research people doing some work on Enigma. OKW/Chi head Dr Eric Hüttenhain mentioned the possibility of a solution resulting from faulty indicator procedure. He thought that a general solution might be theoretically possible by the use of an E-strip as in the case of commercial Enigma. But this would be slow and was never attempted by the Germans. OKW/Chi's final general judgment on the plugboard Enigma seems to have been that 'the device was secure if used according to regulations.'

The Germans were aware that solution might be possible by means of stereotyped beginnings, stereotyped messages or a number of messages in depth. No texts of messages actually transmitted in the field were ever made available to OKW/Chi by any branch of the armed forces. However, early in 1944 the Navy became concerned about security as a result of heavy U-boat losses and a naval lieutenant called Frowein was given the task of studying naval Enigma, which had four rotors. TICOM reports that 'Frowein broke the naval machine with known wheels on a crib of twenty-five letters'. OKW/Chi's cryptanalysts 'had a general uneasy feeling about the security of the chief German ciphers'. In a lecture in autumn 1944, Lieutenant Dr Stein told a conference that no German system was secure if the cryptographic regulations were violated. Without any authority to monitor actual traffic with a view to finding out how well the regulations were observed, all German cryptographic agencies were driven from security scrutiny to an attempt to develop cryptographic devices with a higher degree of theoretical invulnerability.

OKW/Chi's contribution to increased Enigma security was a suggestion that the wheels be redesigned so that they could be given an irregular motion, and a device known as the 'changeable turnover rotor' (Lückenfüllerwalze) was developed. It meant that every Enigma machine would have to be supplied with a new set of wheels, but they were never produced in great enough quantity so that the system could be changed. An effort was also made to replace Enigma entirely. One such device, the

SG-39, built by Telefonbau und Normalzeit, a kind of combination of Enigma and Hagelin principles, was scheduled for production in 1939, but because of technical difficulties, lack of clarity in the operational requirements and the bombing of factories capable of producing the device, the first experimental models were not ready for delivery until February/March 1945, and never reached their destination in Berlin. The device seemed to have been mainly developed by the Army. Senior Inspector Fritz Menzer seems to have had the most fertile mind in OKW/Chi in the development of cryptographic devices. Between 1937 and 1939 he produced a purely mechanical machine called the M-40 and about thirty models were built. It was tested by the Army and found 'moderately secure' but was never used. One variety was to have been adopted for automatic Morse transmission.

An invention of Menzer of great practical significance was the SG-41, a purely mechanical machine wherein the wheels had an irregular interlocking motion. It was considered that with the SG-41 a fundamental weakness of Hagelin had been overcome. Like all machines of the Hagelin type, the SG-41 can be read in depth, but the setting of the machine cannot be recovered even from a very considerable length of key. The SG-41 was used by German agents but was never authorised for the Army, largely because of inter-departmental differences of opinion, which seem to have been typical of the German signal intelligence set-up, where the link leading from the cryptologic experts to the troops in the field seems to have been unusually long and tenuous. The cryptographers spent a great deal of time discussing whether the order of letters on the printing wheel should be alphabetical, but Army Chief Signals Officer General Erich Fellgiebel decided that he wanted a machine with a keyboard, so the alphabetical arrangement on the printing wheel was not required and a mixed alphabet was used instead as adding some slight extra security. A thousand machines were built.

Then all the officers in the Army Signals Department decided that they wanted a smaller machine without a keyboard for use below the regimental level. On such a machine an alphabetical arrangement of letters on the printing wheel was necessary – if such a machine was to be used with the keyboard machines, they too would have to have a regular alphabetical arrangement on the printing wheel. As a result of the changeover delay, the machine was never turned out in sufficient quantity for wide use, but a model with ten digits rather than letters was produced for the use of the weather services.

The Army medium-grade system was Double Playfair, but it had weaknesses. As such, the 'Raster' transposition system was developed and replaced Double Playfair. However, the transposition system proved awkward for field use because the original metal grilles could not be turned out because of a shortage of material, and paper grilles required constant replacement. Menzer then developed the 'Key Box' or Schlüsselkasten, which looked like a slide rule with wheels. It was found to be very satisfactory for medium-grade use.

Teleprinting security devices also came under scrutiny. Two series of such devices were produced, the first series, distinguished by the letters SZ, were cryptographic devices separate from the teleprinter and attachable, with encipherment effected by twelve mechanical pin wheels. The second series were built into the teleprinter and were designated by a number prefixed by the letter T. Encipherment was by ten wheels with fixed pin patterns. The SZ series began development by Lorenz in 1937. The first model was the SZ-40, which was shown could be broken on a crib of a thousand letters of text without cribs or other assistance. Only about a hundred of these machines were produced, but even the later model SZ-42 was 'by no means impervious to cryptanalytic attack' and variations designated SZ-42 A, B and C were developed. The T-52 A and B, produced by Siemens, were shown to have 'an extraordinarily low degree of security and could be broken on a hundred letters of cipher text without a crib.' Changes in design were suggested including non-uniform turning of the wheels, but for engineering reasons Siemens refused to accept these suggestions. Instead, the T-52 was produced, which overcame some of the more obvious disadvantages of the earlier models. However, the T-52 C was shown to be breakable on a text of one thousand letters, and led to the production of the T-52 D, which again had faults, so the T-52 E was produced. But Hüttenhain knew that T-52 D and E messages could be read on a depth of ten without a crib. But the earlier models were still being used on the supposition that teleprinter traffic could not be intercepted, but evidence of line tapping in Paris in 1942 and 1943 aroused the Army signal authorities to the need for teleprinter security. But again, the Germans were too late with their cipher development and the new machines could not be generally introduced.

Regarding ciphony, in the summer of 1943 all authorities and firms engaged in developing speech encipherment were called together by General Fellgiebel to end the overlapping of this work. In November

1944, Fellgiebel's successor as Army Chief Signals Officer (he was shot as a conspirator in the Hitler Bomb Plot), General Praun, commissioned OKW/Chi to check developments in ciphony, but again it came too late because of the general war situation.

Assuring a high degree of cryptographic security involves three steps:

- the systems in use must be put in the hands of skilled cryptanalysts who are able to judge their effectiveness;
- they must be thoroughly examined by these cryptanalysts, and if accepted as usable, regulations for their use must be produced by experts; and
- the recommendations of the cryptanalysts regarding acceptance or rejection of systems and regarding the use of systems finally accepted must be adequately enforced.

On the first point, the Germans were largely a failure. When the war began, the administration of German cryptographic systems 'was in a chaotic state'. The signal authority of each branch of the armed forces did much as it pleased, at times without regard to the recommendation of the cryptanalytic authorities. For example, prior to October 1943, OKW/Chi had no authority whatever to examine systems used by the armed forces. The order of Field Marshal Keitel of October 1943 that the opinion of OKW/Chi was required before any system was adopted by any of the separate branches, was apparently 'very incompletely observed'. An attempt late in the war to establish OKW/Chi as a security authority for the separate branches came too late.

On the second point, despite the lack of any real authority in the matter, OKW/Chi did manage to examine fairly thoroughly at least the leading Army and Air Force systems, and correctly appraised the weaknesses of the commercial and 'counter' Enigma models, and at least saw that the plugboard version was not invulnerable to attack.

On the third point, academic aloofness by OKW/Chi was probably only partly responsible for the complete German failure with regard to this point. There was a 'curious lack of interest' by German cryptographers in the size of the Allied cryptographic attack against them. They knew of the Deuxième Bureau, but nothing of British efforts, and on US cryptography they knew only of the inter-war Black Chamber.

Miscellaneous operations

a. Broadcast monitoring

Located at the Fehrbelliner Platz in Berlin it put out a daily newspaper called Chi Nachrichten or Chi Reports, which could only be obtained after Stalingrad as the news deteriorated, with Keitel's permission. In addition, the monitoring section published special reports such as Russian news.

b. Attacks on ciphony devices

One of the most interesting items to appear in the Chi Reports was conversations between Churchill and President Roosevelt conducted over a radio-telephone link between London and Washington. German informants stated that this link was evidently not intended to have any very high degree of security since an operator warned the two leaders whenever the talk approached highly secretive matters. The transmission was scrambled and the intercept took place at the broadcast monitoring station at Ludwigsfelde by means of a descrambling apparatus which was said to be completely effective. Changes in the key of the scrambler could be easily followed by turning a few knobs. The Germans constructed apparatus used to restore the 'scrambled' radio circuits in use between Britain and the United States to complete intelligibility, and by 1942 the equipment was working on a twenty-four hour basis at Kelheim in the Munich area.

In June 1944, at the experimental intercept station at Staats, study began of the Russian scrambler known as X2, but this was unsuccessful. Interest was aroused by a ciphony device recovered intact from a crashed American Mustang plane. Investigations of the device was said to be inconclusive, although it was possible to reconstruct the key setting from intercepted oscillograms. However, it was doubtful whether solution could have been rapid enough to be of any use during an actual fighting operation.

c. Training

Training was a regular part of OKW/Chi and occasionally special courses were given. For language section members the training procedure, which had been followed since 1930, was different. They were introduced to cryptanalysis gradually, concurrently with their work as linguists.

OKW relations with other cryptologic agencies

Relations with the Army, Navy and Air Force Signal Intelligence Services

OKW/Chi left the Army, Navy and Air Force systems almost completely alone and worked on diplomatic and military attaché traffic. There was liaison and co-operation with the Services but OKW/Chi did not control the activities of the other Signal Intelligence Services in this field. In general, no material was passed from the branches to OKW/Chi and this arrangement seems to have held throughout the war with some exceptions. However, even in the case of the British Typex and the US M-209 machines, OKW/Chi was not called in by the agencies working on them. A certain amount of co-ordination seems to have been made on interception, and OKW/Chi was the intercept clearing house – when needed – for all the Services. Plans for an extensive inter-Service intercept structure 'remained a dream'. The development of cryptographic devices for use by troops was originally left entirely to individual branches, and development was partly taken over by the Army in autumn 1944, but the other branches kept their right to originate until the war's end, although OKW/Chi had the right of review.

OKW/Chi's greatest effort to assert its authority was as a co-ordinating agency on security scrutiny. Despite Field Marshal Keitel's order of October 1943, little effort was made to assume effective supervision of the security of all branches until a year later, but by August 1944 there was insufficient time left to overcome the difficulties caused by the neglect of five years. During this period no new devices were submitted to OKW/Chi.

On relations with other Signals Intelligence Agencies, the closest was with the Army. OKW/Chi specialists were never allowed to know precisely what was going on in the field and Army cryptanalysts apparently laboured under the same difficulties. For instance, the Army had been using an 'amazingly insecure system' known as the Barbara Keys (Barbaraschlüssel) for weather traffic from 1939 to 1944, and it was not until late 1944 that OKW/Chi heard about it, and presumably the Army cryptanalysts had not heard about it either. Contact with the Air Force was more lax. Lieutenant-Colonel Friedrich, head of the Air Force Signal Intelligence Service, told interrogators decoded traffic from OKW/

Chi was of no use whatever and he stopped reading it. Dr Ferdinand Voegele, Air Force chief cryptanalyst, said on liaison that he had worked on the British Government Telegraph Code and later received a copy of it from OKW. In 1940 and 1942 he had exchanged traffic in the Inter-Departmental Cypher, results of the reconstruction of the recipher book used with it with OKW as with the Navy. In 1945, messages and items in an American code were exchanged with OKW and the Army. OKW/Chi also gave some assistance to the Air Force weather service in their attack on a British meteorological system, putting at their disposal the digraph 'weight' recorder (Bigrammsuchgerät), but the cipher was not solved. With regard to liaison with the Navy, no naval research problems were referred to OKW/Chi. However, it was through OKW/Chi that the Navy learned that the Polish Government-in-Exile used a stencil system similar to the Royal Navy system.

OKW/Chi and other German high-level Signal Intelligence Agencies

OKW/Chi was the competitor of Goering's Research Bureau (the FA, or Forschungsamt) and Pers ZS – the Foreign Office Cryptanalytic Section. Since 1933 the FA had given some attention to diplomatic material and since World War One the Foreign Office had maintained a cryptanalytic bureau dealing largely with diplomatic traffic. So OKW/Chi was competing with two agencies which had been longer in the field. Hermann Goering was scornful of OKW/Chi which he described as 'the most junior member of the family'. On the other hand, the scorn was reciprocated by OKW/Chi. One OKW/Chi operative said that the FA knew little about cryptanalysis and employed no mathematicians. However, by Spring 1944 one-third of the raw traffic reaching OKW/Chi came from the FA. Intelligence obtained by the FA from cryptanalytic and other activity was passed direct to OKW, bypassing OKW/Chi. Foreign Office (Pers ZS) felt most strongly against OKW/Chi, and was one of 'mild contempt'. They were the older organisation, felt they had more able people and were bitter because they felt their efforts were unappreciated in higher quarters. However, a high degree of co-operation was achieved, and the delicate problem arising from the fact that both bodies were committed to the same material were partly met. When both bodies were breaking the older Japanese cipher machine, OKW/Chi worked on odd days and Pers ZS on even days, although Pers ZS made the initial break. Results were exchanged, and the debt of OKW/Chi to Pers ZS was probably considerable. South African codes were worked on jointly by both agencies, Pers ZS taking the lead. Where quality and expertness were primary considerations as in initial attacks on cipher systems, and in more difficult book-breaking problems, Pers ZS was superior.

Liaison with foreign signal intelligence agencies

Regarding liaison with the signal intelligence agencies of Germany's allies, the authority of OKW/Chi seems to have been partly recognised.

Austria: Before annexation, Austria was said to have had a small but efficient cryptologic office. It handled traffic of Italy, Rumania, Greece, Yugoslavia, Bulgaria, Turkey, Poland and Czechoslovakia. After the Anschluss the Austrian personnel were sent to Berlin to join OKW/Chi.

Japan: Astute sparring between German and Japanese Sigint. In 1942, a leading Japanese cryptanalyst Colonel (later General) Hayashi, was in Berlin and unable to get home, became military attaché in Budapest. He had arranged an exchange of material with OKW/Chi which lasted throughout the war. When OKW/Chi found that the non-pluggable Enigma was readable it was suggested to Army signals chief General Fellgiebel that the Japanese be given plugboard machines, but 'he vacillated'. There was a plan to send a cryptographic team to Japan by submarine in winter 1944-1945, but so little was known about Japanese cryptanalytic activity that they did not know where they were to go in Japan or to whom they would announce their arrival. The first contact was to be the Abwehr in the Far East, but it was believed only one of the delegation members spoke Japanese. German liaison with Japanese was not considered good, and German officers who visited Japan had to wear civilian clothes 'so that they would not embarrass their Axis partners'.

Italy: Liaison is believed to have begun at the start of the Abyssinian war, but does not seem to have been much closer than that with the Japanese. Certain Italian IBM equipment was exchanged for German IBM equipment to enable the Italians to use the machinery in their cryptographic work. OKW/Chi chief cryptanalyst Dr Eric Hüttenhain recalled how the Germans broke an Italian cipher, but the Italians refused to believe it, so a cryptographer was sent to Rome and locked in a room until he had done so!

Hungary: Liaison with Hungary had begun in the early 1920s and there was a regular exchange of material during the war. In spring

1944, OKW/Chi was receiving about one-eighth of its raw traffic from Hungary. In return for traffic, the Hungarians were given methods of solution for Italian, Rumanian and Polish systems, the only countries of interest to Hungary. Hüttenhain tells a story of how, in summer 1944, they broke a Turkish code and gave it to the Hungarians, who sold it to SS chief Heinrich Himmler's security service, the RSHA, which brought it proudly back to OKW/Chi!

Finland: Liaison with Finland began around 1938 and intensified after the first Russo-Finnish war and both military and diplomatic traffic was exchanged. Relations with both Hungary and Finland were of great assistance in restoring the archives of OKW/Chi which had been destroyed in an air raid of November 1943.

Bulgaria: The only liaison evidence is that in spring 1944, several Bulgarians were given a course in elementary cryptography by OKW/Chi.

Spain: Spain received French and general military traffic sent to North Africa, and in return, gave cablegrams about ship movements, probably originating with commercial attachés. About cryptanalytic material they supplied nothing, and this was because the Germans believed they knew nothing.

OKW/Chi disintegrates

The reorganisation plan partly put into effect in November 1944 is the final organisational expression of German ideas on high level signal intelligence. Later organisational changes were ad hoc, forced by the pressure of looming defeat. In February 1945, plans were made to move OKW/Chi out of Berlin and the following month most personnel were moved to Halle along with the cryptanalytic machinery. Operations began at the Army Signal School while the archives were moved to Lauf. Section III moved from Dresden to Halle but did not begin operations there.

On 10 April 1945 most of the unit moved to Ammersdorf and the train was routed to the Chiemsee via Falkenberg, Dresden, Prague and Pilsen. Most personnel reached Werfen near Salzburg and some personnel from the Treuenbrietzen intercept station also reached there. The Lauf station with archives arrived at Schliersee, south of Munich, on 10 April and operated for three days. On the thirtieth, orders were received for some staff to proceed with one-tenth of the equipment to Werfen. Those who remained dumped the rest of the equipment and the archives in the lake.

Others joined the remnants at Werfen and the OKW/Chi personnel were finally captured by the Americans, some of whom worked for the Americans until the end of May, after which they were moved to Heufeld near Bad Aibling, whence they were released. Others such as chief cryptanalyst Erich Hüttenhain ended the war in the north, where they, too, were captured.

Chapter 10

Army High Command Sigint

Army Signal Intelligence Service history

Pre-Hitler period (1919-1933)

This period is very obscure but it appears that a codes and ciphers section of the Defence Ministry (Reichswehrministerium) was maintained in skeleton force from the end of World War One. The head of this section also controlled the Ministry's intercept network, which dated from 1923-1924, when the first intercept stations (Feste Horchstelle, or Feste) were established. At least seven such stations operated before 1933, of which six dealt with foreign military traffic, at Stuttgart, Munich, Münster, Königsberg, Liegnitz and Breslau and one of foreign diplomatic traffic at Treuenbrietzen.

Pre-World War Two period (1933-1939)

In 1933-1934 three more intercept stations were set up, at Hersbruck (later moved to Lauf), at Striegau and Chemnitz. These ten stations intercepted foreign Army, Air Force and diplomatic traffic. In 1933-1934 the Defence Ministry set up set up its own military code and cipher section called the Intercept Control Station (Horchleitstelle or HLS) and drew a few trained cryptanalysts from the War Ministry (Reichskriegsministerium) codes and cipher section. Foreign Army traffic intercepted by the Defence Ministry went to the HSL, Air Force traffic to the SIA of the C-in-C Air Force (Chiffrierstelle des Oberbefehlshabers der Luftwaffe or Chi-Stelle OBdL), established in 1937. Diplomatic traffic went to both the Defence Ministry codes and ciphers section (after 1934 called the War Ministry – Kriegsministerium) and the Foreign Office Cryptanalytic Section (Sonderdienst des Referats Z in der Personalabteilung des Auswärtigen Amts – or Pers Z).

Early World War Two period (1939-1941)

During the early years of the war the main developments were as follows:

- Narrowing of the mission of the intercept service to include only Army traffic. In 1939 OKW/Chi took over foreign diplomatic interception, and the Army gave it two of its intercept stations – at Lauf and Treuenbrietzen;

- Establishment of five signal intelligence regiments (Kommandeur der Nachrichten Aufklärung or KONA), which were sent into the field as complete intercept and evaluation units attached to Army Groups. KONA 1, 2 and 3 were assigned to the Eastern Front. KONA 4 was not attached to any Army Group but assigned to the Commanding Officer, who controlled the Armies in the Balkans (Befehlshaber Südost), while KONA 5 was assigned to the Army Group on the Western Front.
- The introduction of mathematicians and linguists, who were drafted into the Army in 1939 and assigned either to the various field units or to the Intercept Control Station.
- An increasing Army interest in the security of its own systems, which gave rise to the Army Signal Security Agency, designated as Group IV of Inspectorate 7 (Inspektion 7 Gruppe IV or 7/IV), which was subordinated to the Chief of Army Equipment and Commander of the Replacement Army (Chef der Heeresrüstung und Befehlshaber des Ersatzheeres or Chef H Ruest u. Bde). 7/IV comprised mathematicians and former actuaries whose function was the examination of cryptographic systems used by the Army, and the preparation, printing and distribution of codes and ciphers.

Middle World War Two period (1941-1944)

In 1941 increased traffic because of the war found that the small staff at the HSL led to the establishment of two central stations to replace it: a central cryptanalytic agency at Berlin designated as Inspectorate 7/VI of the Chef H Ruest u BdE, and a central evaluation agency at Zossen designated as Control Station for Signal Intelligence (Leitstelle der Nachrichten Aufklärung or LNA). During the first few months of its existence, In 7/VI Russian cryptanalytic work was included in its work and Russian evaluation was included in the LNA evaluation. In late 1941, in order for Russian traffic evaluation to be closer to the forward echelon of the Field Army in East Prussia, cryptanalysts and evaluators were detached from In 7/VI and LNA and sent to Loetzen.

These cryptanalysts and evaluators became the nucleus of Intercept Control Station East (Horchleitstelle Ost) and until November 1944 signal intelligence activities were sharply divided into Russian signal intelligence, carried on by HLS Ost, and non-Russian signal intelligence, carried on by In 7/VI and LNA. In Autumn 1943, In 7/VI was transferred to the newly created General Army Office Department of Signals and renamed Signal Intelligence, Department of Signals, General Army Office, Army High Command (Oberkommando des Heeres/Allgemeines Heeres Amt/Amtsgruppe Nachrichten/Nachrichten Aufklärung or OKH/AHA/AgN/NA).

Additional units were placed in the field, and in 1942, eastern KONA 1, 2 and 3 were supplemented by KONA 6, formed to cover the Caucus campaign. KONA 7 was established in February 1943 and subordinated to C-in-C South (Oberbefehlshaber Süd), who controlled Army Group C and German forces in Italy.

Late World War Two period (1944-1945)

In October 1944, the organisation of the German Army signal intelligence service was completely changed through the amalgamation of the three central agencies, In 7/VI (latterly AgN/NA), LNA and HLS Ost, into one central cryptanalytic and evaluation agency, the Army High Command SIA (Oberkommando des Heeres/General der Nachrichten Aufklärung or OKH/GdNA). This was the logical result of the retreat of HLS Ost and the German Army from East Prussia to Zossen, where In 7/VI and LNA were situated, and KONA 6 was moved from the eastern to the western front. The KONAs were not greatly affected by this amalgamation.

The main changes in Army signal intelligence field organisation resulted from D-Day and a senior signal intelligence commander was set up to co-ordinate and control KONA 5 and 6. In late 1944 and early 1945, two extra KONAs were formed in the east, KONA 8 and KONA Nord. KONA 4 was transferred to the west at the end of the war. Because of the lack of detailed information concerning German signal intelligence at the end of the war, it is difficult to appraise the effectiveness of the final reorganisation of November 1944.

The full organisation existed as an integrated unit only from November 1944 to February 1945. From then until the surrender, OKH/GdNA was almost continuously on the move, seeking refuge in southern Germany. Most of the groups moved from Zossen to Bad Reichenhall, either directly or via Erfurt. Somewhere between Erfurt and Bad Reichenhall in the Weimar area, the IBM section was lost. Group VI, which had been located at Potsdam, went first to Stuttgart and then to Rosenheim.

German Army Field Sigint Organisation

Typical signal intelligence regiment organisation

The basic element of the Army signals field regiment was the KONA which was provided to each Army Group which had control over all signal intelligence units in its area. The typical component parts of a KONA were a Signal Intelligence Evaluation Centre (Nachrichten Aufklärung Auswertestelle or NAAS), designed to work with KONA HQ at Army Group level; usually one Stationary Intercept Company (Feste Nachrichten Aufklärungstelle or Feste), designed to work at Army level; usually two Long-Range Signal Intelligence Companies (Nachrichten Fernaufklärung Kompanie or FAK), designed to work at Army level; and usually two Close-Range Signal Intelligence Companies (Nachrichten Nahaufklärung Kompanie or NAK), designed to work at Army Corps level. Each Close-Range Company usually had two or three Close-Range Platoons (Nachrichten Nahaufklärungszug or NAZ), designed to work below NAK but still at Army Corps level.

In 1944, the Signal Intelligence Battalion (Nachrichten Aufklärung Abteilung or NAA) was introduced into the KONA organisation. They were small administrative units which acted as co ordinating units at Army level.

Army Intercept Operations

Intercept operations 1923-1933

Intercept coverage 1923-1933 was made by the Codes and Ciphers section of the Defence Ministry, and was established on a geographical basis. Material intercepted daily was studied by the traffic analysis section of the Feste and incorporated into daily reports. The first real military activity was the monitoring of the Riff War in the mid-1920s when the deployment and operational tactics of the Spanish and French were learned in detail through decoding radio messages.

Intercept operations 1933-1939

In 1933, the Army High Command (OKH) assumed general control of the intercept organisation and the Intercept Control Station (HLS) directed intercept coverage. Three new fixed intercept stations were established at Striegau, Hersbruck and Chemnitz. In 1935, the first mobile Signal Intelligence Companies were activated and at this time the Army was intercepting all Army, diplomatic and Air Force traffic. In 1935 the Air Force began to organise its own Signal Intelligence Service, and by 1939 the break between the Army and Air Force was complete. At the same time, OKH also set up its own intercept service for diplomatic traffic, intercepted at Lauf (formerly at Hersbruck) and Treuenbrietzen, two intercept stations which the Army had given to the Armed Forces. From this period on, the Army intercept service confined itself to intercepting foreign Army traffic.

From 1933 to 1939 the Army intercept service centred around the various international crises. In 1934, at the time of the Austrian revolt, Munich monitored all Austrian traffic including internal communications. It also monitored the Italians and discovered that they were massing troops at the Brenner Pass brought about by the timely withdrawal of Germany from the affair. In 1935, Munich was monitoring French traffic at the time of the occupation of the Rhineland. As a result of the intelligence derived, German troops marched in without fear of reprisal. From 1933 to 1936, the period of the Abyssinian War, OKH monitored Italian traffic without cessation. From 1936 to 1939, Munich and Stuttgart monitored both factions in the Spanish Civil War. During this period, the first mobile signal intelligence company went into the field attached to the Legion Condor, and became the most important intelligence instrument of the Legion Condor.

Intercept operations 1939-1944

Before 1939, the German General Staff had placed very little emphasis on intercept in the field, but with the approach of mobile warfare, intercept operations also became mobile. The new emphasis on field intercept led to the formation of the KONA, and the adaption of the Signal Intelligence Regiments to meet the needs of the Field Army was one of the chief accomplishments of the Army signal intelligence service.

Control of intercept coverage 1939-1944

Control of intercept coverage during the war stemmed from the Intelligence Officers of the Eastern and Western Armies Branches. In the last year of the war the chain of command is clear. The Eastern and Western Armies Branches Intelligence Officers briefed the chief of the Understaff of OKH/GdNA, who controlled the KONA and who issued them their directives for intercept coverage. In the West, the Understaff worked through the Senior Commander of Signal Intelligence (Hoeh Kdr d NA), whose function it was to co-ordinate the intercept coverage of KONA 5 and 6. With the other KONA, the chain of command from Understaff was direct. The Signal Intelligence Evaluation Centres (NAAS) of the KONAs issued the directives for intercept coverage to all units subordinate to the KONA. In 1941-1944, prior to establishing the GdNA, the chain of command appears to have been that non-Russian interception was directed by Western Armies Branch through the Control Station of Signal Intelligence of the Army High Command (OKH/LNA). Russian interception was directed by Eastern Armies Branch through the Intercept Control Station East of the Army High Command (OKH/HLS Ost).

Western intercept

Traffic from Britain was considered the most important of the Western traffics, and had been monitored intensively since August 1939, when a Long-Range Signal Intelligence Company (FAK 620) was sent to the Atlantic coast near Norderney Island to monitor British Army manoeuvre traffic. Although FAK 620 was later sent to the East, British traffic continued to be monitored by the following units of KONA 5 from 1939 to 1944:

- Long-Range Signal Intelligence Company FAK 613, located at St Malo exclusively for radio traffic;
- Feste 2, a Stationary Intercept Company located, until November 1943, at Husum in Holland, afterwards at Lille;
- Feste 9, formed in June 1942 at Frankfurt and sent to Norway, first stationed at Trondheim, later at Bergen. In Spring 1944 it moved to Ski near Oslo. Its main task was intercepting British Army traffic in Northern England, Scotland and Faroes;
- Feste 12, a Stationary Intercept Company attached to the Evaluation Centre of KONA 5 and located at Louveciennes.

The traffic of the US and Iceland and US troops in Britain was monitored chiefly by Feste 3 at Euskirchen and Feste 9 at Bergen. Feste 3 concentrated on US traffic. After Autumn 1943, Feste 3 had a special intercept unit for US non-Morse radio teletype traffic, designated by the Germans as FF5 – Funk Fernschreib 5. From Feste 9, US traffic in Iceland was monitored and watched for short-wave radio traffic from London to Washington via Ireland, but without success. Traffic of Spain, Portugal and the Brazilian Army in Italy was monitored from 1939 to

1942 by Feste 3 at Euskirchen. In early 1943, FAK 624 was formed at Montpelier, to intercept this traffic.

In January 1944 this traffic was shared with FAK 624 by Feste 12. Two other minor traffics were monitored: Swedish Army and French police, originating in Corsica. Swedish traffic was intercepted by a subordinate unit of Feste 9, stationed at Halden in Norway. French police traffic was monitored at Montpelier.

South-Western intercept

Before 1943, the German Army appeared to have had no signal intelligence unit in Italy, but in February that year KONA 7 was established to handle traffic from Italy and North Africa. FAK 621, which was attached to KONA 7, was originally designated as Army Signal Company 3 (Horch Nachrichten Aufklärung (HNA 56). This unit, which was particularly active in North Africa, was captured, in part, in July 1942, and in May 1943 the entire unit was captured at Tunisia. It had monitored British, French and US troops and the Egyptian Army and Camel Corps.

Intercept service 1944-1945

Intercept operations of OKH/GdNA

The years 1944-1945 saw the centralisation of Army Sigint and its catastrophic dissolution in the months prior to capitulation. In centralising the service, OKH/GdNA assumed responsibility for the intercept and evaluation of the foreign press, special high grade machine ciphers and wireless photography. Western monitoring of foreign press was confined to the BBC London Service, news monitoring to the Reuter and Tass agencies. Interception and evaluation of special high grade machine ciphers of Britain, USA and Russia was assigned to OKH/GdNA Group 6 at Potsdam. Section 1 dealt with Russian traffic and Section 2 with British and American high grade machine ciphers, conducted by Feste 3 at Euskirchen until the establishment of GdNA, when responsibility was transferred to the central agency. Wireless photography was carried out worldwide, but the non-Russian channels were said not to have yielded any useful information.

Intercept service in the field

The intercept service in the field during the last year of the war maintained its geographical distribution. With the pressure of the Allied invasion, western intercept assumed of necessity a position of greater importance. KONA 6 had been reassigned from the East to the West and KONAs 5 and 6 were subordinated to a Senior Commander of Sigint, who was responsible for all Sigint operations in the West. Upon these two KONAs fell the task of intercepting the traffic of the invading armies.

Disintegration of intercept operations

During the last months of the war, KONA 1 withdrew from the East into Czechoslovakia and was found by the invading forces at Novy Jicin (Neutitschein); KONA 2 retreated from Grodno to Ortelburg in Prussia, Danzig, Holstein and finally the Wismar area; KONA 3 was caught by the Russians in a pocket at Kurland and captured; KONA 8 withdrew, first into Rumania, then Croatia, and finally to Lenz. KONA 5 in the West withdrew from Louveciennes in mid-August 1944 and went first to Viggingen near Metz, and at the beginning of September it moved to Krofdorf near Giessen, where it stayed until March. From there it went to the Rhoen and finally to Dischingen in the Donauwoerth area. Of the component parts of KONA 6, less is known. The south-western unit, KONA 7, and its subordinate units retreated into northern Italy.

The constant shifting of the KONAs, and in the late months of the war, the disruption of internal communications between the various parts of the KONAs and between KONAs and GdNA had a disastrous effect on the whole problem of enemy intercept. During the last months of the war, the intercept units of the GdNA were also disrupted. Units of Groups I and V moved with other GdNA Groups to Erfurt and then to Bad Reichenhall. Group VI's intercept unit, which had been covering high grade machine traffic at Potsdam, moved to Stuttgart and then to Rosenheim. The equipment was buried in the cellar in the surrounding neighbourhood of a house, the Pioneer-Kaserne in Rosenheim, where it was later found by TICOM interrogators.

Functions of the KONA units

The purpose of the KONA was to supply intelligence from original sources to the intelligence sections of the Army Corps, Armies and Army Groups. A typical KONA consisted of one Regimental Evaluation Centre and of five or six intercept and intelligence companies. Close-Range Signal Intelligence platoons intercepted very low level traffic, evaluated what they could, kept the intelligence organisations of their assigned Army Corps informed of all intelligence derived and passed back to an evaluation platoon at company HQ all their results and presumably their intercepts.

Long-Range Signal Intelligence companies intercepted higher level traffic and did some evaluation, the results of which were given to the intelligence section of their assigned Army HQ, and passed back evaluation reports and intercepts to the regimental Signal Intelligence Evaluation Centre (NAAS). The Stationary Intercept Companies operated in an almost identical manner, with primary emphasis on enemy unidentified traffic. The NAAS evaluated the reports and intercepts from all companies of the regiment and passed their results to the intelligence section of Army Group.

Functions of the NAAS

Functions of the NAAS included evaluation and traffic analysis, cryptanalysis, dissemination of intelligence and direction of intercept cover. The NAAS passed its results to the Intelligence Officer of the Army Group to which the KONA was attached, and reported its findings to the Army High Command Signal Intelligence Agency (OKH/GdNA). The NAAS had a key position in the direction of intercept cover and controlled the intercept coverage of all the lower elements of the KONA, following the overall co-ordination exercised by the OKH/GdNA. Certain items were passed unprocessed through the KONA to the GdNA.

Functions of the Feste

The functions of the Stationary Intercept Companies (Feste) were designed to work at the next lower level to the NAAS, that of Army. They were pre-war Army intercept stations. The interception and study of unidentified traffic were the main functions of the Feste. A cryptanalytic section contributed to the interpretation of unknown traffic by the identification of keys, translated plain-text messages and did some solution. The Feste had a DF platoon which carried out the requests of the companies.

Functions of the FAK

The Long-Range Signal Intelligence Companies (FAK) were distinguished from the Feste in that mainly they were concerned to a much greater degree with identified traffic. In their interception of identified traffic, the coverage of the FAKs was directed – as was that of the Feste – by the cover control section of the NAAS. Plain-text messages were translated and traffic of known codes decoded by specialists assigned to the unit. A general section was devoted to card indexes and lists.

Functions of the NAK

The Close-Range Signal Intelligence Company (NAK) worked at Army Corps and Army level and its main responsibility was to pick up and work on low-level two-figure, three-figure and possibly some four-figure traffic. Each company was divided into four platoons: intercept, DF, evaluation and communications. Intercept coverage was directed by the NAAS. A normal programme of intercept called for about twenty receivers. The organisation of the DF platoon was that for one company there were about eight outstations, separated from each other by five to ten kilometres and parallel to the front at a distance of from one to several hundred kilometres. Each section had about five men.

Direction Finding

The NAAS evaluation section was fed by the DF sections from both the FAK and the NAK. Long-range DF sets were located 200-350km behind the front line and two to three DF sets constituted a DF group. The Close-Range sets were located with the NAK platoons. While, generally, Long-Range DF operations could fix a station within fifteen kilometres, Close-Range platoon DF operations could narrow the possibility to two or three kilometres.

Radio Finger-Printing

Radio Finger-Printing was used to identify particular radio stations and to register the incoming traffic in the form of an image on a cathode ray tube and analyse the image. The apparatus was attached to a normal intercept set and the individual characteristics of the transmitter could be recorded graphically by means of tracings, or in the form of photostats, in a card index.

Chapter 11

Army Cryptanalysis against Russia

Organisation of cryptanalytic effort against Russia

During the first Russo-Finnish war, the Germans were able to break a number of two, three and four-figure codes. In addition, a copy of the Russian five-figure code was obtained from the Finnish General Staff, and was used by the Russians in the first year of the war with Germany. The Intercept Control Station (HLS) was replaced in 1941 by two agencies – Inspectorate 7/VI, serving as a cryptanalytic unit in Berlin – and the Control Station of Signal Intelligence (LNA) in Zossen. The section for Russian cryptanalysis that had been part of HLS remained attached to In 7/VI during the first few months of its existence, while Russian evaluation was done at LNA.

However, it was accepted that cryptanalysis and evaluation should be done further forward, and late in 1941 the Russian section of In 7/VI was sent to Loetzen in East Prussia. This section formed the nucleus for a third central agency, the Intercept Control Station East (HLS Ost). From then until November 1944, German Army Signal Intelligence activities were sharply divided between non-Russian (In 7/VI) and Russian (HLS Ost and LNA). In October 1944, HLS Ost and LNA were amalgamated with In 7/VI Army High Command Signal Intelligence Agency (OKH/GdNA), the one final central agency of the war. The amalgamation was necessitated by the retreat of the German forces in the face of the Russian advances.

Review of Field Office organisation

While preparations were made for the attack on Russia, it was found that there was an acute shortage of cryptanalysts available for field work, and they were culled from the fixed intercept stations and trained by the new KONA. Five regiments were sent into the field as complete low level intercept and evaluation units attached to Army Groups, two went to the western front and KONAs 1, 2 and 3 were assigned to the eastern front, which were supplemented in 1942 by KONA 6, sent out to cover the German campaign in the Caucasus, which was attached directly to

HLS Ost. Low level cryptanalysis and evaluation was also done by KONA 8 and KONA Nord, which were made up from other eastern front signal intelligence regiments, and activated in late 1944 and early 1945. Cryptanalysis was done on all levels of field operations and the central offices almost interchangeably, from the lowest level to the highest – where it involved pure mathematics and the assistance of IBM machinery.

Cryptanalysis achievements against Russia

Two, three, four and five-figure codes were used by the Russian Army, Air Force and NKVD (secret police) and by some small independent special units. Two figure codes were not always in use but were constantly read. Much assistance was gained by Russian operator security breaches, but solving two-figure traffic was never really difficult. By the time of Stalingrad, practically every Army engaged in the battle had its own three-figure codes under various circumstances. Like the two-figure system, the three-figure system consisted of a code book and an enciphering table.

A good deal of plain-text was inserted in three-figure codes and was eighty percent readable, particularly Air Force ground-to-ground messages. From Spring 1943 to 1945, two and three-figure traffic was regularly decoded. In 1943 three-figure codes were superseded by three-figure Signal Codes, and there is no evidence that these were any more difficult to solve.

Some four-figure codes were captured in the Russo-Finnish and Russo-German wars, but all these systems were recovered by cryptanalysis before their capture and were made completely and currently readable. The breaking of the five-figure reciphered code was described by one German cryptanalyst as the most outstanding cryptanalytic achievement of In 7/VI. However, the TICOM report adds: 'Certainly the evidence from other prisoner-of-war interrogations pointed conclusively and without a doubt to an almost complete failure on the part of German cryptanalysts to make any real progress with the solution of the five-figure code.'

One interrogation revealed that the five-figure code was breakable if at least three messages had the same additive applied or the code had been captured. Further, all the newly appearing versions of the 'cipher-code' were captured, and always so soon that the originals were almost always in the hands of the cryptanalysts at the instant of their being put into use by the Russians. Another German cryptanalyst interrogated said that five-figure and five-letter messages were not touched at all, and were only used to identify units and only read if codebooks had been captured. The Russians introduced a new five-figure code on 1 April 1942, but the changeover was faulty, and it was possible to establish 2,000 groups of the new code within a week. The number of Russian ciphers of all sorts broken was about 3,000.

Russian cryptanalysis: successes and failures

The effect of the administration, both of the central office and the sub-divisions, was mostly to hinder and not to forward the work. Because the NAAS worked closely with Army Group commands, the NAAS and its technical direction tended to correspond more closely to the desires of the Army HQ rather than to their own central office. Moreover, the division of cryptanalysts between the central office and the NAAS resulted in an enormous amount of 'paper warfare' where the work of cryptanalysis and exploitation was carried on with almost complete duplication. Multiplication of effort also resulted from the erroneous ambition of administrators at individual stations due to 'competition'. The most serious interference with the actual work, however, both in the central offices and all its branches, was doubtless brought about by the purely military 'manipulation' of this set-up, involving treatment according to rank, not skill or competence, military exercises, field manoeuvres, etc.

The only major failure of the German Army vis-a-vis the Russian systems was the failure to solve and read currently the five-figure codes. TICOM comments that, from prisoner-of-war interrogations, it was apparent 'that the five-figure code was not read currently and that, even if the book had been captured, the encipherment by almost exclusively one-time pads rendered actual solution practically impossible.' POWs admitted that there was no trouble in reading two and three-figure traffic of all sorts, and only a relative difficulty with four-figure traffic. On NKVD codes, a great deal of information seems to have been gathered.

TICOM says that the amount of cryptanalysis achievement by GdNA and HLS Ost was 'impressive'. Finally, the importance of the apparently large amount of captured codebooks and tables cannot be overestimated. The German Army read 'a tremendous amount of material purely cryptanalytically' which, though only rarely of high level operational importance, produced a steady flow of tactical and strategic intelligence. One German cryptanalyst drew up a table of successes for 1944 as follows:

Type of Message	Intercepted	Dealth with	Percent	Remarks
2-figure	140	125	90	
3-figure	6,000	2,600	43	
4-figure	5,000	1,900	38	
Mixed	2,350	865	37	
Total	13,500	5,500	41	
Clear Text	6,000	6,000	100	
Practice	500	500	100s	
Grand Total	**20,000**	**12,000**		
Plus				
5-figure & NKVD-5 figure	8,000			Not studied at KONA 1
NKVD	2,000			Only partially studied at KONA 1
GRAND TOTAL	**30,000**			

The following Russian systems were said to have been worked on and solved:

- Operation systems carrying text concerning operations and traffic technique; PT-35, PT-39, PT-41: there was a large volume of messages in the PT systems which were superseded by 'small codes' in 1944;
- Signal Codes: used in the second half of the war and were 3 and 4-figure codes called CYB or 'front' codes. Partially solved, but rarely completely worked;
- Address Codes: used by any unit in the 'front' Commands. Interpretations were hard to make because of the Russian use of cover names. It was difficult to solve the encipherments;
- 'Conversion' systems: these included codes, code tables and extended substitutions. Among those specially mentioned were the Air Force General Code (1934-1937) carrying information on landings, take-offs, weather etc. The BAK-38, the last general Air Force system used to the end of 1939. The Army and Air Force 'General Commanders' Code OKK-5 to OKK-8 (1939-1941) and OTSKK-7 General Commanders' Code used in rear areas. All conversion systems were considered CYB or 'front' systems;

- Transpositions: pure transpositions were used in the Army and Air Force only for practice traffic;
- Number codes (called 'cipher-codes' by the Germans) were 5-figure codes for relaying radio reports of operational or tactical content, direction of troops on the highest networks. Specifically mentioned were 011-A (19,000 code values in 390 pages); 023-A, 045-A, 062-A, 091-A (23,000 code values in 340 pages), used until the capitulation. All these books were captured, but the encipherment of Blocknots (one-time pads) made solution practically impossible – there was almost complete security in these systems.

NKVD:

- Operational systems: used by individual units in 1939, when a general operational system (mono-alphabetic substitution – no description was given) was introduced;
- 'Conversion' systems: a 4-figure code was used in the Kasakhastan area. Three 4-figure codes were in use by 1939; three 4-figure codes were in use at the time of capitulation – ZERNO, NIVA, VIZA; a 5-figure railway code was also in use;
- Transposition systems: Not used by the NKVD with the exception of one 4-figure code (used in the Arctic Ocean district and on the Finnish-Russian border) which was enciphered by a transposition. It was read currently in part;
- Number series: From 1940 on, a 4-figure code was enciphered by various methods, monographic letter substitution, sliding number sequences and Blocknots. They were read currently to the end of the war.

Agents and Partisans systems: these were transpositions (single and double), grilles and keyword substitutions. Although TICOM says there was no statement of cryptanalytic achievement, apparently great difficulty was encountered in achievement, and not much success was achieved.

Chapter 12

Miscellaneous Army Cryptanalysis 1919-1945

Army cryptanalytic effort 1919-1933

Prior to 1938 there was no Army High Command and consequently no separate Army Signal Intelligence Service. The Defence Ministry handled the cryptanalytic work on foreign Army systems and any security work on German Army systems.

Army cryptanalytic effort 1933-1939

In 1933 the new Army High Command (OKH) set up its own central agency to handle foreign Army traffic. Known as the Intercept Control Station (Horchleitstelle) it was staffed by a few trained cryptanalysts drawn by the Army from the cipher section of the Defence Ministry, divided into geographical units. During this period, continuous and significant successes were obtained. In the crises of 1937 and 1938, the Germans read the systems used by the French on the wireless net which radiated from Paris to the static French formations within France. Known to the Germans as F-90 and F-110, they were based on a four-figure code. The complete Battle Order of the Belgian Army was known in 1939, partly by reading Belgian systems, which used a three-figure code. The Dutch Order of Battle was also known through reading their principally double transposition ciphers. Switzerland was only casually monitored, and there was very little success against British systems. The British Army Order of Battle was built up from DF information and evaluation of call signs or other radio procedure.

Army cryptanalytic effort 1939-1941

In the early years of the war the Intercept Control Station was unable to cope with the added traffic. British systems could not be solved and French systems required the help of OKW/Chi. The British section comprised six people and in 1940 moved to Bad Godesberg, where no success was achieved despite an abundance of material. No cryptanalytic success was recorded during this period. However, in 1940, the British section received a copy of the War Office Code, captured in Norway, and a second copy was obtained at Dunkirk. Success with this system was therefore possible as Britain continued to use it until 1943. France changed its F-90 and F-110 systems and the Army had to ask OKW/Chi for help, and the new system was read until the German offensive of spring 1940, when the French began to use systems in the forward echelons which the Germans were unable to solve. Army cryptanalysts concentrated on two machine systems, the C-36 and B-211, but were unsuccessful. In the winter of 1939, the dearth of field cryptanalysts became apparent to the German Army. When the Signal Intelligence Regiments (KONA) were preparing to move into the field, the Army had no trained cryptanalysts to send with them. In this period the Germans realised the inadequacy of their personnel and effort, and set about correcting them.

Army cryptanalytic effort 1941-1945

The experience of 1940 showed that considerable expansion in Army cryptanalytic effort was desirable, and in Spring 1941 a new Army cryptanalytic and evaluation agency to replace the old Intercept Control Station was set up – Group VI Inspectorate of 7 (Inspektion 7 Gruppe VI or In 7/VI). A large number of mathematicians and linguists were recruited and the number of countries covered increased greatly. Western and South-Western cryptanalysis was handled by 7/VI British section, whose main success was with the captured War Office Code, including reading North African traffic encoded with this system in Spring 1941. A considerable volume of traffic was read with this system during the Cyrenaica offensive of the Eighth Army under General Wavell. The War Office Code with an enciphering table was almost exclusively used during the first siege of Tobruk and was read by the Germans. As a result of this success a special detachment of eight cryptanalysts was sent to KONA 4 in Athens to short circuit information being sent back to Berlin, but difficulties at this time were encountered with the War Office Code which prevented its solution for eight or nine months. Then, in 1942, the Signal Intelligence Company 621 was captured in North Africa. Captured information revealed to the British that their code was being read.

From 1942 to the end of the war, the only success against Britain was low-level traffic, particularly Slidex, which was used by the British, American and Canadian Armies in front line units and Air support networks. The Germans called Slidex the 'Englische Code' or 'EC' followed by a number to denote variations of the basic system. EC30/3, for example, was intended to be used specifically for D-Day and thereafter, but had been used by Air liaison links in the UK during May 1944, and had already been constructed at the time of the invasion. This enabled the Germans to reconstruct the Allied Order of Battle at Corps level. The system was currently and easily solved, and was aided by captured tables, enabling the system to be solved so quickly that it could be handled like plain text. Slidex was used by the Americans after D-Day and by US Military Police units, enabling the deciphering of Army units which passed their control points. Slidex was also useful for identifying bombing and artillery targets. The Slidex messages were being solved in one to three hours if the basic cards were to hand, five to six hours if they were not and sixty-five percent of the work was said to have been done with the cards available. Another British system, Maplay, was worked on but was founder harder to break than Slidex. Codex was solved largely with the help of a captured specimen which had been in German hands since the invasion of Leros, part of the Dodecanese Islands, in November 1943. A 'Tiger' code – so-named from its use during the 'Tiger' pre-invasion exercises in England) was solved after six months, and made possible by the transmission of a long report in a British paper giving the names of units, officers etc. Another British system – the '999' – used during the pre-invasion period, was solved, but it was never used operationally.

The outstanding failure of In 7/VI British section, was not being able to solve the 'big machine' – Typex. A senior cryptanalyst, Mettig, told TICOM that Typex was read in North Africa in 1942 until the autumn, after which they had no more success. TICOM states: 'This fact, coupled with some information from Ultra sources to the effect that FAK 621 in North Africa had been reading Typex at the time of its capture in North Africa in July and November 1942, brought about a thorough investigation of this subject by the interrogators.' Briefly, in June 1943, a German prisoner claimed that he had worked on British machine methods from 1937 to 1940 and that messages which could not be decoded by FAK 621 in North Africa were sent to In 7/VI in Berlin. Two other FAK 621 prisoners stated that all high grade traffic was handled by a Warrant Officer Wagner who had at his disposal one or more Typex machines captured at Tobruk. Certain documents were used to solve settings, either captured British cipher documents or machine settings compiled by In 7/VI from three or four years of traffic. However, this evidence was contradicted by high-level German cryptanalysts after the war. Much effort was expended on Typex from 1940 and in 1941 some mathematical studies were made.

In January 1942 one study concluded that it was similar to Enigma, according to single frequency counts based on 10,000 cipher letters, and certain relationships between two message settings frequently existed. Some documentation from a British security officer pointed out frequent breaches in the strict regulation that Typex rotors should be turned at random after a message was enciphered. There seems to have been no knowledge of how many rotors Typex had – one estimate was twenty-five. The whole idea was apparently abandoned in 1943.

KONA 4 solved traffic from the Transjordan Frontier Force which gave valuable information about British troop movements in the Middle East. Even when this code was changed in July 1942, solution proceeded regularly after a few hours' work.

Work on US traffic 1941-1944

The US section of 7/VI was set up after America entered the war in December 1941, and although there were initial problems, order was established by reading call signs and sorting of discriminants. The section's first major success was in summer 1942 with the solving of the M-94, which was succeeded in 1943 by the M-209, solved by the Germans in autumn 1943, and solved with some success throughout the remainder of the war. Solution was aided by the fact that the US government had bought the Hagelin machine which had been offered to the Germans! The Germans knew of a 'big American machine' but it was never solved and In 7/VI had no idea of its construction.

However, the Germans were successful with US codes. A code of no strategic value – a US Army administrative code – was captured in 1939 and copies distributed to all field cryptanalytic units. Simple codes used by US Army units in Iceland and the Caribbean were also broken, as was the Air Transport Code used for air cargo and passenger transport circuits to Africa and South America. In 7/VI was successful on US low-grade ciphers and medium ciphers such as M-94 and M-209.

Work on French traffic 1941-1944

French traffic during this period was of two types – Vichy French and Free French. The former traffic was under the direct control of the French Armistice Commission at Wiesbaden and was monitored by 7/VI French section. By agreement with the Vichy government, the French were to inform the Germans of their code and cipher procedures, but watch was kept on their traffic. Work on Free French traffic from Syria and North, West and Equatorial Africa, was carried on by 7/VI and KONA 4 at Athens, where the traffic was intercepted.

To these must be added the de Gaulle systems, two of which were Control Bedouin and Service Politique. French systems used in Syria were read and a complete picture obtained of the French armed forces. Several Free French systems from North Africa were also read. French section of 7/VI had solved the C-36 and B-211 in 1940 and de Gaullist troops in North Africa and Corsica began to use the C-36 machine and it was easily solved by 7/VI in 1943. French section was greatly aided by fundamental weaknesses in French cryptography. These were:

- The extraordinary conservatism regarding construction of their code systems or reciphering methods;
- The habitual use of stereotyped message beginnings and endings which facilitates breaking into the system;
- The idiosyncrasy of communicating cipher matters or key changes by radio.

Work on Swiss, Spanish, Portuguese and Brazilian traffic

The volume of this traffic was always extremely small and unimportant. The Germans had solved the Swiss (or Commercial) Enigma, but easy solution was precluded because the Swiss did their own Enigma wheel wiring and changed these frequently. Spanish military transpositions and a Spanish digit system with variants were read, and of seven known Brazilian systems, five of which were read.

Work on Italian traffic 1941-1944

Security of Italian systems was a constant concern to the Germans, who feared that Germany Army troop movements to North Africa were being betrayed by Italian insecurity. By late 1942, the general impression among the Germans was that the Italians were incapable of improving their own systems, even with German monitoring, and the 7/VI Italian section was disbanded in 1942 on Hitler's orders, but was resumed when the Italians changed sides, but was again disbanded in November 1943. However, from July to November 1943, the section worked on two codes – the Ellade and Piave – which were decoded with the help of an enciphering table captured by the Germans in Athens under dramatic circumstances. Apparently, when told of the Italian armistice, some German officers went to the Italian HQ and collected material from the code office, but when the Italians became threatening, they withdrew. Traffic was read on the Piave code and the Ellade code was partly reconstructed.

Work on Swedish traffic 1941-1944

Work on Swedish Army traffic in this period was handled by a special detachment of Feste 9 called Out-Station Halden (Aussenstelle Halden) with a number of successes. The Germans were able to build up a complete tactical picture of the Swedish Army during the late years of the war.

Work on South-East European traffic 1941-1944

This traffic was handled at 7/VI by the Balkan Section and in the field by KONA 4 and involved Greece, Hungary, Rumania, Yugoslavia, Albania, Turkey and Bulgaria as follows:

Greece: The first Greek messages broken were Air Force, but Greek Army and Navy systems were not broken until codes were captured which were used by the Greeks during the attack on Crete. Greek partisan traffic was also read and gave an almost complete picture of the organisation and composition of the Greek People's Army of Liberation (ELAS) and the National Liberty Front (EAM). The systems provided the Germans with many planned military and political actions, acts of sabotage, ambushes, dynamiting etc. It also provided the the location of Allied airfields in the Greek mountains, the position, strength and activity of the Allied military missions and various British commando troops, about Greek internal and inter-allied crises and struggles, about the British tactics for the occupation of Greece, etc.

Hungary: The Hungarians used the commercial Enigma, whose rotors were made by Konski and Krueger, but Hungarians connected with the firm took the rotors at night and changed the wirings enough to make the firm's records incorrect. No effort was made to recover the wirings, so evidently the Germans did not consider the traffic worth causing embarrassment to the Hungarians. However, during spring and summer 1941, the radio signals of the Hungarian Railway Administration were monitored and its Raster code was read. In 1943, some members of Feste 6 were sent to Hungary but such was the tenseness between the Hungarians and Germany that they had to wear civilian clothes.

Rumania: Little is known of the work of the Balkan section on

Rumanian traffic, although a transposition system was decoded with comparative east.

Yugoslavia: Various types of traffic were monitored including the friendly Croatian Regular Army (Domobrani) and its secret police (Ustashi), military units of the German puppet government installed in 1941, anti-German Chetniks under General Mihailovitch, Yugoslav partisans under Marshal Tito and the Croatian Resistance Movement led by Dr Matchek. The pro-Nazi Chetniks used the commercial K-model Enigma, easily readable, and the Germans read almost all the traffic from the beginning. The Mihailovitch traffic was entirely double transposition with fixed key length and key word and was regularly, if slowly, solved, taking one to three days to break a message. The Tito systems were far more varied, mostly of Russian origin, and several were broken. Croatian Resistance Movement traffic was also broken. In general, work on Yugoslav systems was successful, with the Tito and Mihailovitch systems the most important.

Turkey: Turkish Army codes were broken as well as the special code of the President of Turkey when sailing on the State yacht Savarona. Turkish diplomatic traffic was read continually and was used by military attachés for their reports from Russia, Bulgaria and Italy, and proved a very valuable source of information about Russia. Despite warnings from Britain that the traffic was being read, Turkey failed to change the system.

Bulgaria: Very little work was done on this traffic although messages of the Bulgarian military attachés were read.

Agents' traffic 1941-1944

In 1942 a special section for the traffic of agents was set up with In 7/VI. Prior to this the activities of this section consisted of radio security inside Germany and monitoring of illegal transmissions was conducted by Section III of the Armed Forces Communication Branch (Amtsgruppe Wehrmacht Nachrichten Verbindungen, Funkwesen Gruppe III, abbreviated to AgWNV/Fu III or Fu III). It was known as Vauck's section after its head and consisted of twenty people in the main section, ten at outposts in Paris and Brussels and other cities and eight lent to the Polish section of OKW/Chi. The section's activities were as follows:

Czech agents: Work was conducted on the Czech Resistance Movement and the breaking of two links in 1941-1943 running to England made possible the arrest of British agents in Czechoslovakia. The greatest success was the interception of wireless communications of the Czech Resistance Movement in London. In September 1942 the Czechs planned to move to a new system but foolishly named in the old system the book to be used for enciphering in the new system. Messages concerned reports on the political situation and activities of the resistance which was so important that for a long time the W/T traffic was allowed to continue unhindered.

Yugoslav agents: Described above.

Agents in southern France and Spain: Traffic emanated largely from the US, Britain and Spanish Republican agents who were in radio contact with stations in Spain. A camouflaged branch station was set up in Madrid and results of the traffic were very good.

Russian agents: There were three important Russian agent networks – Rote 3 (Red 3), the Schulze-Boysen net operating in Berlin in 1942 and two links running from Brussels, but the last named traffic was not believed to have been solved. The Rote 3 traffic was broken and in the autumn of 1944, the exact sending position of the net was found to be in Switzerland. The Swiss forestalled a German planned attack on the net, and the station was subsequently evacuated and destroyed. The home of Dr Schulze-Boysen was the centre of a large-scale communist network. One of the Vauck section, called Haymann, actually frequented the house, and warned Mrs Schulze-Boysen. He and Dr Lenz, another Vauck section member, were arrested. Haymann was sentenced to death and Dr Lenz was sent to Paris, as all he had done was mention the name Schulze-Boysen to Haymann. The Gestapo arrested around eighty people of whom seventy were condemned to death. The case was kept secret because some of the accused were employed in various war agencies and were betraying secrets to the Russians.

Polish Resistance Movement: The most notable results of the Agents' section was the solution of this system, particularly during the Polish uprising in Warsaw in 1944. The disposition of Polish troops as well as friction between them and the Russians, was established. Because of the traffic's importance, eight members of the Vauck section were transferred to the OKW/Chi Polish section. All wireless traffic between the Polish government in exile and its organisations in Poland were solved. Four systems were broken and most of them were simple two-figure substitutions used without an indicator, with some variations in development and the use of basic keys or key phrases.

Mathematical Research 1941-1944

A Mathematical Research Section had three tasks: handling research on foreign systems and dealing with the security of both German Army hand and machine systems. It apparently did excellent work in solving more simple machine systems such as the Russian K-37, the Converter M-209, the French B-211, the de Gaulle traffic enciphered on the French C-36 and the solution in 1944 of the Swedish Hagelin BC-38. The C-36 had also been previously solved by OKW/Chi in 1940. Partial success was also achieved on Russian four and five-figure enciphered codes.

Use of IBM in cryptanalysis 1941-1944

The IBM section of In 7/VI was derived from the IBM section set up in 1939-1940 by the German Security Agency (7/IV). It was mainly of German make although some captured French IBM machines were included. In 1943 the unit consisted of thirty or forty women key punchers and twenty to thirty soldier mechanics. There is no exact information of the number or types of machine used, but it is believed that in 1944 there were thirty key punchers and two tabulators. The special contribution of In 7/VI to IBM work was adapting machines to various tasks by special wirings. In 1943, a special workshop for the development of improved wirings was set up with the IBM firm Lichterfeld, and the major success was on Russian five-figure traffic. Early in the Russian campaign, it was fairly easy to establish depths in these messages without the use of IBM, but by 1943 IBM was indispensable for locating depths.

No tasks were undertaken by the section which could have been done by one hundred people. Lack of IBM machinery spurred the analysts at OKW/Chi to develop new and better types of analytic devices while 7/VI remained content with inferior IBM adaptations. An Army cryptanalyst stated that Enigma could probably be solved by a large enough array of IBM machinery 'but it never occurred to him, evidently, that such would be contemplated by the enemy'. Towards the end, the In 7/VI machines were outworn, outmoded and irreplaceable. The factories were bombed out and, as the machines wore out, their work became inaccurate, and In some work by machine was abandoned.

Army cryptanalytic effort in 1945

With the establishment of the GdNA in late 1944, all operational cryptanalysis was carried on by sections 2, 3 and 4 of Group IV. Section 2 dealt with Western Europe and probably Hungary, Rumania and Italy. There were three sub-sections: 2a – Britain, the US and Sweden; 2b - France and 2c, the Balkans. Section 3 had four sub-sections: 3a – NKVD; 3b – Russian Army; 3c – Russian Partisan traffic and 3d – Russian systems general research. From February 1945 until the end of the war, GdNA Group IV was constantly moving, seeking refuge in the south from the Allies.

Chapter 13

Air Force Sigint

The Service in General

Introduction

The outstanding achievement of the German Air Force Signal Intelligence Service from its beginning in 1937 was its development of signal intelligence without cryptanalysis. The exploitation of every radio manifestation, including radar and beacon monitoring, evaluation of tuning transmissions and chatter, highly efficient direction finding, radio-telephone monitoring and traffic analysis, provided valuable strategic and tactical intelligence. The Service expanded from one officer and twenty civilians in 1937 to 13,000 personnel in 1945, of which 6,600 were in the West, 4,000 in the East and 2,400 in the South.

Objectives

Strategic evaluation after the fall of France gave a coherent picture of RAF Order of Battle and long-range intentions. As Allied raids intensified in 1943, tactical evaluation again became important to provide early warnings of planned Allied raids, for which an intricate system of reporting centres and a central warning unit were established in 1944.

Brief outline of achievements

Great Britain: RAF systems produced the greatest amount of intelligence on air-ground circuits. Syko, Rekoh and Slidex and the Bomber Code were currently solved. Although the RAF four-figure code was changed in November 1942, rendering it more difficult, it was read up to that time. Both on the strategic and tactical level, there were notable results on RAF traffic. In the West, it was possible to reconstruct accurately the Order of Battle, deployment, strength, equipment and intentions of the RAF, and through it, the ground organisation. In order of battle, the following RAF units were continually followed throughout the war:

- Bomber Groups: Nos. 1, 3, 4, 5, 6, 8, 91, 92, 93
- Fighter Groups: Nos. 9, 10, 11, 12, 13, 82, 100
- Coastal Command Reconnaissance Groups: 15, 16, 17, 18, 19

- 2nd Tactical Air Force
- RAF Transport Command

Tactically, the monitoring of RAF VHF and centimetre radar transmission and navigational aids permitted the Luftwaffe Signal Intelligence Service to achieve the following:

- Give accurate, long and short interval, early warnings of both daylight and night raids of heavy bomber formations;
- By continuously tracking heavy bomber formations, to provide to fighter defence a lucid picture of the air situation from take-off to landing of enemy formations; and
- To interpret the air situation picture so as to predict the RAF strength in formation, depth of penetration, targets and deceptive tactics.

In the Mediterranean it was possible to chart RAF operations throughout the war, and in the first years of the war it was possible to break 'the most frequently used cryptographic systems ... to read the bulk of the messages intercepted'. The extensive use of radio communications permitted a minutely accurate reconstruction of RAF Order of Battle, strength, equipment and intentions, down to squadron level. The following units were monitored:

- 414th and 416th Night Fighter Squadrons;
- South African Air Force 8th Fighter Group;
- Various groups of the RAF Desert Air Force (MASAF);
- Various elements of 90th Mediterranean Allied Photo Reconnaissance Wing;
- RAF Mediterranean Allied Coastal Air Force (MACAF);
- Various components of RAF Middle East, the RAF Balkan Air Force and RAF Air HQ Greece, Eastern Mediterranean and Air Transport Command.

Russia: Throughout the war eighty-five per cent of Russian Morse ground-to-ground traffic of the Soviet Air Armies, Corps and Divisions and supporting ground organisations was deciphered. Ground-to-ground radio traffic, such as fighter control, consisting of simple word encodements was continuously solved. Air-ground traffic of Soviet long-range bomber formations, although only partially deciphered, permitted warning of air raids in time to give adequate warning. The Air Sigint was able to provide an accurate and current listing of the Soviet Air Order of Battle on the three operational fronts, and the deployment of

Russian ground forces to which their Air Forces served as an adjunct. This provided timely warning of air raids, route-tracking of bomber formations and indicated long-range intentions of both Soviet ground and air forces as well as information on supply and economic conditions. Although until Stalingrad, Sigint warnings had not been heeded, when the Sigint unit on the Southern Front correctly advised that the Russians had assembled five air armies in that sector, Sigint was held to be the main source of intelligence.

United States: The chief success against the US was made possible by alert traffic analysis. Although air-ground systems, used jointly by Britain and the US, were read in many cases, the effectiveness of cryptanalysis was definitely limited. For example, whatever success was achieved with M-209 was usually too late for exploitation. Traffic analysis provided a comprehensive and continuous picture of the battle order and deployment of the US Air Force in Britain, later on the Continent and the Mediterranean, and numerous predictions were made of long-range Air Force intentions. Tactically, traffic analysis of all radio manifestations, including everything from radio signals to beacons, gave immediate and timely warning of US air raids. In the West, the Germans reconstructed the organisation and strength of the 8th USAF, and its bomber and fighter commands, the 9th Air Force and the Allied Expeditionary Air Force, comprising the US 9th Air Force, the 1st US Tactical Air Force and the 2nd RAF Tactical Air Force. The US 1st Tactical Air Force Allied Air Transport units and other Air units were also successfully monitored. Major long-range operations, such as the invasion and breakthrough at Avranches were – with some degree of success – correctly forecast. Tactical monitoring of US Air support parties yielded much more information about Allied Order of Battle than did the regular Army networks, since the Air support parties acted in conjunction with specific ground units.

In the Mediterranean and Middle East, Air Signals Regiment 352 reconstructed – with minute accuracy – the 9th Tactical Air Command, the 57th Medium Bomber Wing, the 5th, 47th, 49th, 55th and 304th Heavy Bomber Wings, the 15th Fighter Command and the Mediterranean Air Transport Service.

The accurate reconstruction of Allied Order of Battle attests to the effectiveness of the German analysts. In general, American assessments of German Air Sigint was that it was a 'most scientific, professional and able organisation, performing a valuable, meticulously complete and reliable service for the enemy'. Operational strengths were, in the main, correctly estimated, and the precision with which unit movements were followed is said to have been 'truly impressive'. US intelligence evaluations of Sigint operations against the US 9th Air Force came as an 'uncomfortable surprise'. However, the Luftwaffe Sigint information was not exploited by operational units, which were sluggish in acting upon the intelligence provided. According to one interrogated Luftwaffe Sigint operative, 'it was a course of bitter chagrin' that the German Command lacked the resources to translate its realistic intelligence into offensive action. This Sigint success was achieved despite, rather than because of the organisation's administration. Interminable disputes prevented the smooth functioning of the service. These disputes, when settled at all, were resolved by compromise and appeasement.

Development of Luftwaffe Sigint

January 1937-September 1939

On 1 January 1937, a Signal Intelligence Agency was established by the Luftwaffe. Prior to this, all intercept and evaluation of foreign Air Force traffic had been conducted by the Army. Fixed intercept stations were established in 1937 and given the cover name of 'Weather Radio Receiving Stations'. They were supplemented by DF stations called 'Weather Research Stations'. In addition, mobile intercept platoons were established to operate in the field. Field evaluation centres of company strength were later established under the cover name of 'Weather Control Stations'. In 1939, after several experiments at reorganisation, the fixed and mobile Sigint units were combined into signal intelligence battalions, removed from Chi-Stelle administrative control, and attached to local Air Force signals regiments. Each was composed of an evaluation unit, two mobile intercept companies and three fixed intercept stations. So, by September 1939, the Luftwaffe had a 'quite accurate picture of the Air armament, deployment and strength of foreign Air Forces, as well as their organisation and expansion'.

September 1939-November 1944

Germany's early lightning successes in the war were a 'great handicap for future development' as a British Air Ministry report put it, 'for they rendered almost superfluous the help which it could have given if duly appreciated and developed. All that seemed necessary was to listen to enemy R/T traffic while the German armies and the German Air Force were hammering their way forward ... '. But in December 1939, Luftwaffe Sigint enabled German fighters to destroy a large Wellington formation over northern Germany by supplying Fighter Command with the location, height, speed and size of the raiding force. 'The result of this signal intelligence success was the realisation that signal intelligence had an important place in Germany's air raid defence.' In 1940 and 1941 there was a great expansion of Air Sigint, and as Allied air raids became more frequent in 1942 and `1943, the tactical air raid warning aspect of Sigint was exploited.

The development of airborne and navigational radar by the Allies made necessary the creation of both a radar observation and a radar jamming service. From the outbreak of war until the middle of 1944, operations of both the central and field units were sufficiently developed to provide a continuous flow of information to the Luftwaffe High Command. However, the many channels of tactical and operational command to which these units were subject, and the growth of their work, compelled a reorganisation in the last stages of the war, and constituted the most coherent form of the Luftwaffe Sigint service, and is described below.

Staff level reorganisation in November 1944

In spring 1944, the first of these reorganisations took place and all Sigint units, including the Chi-Stelle which had been under the Air Ministry, were placed under the tactical command of the Chief Signal Officer, 3rd Division, in order to unify operations under a central command, but led to difficulties in guidance and supply. In autumn 1944, after an abortive order by Goering to unify all Air Sigint units, a new comprehensive organisation was finally created. It unified all home and field units into independent Air Signals regiments and battalions with numbers ranging from 350 to 359. This provided for centralised control in the Chief Signal Officer.

The Chi-Stelle

The Chi-Stelle – the Sigint Agency of the C-in-C Luftwaffe (Chi-Stelle/OBdL) – was the highest authority of the Luftwaffe Sigint service. From its origin in 1937 until 1940 it was located in Berlin, but right after the start of the Polish campaign it moved to the Marstall, the riding academy of Frederick the Great in Potsdam-Wildpark, where it remained until just before the war ended.

Section A: Staffing, Allocation and Employment: This section was divided into operational planning, personnel, war diary, procurement and research.

Section B: Evaluation West: This section made a significant Sigint contribution. Pre-war it had provided a comprehensive picture of RAF organisation, location, strength, aircraft types, personnel and supply. One of its most important functions was the control of listening activities.

Section C: Evaluation South: This section has been described as the least capable of all the Allied units or activities. Another two especially successful sections handled press reports and POW intelligence, the other point-to-point networks. There were also sub-sections handling traffic in Turkey, Sweden and Free France.

Section D: Evaluation East: In peacetime this section evaluated traffic intercepted from Russia, Czechoslovakia, Poland and the Balkans, but after occupying eastern Europe, concentrated on Russian messages. The majority of enciphered messages could be read, which placed Sigint work on this Front in a quite different aspect. Moreover, while in the West there was a new and revolutionary radio or radar technique every month, in the East there were relatively few technical innovations.

Section E: Cryptanalysis: This section was formed within Chi-Stelle after the Luftwaffe Sigint service was formed in 1938. At the outbreak of war there were only fifteen to eighteen cryptanalysts. Towards the end of 1942 it reached its peak strength of about 400 men. Although fit men were released for active service, even in January 1945 it is said to have broken 35,000 messages in the West and 15,000 in the East.

Field Units – Organisation and Operation

Operations in the West

The final Luftwaffe Sigint unit in the West – Air Signal Regiment 351 – was the result of four years of continuous operation against Britain and, eventually, the Western Allies. Intercept missions were assigned by Section B of the Signal Intelligence Agency, and also directed search cover, including the employment of the search receivers and the identification of new traffic. Evaluation was performed at all levels. As Germany's position deteriorated, the communications systems were enlarged to accommodate the ever-increasing flow of intelligence. The objectives of strategic evaluation were to establish the Order of Battle of the opposing Air Forces, to determine the Order of Battle and intentions of the ground forces as revealed through Air Force communications, and to predict long-range intentions of the opposing Air Forces. Success was most remarkable in establishing the Allied Order of Battle, providing a continuous and highly accurate picture of the Allied Air Forces in Britain, the Mediterranean, the Near East, and, later, the Continent. 'Frequently, the reconstruction was precise to the most minute detail, and call signs, frequencies and networks were in the vast majority of cases absolutely accurate.' The reconstructed Order of Battle for the RAF and USAAF show the 'meticulously careful work of the traffic analysts'. Establishing ground forces Order of Battle was more difficult, but after the invasion, when the Air Force was acting in direct support of ground operations, much information was disclosed of value to the Germans. Indications of coming events were frequently derived from strategic evaluation. The extent to which the Luftwaffe Sigint organisation was able to forecast the Dieppe raid and the invasion etc., has already been noted.

Tactical evaluation was far more important than strategic. The primary purpose of tactical evaluation was to provide a prompt and efficient warning of Allied air raids, and demanded alert interception of all possible signal manifestations – signals, radar, beacons, noises and silences etc., - prompt and reliable evaluation, and immediate dissemination of the intelligence derived to the operational units and the defence organisations concerned, and achieved outstanding success. 'If Germany was not able to counteract the attacks it was not the fault of signal intelligence which gave the warnings. So efficient was the operation that it won the attention of the very highest commands, and Goering was proud of the listening service.' Realisation that Air Force Sigint could produce tactical intelligence came as a result of a successful prediction of a Wellington raid in December 1939. Anti-aircraft units had been relying on ground observer service of the old type, visual and acoustic. It supplemented that service with its own troop units of ground observers, and later with its own radar.

As a unified command for route-tracking purposes became necessary, a new office was created – Chief of the Air Raid Warning Service for Germany (FAF), who was put under Chi-Stelle for operational purposes. Among his tasks was the tracking of Allied strategic Air Forces. The

Central Reporting Centre for Germany was known as the Central Air Raid Warning Unit (ZAF), and evaluation of the ZAF was primarily the tracking of Allied aircraft. A command post for the jamming of all Allied transmitters was located at ZAF, and this arrangement avoided the jamming of Allied transmitters that were currently producing intelligence.

Operations in the East

The activation of LN Regiment 353, the final Sigint unit in the East, was the last step in the evolution that began in 1936, when a fixed radio intercept station was erected at Glindow, near Berlin. In 1937-1938, five more stations were erected at Breslau, Pilsnitz, Bromberg, Kobbelbude and Hirschstetten, near Vienna, and were responsible for preliminary analysis and evaluation of Russian Air Force traffic, the final evaluation being done by the Chi-Stelle. There was a reorganisation in 1938, which saw the formation of collecting and evaluating agencies known as Wetter-Leitstel or W-Leit, which issued interim reports to the local Air Forces to expedite the flow of material to the Chi-Stelle. In 1939, the W-Leit and the fixed and mobile radio intercept companies were formed administratively into battalions. The years 1940-1942 saw modifications in the organisation of Sigint units concerned with Russian traffic. Organisation remained fairly stable during 1943, but in 1944 an important change took place principally involving LN Regiment 353 to encompass all Sigint activity on the Eastern Front.

Operations within battalions

The operations of LN 353 in the East differed from that of its sister units in the West, and reflected Russian weaknesses, as their cryptographic and radio development was behind that of Britain and the US. The Western Front was the sphere of the traffic analyst, whereas that of the Eastern units emphasised the cryptanalysis of Soviet ciphers. The heart of the battalion was the evaluation company and its seven sections. The importance of the cryptanalysis section is illustrated by the number of persons it contained – twice as many people worked in the cryptanalytic section as in the other combined six sections of the evaluation company, and roughly eighty-five percent of Russian traffic was readable. Although a Luftwaffe unit, LN Regiment 353 was often of tremendous help to the Army, and was a highly successful Sigint organisation. Russian backwardness in communications techniques was a significant factor in this success. Sigint had much influence over the way the Luftwaffe was used. Because of fuel scarcity, flying commands would not send up planes until intelligence gave them a target. The Russian long-range bomber force was independent of the Air Armies and was controlled from Moscow. The long-range bomber evaluation section was alerted with advance warning of bombing operations, and Soviet bombers were usually first heard on take-off. Plentiful R/T and Morse air-ground traffic was plentiful, and allowed DF route tracking, and monitoring of ground control stations also helped locate the bombers. With operations against the Russian Air Armies, out-stations were co-located with fighter and reconnaissance squadrons and groups, often in the same building as the aircraft reporting centre of the HQ of the formation they were serving.

The chief contribution of LN Regiment 353 to Eastern Front tactical operations was the constant supply of intelligence that made possible the economic and efficient use of German aircraft. Once airborne, the ground control kept them constantly informed of the intentions and dispositions of Russian fighters and bombers.

Operations in the South

1938 – August 1943

The last Sigint unit operating in the southern sector – LN Regiment 352 – began in 1938 as a fixed station, W Leit 13, in Oberhaching, and monitored French and British traffic from Africa. In the Mediterranean, LN Regiment 40 was at Athens, and a Sigint platoon from W-13 was at Palermo, with a fixed station, W-Leit 14, at Vougliamend, near Athens. The 9th Company at Athens was formed into one battalion and the W-Leit 2 and its subordinates into another. They reserved the right of final evaluation and their material came mainly from subordinate units that favoured the interception of air-ground traffic that had been successful in their cryptanalysis of point-to-point traffic, especially the RAF four-figure code. During 1943, many radar and VHF intercept out-stations were erected and thoroughly monitored the Allied units operating against the German supply line from Sicily to the Afrika Korps holed up in Tunisia. The RAF four-figure code, which had been read continuously since March 1940, became unreadable, entailing the shift in operational emphasis of concentrating more on traffic analysis, route tracking, R/T and radar evaluation.

August 1943-October 1944

Three days before the Sicily landings, W-Leit 2 was flown from Taormina to Frascati, near Rome, the rest of the unit following close behind. The unit was at Frascati when Italy surrendered, catching it unawares. Just before it moved to Padua, it was so badly mauled in a raid by 170 B-24s that for a time the German Command could learn of the ground situation in Italy only through Allied air support messages, intercepted in southern France. After two months of moving and inactivity, W-Leit 2 was back in action, mainly as a tactical warning service. W-Leit South-East's mission was to cover frequencies heard in the Adriatic in general and the route-tracking of heavy bombers heading into the Balkans. Owing to military reversals, the Sigint unit moved from Athens to Salonika, and in January 1944 to near Belgrade, and when the Russians broke through, moved to Premstaetten.

October 1944-May 1945

After the retreat a new Sigint unit, LN Regiment 352, was formed, combining W-Leit 2 and W-Leit South-East 2. The receivers on hand and task assignments within LN Regiment 352 illustrate its deployment against the Allies in the South, as shown below:

Allied Air support units	65 receivers
Allied radar networks	30 receivers
Command networks : Eastern Mediterranean and Balkans; transport and supply traffic	50 receivers
15th USAAF, 205 Group RAF	25 receivers
VHF air-ground	35 receivers
HF/DF sets	23 DFs
Radar in 15 out-stations	100 receivers

On evaluation within LN Regiment 352, in the early days the emphasis was on cryptanalysis and reconstruction of Allied Order of Battle, but as Allied ciphers became more difficult and Germany went on the defensive, tactical, short-time warnings became the main Sigint commitment. The Germans in the South had more success against the 15th USAAF than the RAF 205 Group, as the latter's use of W/T and R/T and radiating services was much more careful. Operations against the 15th USAAF can be summarised as follows: pre-warning of bomber flights was given by the tuning traffic of air-ground Morse. During the flight to target, bombers sent short messages on a half-hour schedule that could be tracked by DF. Interception of air-ground R/T traffic provided information on flying units involved and their approximate strength during take-off. VHF air-air R/T provided valuable information on fighters accompanying bombers and continuous DF was possible. On the IFF (Identify Friend or Foe) device, the Americans did not shut off their IFF over German territory, so the Germans used a Freya-D radar unit to make the device radiate and measurements and tracking were possible up to 280 miles. On the meteorological observation planes, their cipher systems could be read and their transmissions tracked by DF. The interception of this traffic gave many advance warnings of US bomber incursions. The Sigint units in the South reconstructed the complete Allied Order of Battle and kept it up to date. On the tactical side, the Sigint did a superb job of keeping the tactical units and civilian defence agencies informed of Allied bomber attacks, so that surprises out of the South 'rarely occurred'.

Operations in the North

1940-1943

In May 1940, soon after the invasion of Norway, a group of Sigint personnel were sent from Husum in Germany to Oslo to set up the nucleus of Sigint in the North, W-Leit 5. Its commitments were all Morse and R/T circuits of RAF Coastal Command operating against the West coast of Norway and all North Sea traffic. The first intercept and DF unit (W-Stelle 25) was set up at Trondheim-Skatval and covered mainly the Morse and R/T of 18 Group, Coastal Command, moving to Stavanger at the end of August. By the end of 1942, an Air Signals Regiment had been formed to include W-Leit 5 and covered 15 and 18 Group, Coastal Command and the high frequency R/T of fighters in northern Britain. Beacons and meteorological traffic were intercepted and Coastal Command Syko was read at Husum.

However, when RAF fighter units converted from HF to VHF, a very fruitful source dried up until they could be equipped with proper receivers, but it developed that they never were so supplied. An important development in 1942 was the organisation of DF Base Atlantic, a series of DF stations at Bodø, Orlandat, Noerland, Husum and Brest. The main function was to DF aircraft of 15 Coastal Command on convoy escort and other units on anti-submarine patrol. In Autumn 1942, intercept coverage was expanded to include all Morse and R/T in the North Sea, the Iceland bases and North Sea convoys, but operations in general were hampered by bad atmosphere. The North listening service remained fairly stable throughout 1943 and excellent results were gained from DF Base Atlantic, and coverage was extended to include the traffic of courier planes operating between Sweden and England.

1944-1945

There was a general reorganisation of the entire Luftwaffe Sigint service in 1944. DF Base Atlantic lost its left wing when Brest fell to the Allies, and the VHF experiments dating from 1941 were finally dropped for technical reasons. Good intelligence was gleaned from Coastal Command Morse traffic and RAF and US bomber units, while R/T traffic was picked up when Allied units approached the Norwegian coast. An important source of intelligence on the North Sea convoys was the traffic of long-range reconnaissance and carrier aircraft. The Sigint operation in Norway was fairly successful considering the bad regional atmospherics and the difficulty experienced by the units in the North in obtaining proper equipment.

Chapter 14

Air Force Cryptanalysis

Introduction

Cryptanalysis was directed and carried on by Section E of the Signal Intelligence Agency (Chi-Stelle). In general, the cryptanalysts appeared to feel their efforts did not receive the consideration they deserved. Cryptanalytic units were as far forward as possible. On the Western Front and in the Mediterranean, immediately exploitable Allied systems such as the bomber code, the aircraft reporting code, SYKO and REKOH, were worked on in the field battalions. On the Eastern Front, the battalions of LN Regiment 353 carried on the current analysis of Russian two, three and four-figure systems. All material was returned to the Chi-Stelle for research. Russian five-figure material incapable of solution in the field was studied by the Chi-Stelle.

Successes with RAF systems

Four-figure system: The RAF four-figure system was an enciphered two-part code used for point-to-point communications between units and airfields. The Germans began working on the system late in 1939 and read the system with increasing ease from March 1940 until 1 November 1942, when a code book change reduced the amount of traffic read to fragments. Interception ended in summer 1944. Four-figure traffic originating in Britain was worked on at Potsdam-Marstall without success. In the Mediterranean a small amount of work was done in September 1940 at Taormina, Sicily, and later at Athens. The Luftwaffe surmounted many difficulties in this period, going through two code book and encipherment changes – at times every three to seven days. Traffic totals varied from 600 a day during the heaviest to 100 a day immediately before discontinuing work on the problem. The knowledge gained from the four-figure enciphered code formed the basis for evaluation for the rest of the war.

The basic RAF enciphered code book system had 10,000 groups. The key 'table' was a book of 200 pages, 20 lines on a page, and five four-figure key groups on a line. The line indicators were enciphered by a separate table of 100 groups and appeared as the second group of the enciphered message. The first two digits of the first group made up the control for the indicator encipherment; the third and fourth were nulls. The conversion from plain code to cipher was made by subtracting the code from the key.

Given sufficient traffic, the inherent weakness of this key system soon manifested itself. During the early stages of analysis, when the line indicators were not enciphered, overlapping messages could be identified. On 24 and 31 December 1941, unenciphered messages were transmitted, compromising many groups in the basic book. After the indicators were enciphered, stereotyped traffic made possible overlapping by external cipher 'hits'. The beginning groups of the overlapping messages were always some multiple of five apart, and setting up of the overlaps were facilitated by the fact that encipherment always began at the beginning of the line. The 'hits' were indexed by machine, and their validity tested by the use of known high frequency differences in the code. Once the messages were overlapped, the highly stereotyped context made stripping quite easy.

The reconstruction of the indicator key had to wait until overlaps were set up. Every message that directly overlapped had the same underlying indicator. Therefore, by arbitrarily assigning 0000 as the value for the first plain indicator, all others that followed could be stripped on a relative basis and reduced to the same terms. The German relative table of indicator key was just as good for practical purpose as the British prime table.

Syko Cards: The RAF Naval Code was the basic book of an enciphered code system of which the Syko Card was the encipherment. A copy of the basic code was recovered from a Wellington shot down over Wilhelmshaven in September 1939. The code was not seriously altered for the duration of the war. The daily reciprocal enciphering table was being reconstructed by February 1940. Messages on the daily table could be read by 1600-1700 hours. The introduction of several cards a day complicated the solution slightly, but forty messages sufficed to solve a single card. The traffic, which contained information concerning British and Axis convoys, submarines, naval vessels and meteorological reports, averaged between eighty and 300 messages a day.

Rekoh: Rekoh first appeared in 1942-1943 and was simply a non-reciprocal Syko. Slightly more traffic was necessary to accomplish solution than with Syko.

Aircraft Reporting Code and UCO: The Aircraft Reporting Code (ARC) replaced Syko and Rekoh in July 1943 and was used by reconnaissance planes in the West, and 16th Company LN Regiment 3 in Angers solved the system in February 1944. ETA messages, frequency changes and hourly barometric pressure broadcasts assisted the initial break-in. The ARC had a particular importance in that it afforded a crib into UCO – the ground-air meteorological code. It was broken by cribbing the pressure reports from the ARC. The fixed Sigint station at Husum carried on this work. Lack of intercept in the last days confined solution to the meteorological crib.

Aircraft Movement Code: The Aircraft Movement Code (AMC) was used on ferry flights from Tokoradi to India and totalled about 500 messages a day. The system was composed of pronounceable five-letter code works which were changed every twenty-four hours at first, and later every twelve hours. W-Leit South-East in Athens began work on it in autumn 1942, and reading stopped in February 1944 when too many variants made solution impossible. The AMC UK Code was a three-letter system with serial numbers in clear and repeated indicators passed between the UK and stations on the Belgian-French border. It was never solved and was assumed to be an administrative or supply system.

RAF Two-Letter Bomber Code: Pages of the Bomber Code, used jointly by the RAF and USAAF, were obtained from a crashed aircraft in November or December 1942, and two weeks later the Germans were reading the system cryptanalytically. Traffic averaged 150 200 messages a day with 600 a day as high and 300 messages yielded 50-60 percent of the values. Letters and numbers from messages containing spellers or frequency information afforded the daily break-in. The code changed daily at 0300 and could be broken during the US day raids and used to decode RAF traffic during the night operations. The 8th USAAF were the daytime unfortunates who had their traffic decoded on the basis of code values recovered during the RAF raid the previous night.

Slidex: Slidex was a digraphic substitution system used in the Army and Air support networks. The co-ordinates of the substitution table changed daily, but offered no great problem to the cryptanalysts. LN Regiment 351 began work on Slidex in May 1943 at Bougival, near Paris, and much progress was made during the pre-invasion 'Spartan' exercises in Britain,. By the time the Allies invaded, the Sigint Evaluation Centre (Army NAAS 5) of the Sigint Regiment 5 (Army KONA 5) and 14/3 (W-Leit 3) had had sufficient experience to break the system operationally. The daily strips were recovered by 0700-0900 hours and traffic averaged fifteen to forty messages a daily.

Government Telegraphic Code: Work on this system was begun by OKW/Chi in May 1939 and given to the Luftwaffe in August that year. The traffic, containing mainly casualty and administrative information, averaged 200 messages a month. The system was considered of little importance in the last years of the war.

India Code: This was an unenciphered four-letter code transmitted in five-letter groups. This traffic was partially read until the end of the war.

Inter-Departmental Cypher: The basic book of this four-digit enciphered code system was captured at Bergen, Norway, in June 1940. Air attachés in the Near East, Portugal, Sweden and Switzerland used the system. Switzerland was always one table behind the others. Chi-Stelle received a photostat copy and began work on the system. Traffic was exchanged with OKM and OKW, the volume being about 100 messages a month. Two tables with indicator patterns CVCVC and VCVCV (where V = vowel and C = consonant) were used, and both were broken most successfully in 1940-1941 when the tables changed quarterly. The date breaks occurred at intervals of between six weeks to two months. Work on this cipher was stopped in 1943 because the decodes were useless to Evaluation.

Bentley Code: This code was used by British Overseas Airways and was copied from South Africa, South-East Africa, Egypt and Syria. During the war about 500 five-letter groups beginning with Y were added. One encipherment for confidential administrative traffic was added during winter 1942-1943. The solution was so simple that it was used to train beginners in cryptanalysis, and the whole project was dropped in 1944 because Evaluation was no longer interested.

Weather System: The solution of enciphered meteorological messages was not the responsibility of the Chi-Stelle, but was undertaken to assist the weather service (WENEUB). The Chi-Stelle solved the British Main Weather Code in April 1940, and turned the keys over to WENEUB at Glindow, near Potsdam. In April 1942, the Signal Weather Monitoring Service received the solution of a five-figure Middle East weather cipher from W-Leit South-East. Systems in the Atlantic carrying the indicators 'Whist' and 'Tooth' were worked on by the Signal Weather Monitoring Service without success.

Miscellaneous: There was solution of a British single transposition cipher, involving a ten-column rectangle. The system changed every Thursday at 2400 hours when the new key word was transmitted in the previous system. There was no success with double transposition despite notebooks captured during the early days of the Normandy invasion. They did not find any messages of the same length in the same key.

Typex: Many attempts were made to get into this system, but work was discontinued as it was considered unbreakable.

Successes with US systems

M-209: The M-209 was first read in March or April 1944 and averaged six to eight days of currency each month on the Western Front and one to two days in the Mediterranean. A 'key chart' was captured in October 1944, providing twenty-six to twenty-seven days of currency. Best time on completion of a complete solution was 22 hours and the average time lag was eight to ten days because of delay in receiving traffic. Eventually the Air Force dropped the M-209 job, which was then performed by the Army. M-209 traffic of the US 8th Fighter Command (65th, 66th and 67th Wings), which carried information about the Mustang fighter, was broken in February 1944. After the invasion, battle losses of the 101st Airborne Division were read. The Luftwaffe traffic totals for M-209 solution were about 100 a day in the West and 40 a day in the Mediterranean.

Strip Systems: The Southern Route Strip System was read in May 1942. The introduction of a device increasing security and a gradual reduction in traffic forced the discontinuance of work on this system. It was estimated that 200 messages a day were required as the minimum for solutions of a strip cipher with channel elimination. It took two months to break a strip system using hand methods, but the use of IBM machinery cut the time to from two to four weeks. Solution of the CENEB strip cipher system was very straightforward.

M-94: An M-94 system was read with the indicator URSAL from summer 1942 until December 1943.

Rekoh: One day's Atlantic Ferry Route traffic of sixty messages was deciphered, but the Evaluation Section considered it unimportant and the project was dropped.

Aircraft Reporting Code: This was broken in February 1944. Partial decipherment was possible with 150 messages a day.

Aircraft Movement Code: This was solved and read currently after autumn 1942. Variants changed every twelve hours, and separate British and US editions made the problem increasingly difficult. In summer 1944 solution was considered no longer possible.

8th Air Force/IX Bomber Command Codes: This was nearly always solved by cryptanalysis when necessary. Very often copies were received from aircraft shot down at night and applied to the next day's traffic. The codes were good from 1800 hours of one day until 1800 hours the next day, and so made for an ideal compromise situation.

War Department Telegraph Code: The one-part code feature of this system (indicator TELWA) greatly facilitated solution. The edition produced in October 1943 yielded 12,000 groups by May 1944 and was absolutely current after February 1945.

Division Field Code: DFC-17 was captured in the Mediterranean and helped in the eventual solution of DFC-19, 23, 28 and 29.

USAAF 'Q' groups: The Germans placed no importance on the security of the 'Q' groups. As with the Bomber Code, copies were recovered from shot down aircraft.

Cryptography of Soviet systems

Code in various forms with the transmitted text appearing as numbers was used almost exclusively by the Soviet Air Force. Each Air Army did its own code compilation and had its own rules for use. The table was comprised of letters and words in a predetermined form, usually a square or rectangle with number co-ordinates that could be changed by the use of sliding strips or by the use of digraphic substitution enciphering tables. The code table was a highly specialised medium for use in air-ground communications. The vocabulary was highly stereotyped and limited to meteorological reports, landing and take-off data etc. The code book was the principal cryptographic medium, especially in the ground organisation. The Russians used all variations from small one-part books to two-part books with up to 30,000 values. Extra security could be gained with an additive encipherment of the basic code.

Successes with Soviet systems

From 1937-1939 the Germans gained valuable experience during Soviet manoeuvres. The traffic was mainly practice and dummy, but formed a foundation for later analysis. During the Soviet occupation of Poland in 1939 the Germans had almost 100 per cent success with OKK-5, a code system with a digraphic substitution encipherment – the most common Soviet Air system. During the Finnish campaign in 1939 and 1940, two and three-figure traffic was completely broken and OKK-5 was ninety-five per cent read, and considerable success was attained on the additive enciphered code system used by higher HQ. The Soviets revamped their cryptographic setup after the Finnish campaign.

The Germans captured working directions to Soviet code and cipher officers that made only the barest reference to codes and ciphers being solved. The directions called for a general increase in cryptographic security, and the Soviets made strong measures to correct their mistakes. These changes did not bother the Germans too much, and they were able to follow, step by step, the modifications, and as they were not too radical, they 'kept pace'.

Dealing with Soviet systems

Regarding systems based on some form of table, statistical pictures or frequency counts were first made and would usually reveal the size of the cipher unit two, three or four-figure. The next step was to deduce the number of tables involved and reduce the statistical picture down to the actual size of the table. This involved the elimination of indicator groups, dummy elements and any clear numbers that appeared in the cipher text. In the event, a simple code table with co-ordinates was used, and a simple book reconstruction job was in order. The more complicated table systems, in which use was made of several tables with co-ordinates that were cyclically shifted or chosen from a 10x10 square, unique in its rows and columns (Latin Square), through the use of indicators, was solved by concentrating on each table as a separate entity. Those that stood out in the original frequency distributions were attacked first. Then, as solution of the tables progressed with relative page and row column designations, the designations were equated and the entire indicator, page and co-ordinate system could be reconstructed.

Some traffic could be read with these relative co-ordinates, but the reduction to prime values was very important. The shifting co-ordinates were often based on a Latin Square, or upon the cyclic variation of the same sequence or sequences, and the sooner this pattern could be isolated, the sooner the entire system fell apart. The Soviets used five-figure additive systems on high echelon circuits, including some one-time pads on which the Germans did not waste any time. On non-one-time additives, however, the indicators were not enciphered and overlaps were quickly thrown together, flags of differences made up, columns equated, additive stripped and basic code recovered whenever sufficient traffic was available.

Successes against other countries

Lithuania: The Lithuanians used an insecure grid system, and traffic was read from 1938 until the Red Army entered the country in summer 1939.

Rumania: The Rumanian police cypher was so simple that the Germans considered it 'camouflaged treason' and information on German troop movements was transmitted on this system. The Rumanian Air Force cipher was a simple transposition.

Yugoslavia: This cipher was not difficult to solve and had currency on the system when Yugoslavia was invaded. It was composed of lexicographic tables with thirty columns and sixty lines and the line and column co-ordinates were at first non-random and later random.

France: A code book enciphered with short periodic additives, although it yielded very slowly, was read.

Carpatho-Ukraine: Five-letter monoalphabetical substitution messages were read in Budapest and the security of the cipher was 'nil'.

Poland: Luftwaffe work on Polish traffic began a few weeks before Poland was invaded, but a few take-off and landing reports were the only messages read.

Czechoslovakia: Work began on Czech material in 1937 and five-letter Air messages, much of it practice traffic, was read and a few tactical transposition messages were solved.

Turkey: Turkish Air systems fell into three categories: a periodic substitution system which changed monthly and was broken in two hours; an unenciphered alphabetic code book and single transposition enciphered weather reports. It was extremely simple to read.

Critique of Luftwaffe Sigint

Liaison with other Sigint agencies

Liaison between Luftwaffe Sigint and other signal intelligence agencies was effective, although each service concentrated on its own commitments. Although the Armed Forces Supreme Command (OKW) exercised a control over security, each service was permitted to work out its techniques and policy in its work against foreign countries. The

Luftwaffe operated independently of the Army in its intelligence activities against the Allies. Relations with the Army High Command were on the whole quite good. Collaboration before suspected large Allied moves was especially close. Luftwaffe Sigint had many problems in common with its naval counterpart. The Luftwaffe kept the Navy informed of its intelligence on the Soviet Navy and gave information about the 1810 seaplanes of the Black Sea force. Of special importance was Russian Air reconnaissance traffic, which when intercepted, warned of impending Soviet action against German convoys in the area.

In the northern sector, an R/T unit aboard the cruiser Prinz Eugen monitored Soviet Air units in the Baltic Fleet. In Norway there were direct wire lines to Naval HQ in Oslo, over which intercept information concerning RAF Coastal Command and Atlantic convoys was passed. The Luftwaffe was able to augment the weather service (WENEUB) coverage and analysis. There was liaison with Finland on Russian traffic, but not on cryptanalysis. A very loose contact existed with Italian Sigint, but the Luftwaffe had a 'very low opinion of the Italian service'. Collaboration with Hungary went back pre-war, mainly on radio intercept, but had no capable cryptanalytic brains.

Organisation and Operations

It took five years of war, until October 1944, before the fairly unified Luftwaffe Sigint service evolved as the norm. The final organisation unified operational and administrative control within the Sigint structure at all levels of command. All the field units came under the Sigint agency operational control. There were good reasons for a distinct Air Force Sigint service. Some of its Sigint problems were strictly Air Force commitments, the clearest example of which was in the operations against Allied strategic bombers. But such a distinction could not be drawn in operations against tactical Air Forces, which operated in conjunction with land forces. In Russia, for example, the Air Armies were subordinated to Army Groups, with which they had common communications channels. Moreover, ground support units were linked with ground combat units by radio circuits.

Operational evaluation

The Luftwaffe Sigint service achieved marked success despite organisational difficulties. On the Russian Front, methods remained elementary due to poor Soviet code and cipher security and primitive radio methods.

In the West, advanced cipher communication, radio navigational and radar techniques for the Germans to rely on advanced traffic analysis methods instead of cryptanalysis, and these they developed brilliantly. The German estimate of US security was that the Americans relied too much on good cipher and did not practice sound radio discipline. TICOM notes: 'The German Air Force Signal Intelligence Service could not have been so successful in the West had American personnel been more security conscious'.

Early warning problem

[The following is an edited version taken from the interrogation of Sergeant Gerd Watkinson, Duty Officer, Meldekopf 1, Luftwaffe SIS].

Tracking the RAF

The problem became acute when the RAF began its heavy raids on Germany, made more urgent when the 8th USAAF joined RAF Bomber Command in unrestricted aerial warfare and the Luftwaffe limited itself to a defensive role. Reliable and timely early warning was to be one of the most important Luftwaffe Sigint tasks. The first attempts to obtain clues for advance warnings from Allied radio traffic went back to bomber R/T traffic on 6440 kcs. From tuning traffic between ground stations and aircraft, and from early messages, the strength of RAF night intruder formations was determined. At that time, there were no more than 80-100 bombers involved.

Traffic evaluation was made easier by the separation of operational airfields and OTU bases. After 1943, the HF R/T traffic of combat units gradually decreased, while that of OTUs increased, and so monitoring of RAF Bomber Command R/T traffic yielded no fruitful results. However, since 1943, the monitoring of American bomber R/T on HF frequencies gave very lucrative indications of impending air activity. Later, advance warning was given as early as the evening before daylight attacks of the 8th USAAF on the basis of this R/T traffic.

This advance warning was facilitated because, at the end of 1943, the 8th USAAF used special airfield frequencies in addition to the regular HF 6440 kcs frequency. It remained to determine the call signs of the ground stations, and the intercept operator needed only to have his receiver properly calibrated in order to identify the airfield. In the final period, the efforts of the combat wings to give instructions to their formations on HF instead of VHF were realised. In the beginning of 1943, the first basic attempts were made to find possibilities for early warning in the air-ground W/T traffic and at that time a scrutiny of the radio traffic from the Regional Control Stations (RCS) began.

England was divided into fixed safety areas, with the radio traffic for each divided into fixed safety areas. The radio traffic for each zone was handled by a specified radio station, which was often a bomber airfield radio station as well. During the early afternoon hours, a large number of unidentified call signs would be heard in tuning traffic with those RCSs serving southern England. This would be followed, at night, by a large-scale raid on France or over France into Germany. However, the experiment failed in that the strength of an expected night attack could not be predicted from the number of call signs heard communicating with these RCSs. But around this time, a special phenomenon was noted by good operators engaged in monitoring Allied airfield DF sections. About one hour before the first Allied aircraft was plotted over the sea, certain short whistling tones were heard in varying intensity. In the case of a raid by about 250 bombers, twelve to twenty-five of these whistling tones were heard in short, chronological sequence and specialists explained this phenomenon as the tuning of aircraft transmitters to zero beat. Thanks to these whistling signals, remarkably good advance warnings could be given from April-June 1943. According to the DF section, not only the strength, but also the probable area of attack could be predicted.

In addition, short-interval early warning was always guaranteed through interception of the British H2S. When the whistling signals no longer occurred frequently enough to be reliable, monitoring of the radio station at Graveley airfield (8 Pathfinder Group), near Hitchin in Hertfordshire, furnished accurate clues. Gravely, one of the newer satellites of Wyton, near Huntingdon in Cambridgeshire, was seldom heard by day. The radio station at every other bomber airfield sent its call sign and the time every fifteen minutes for check purposes. Graveley was the only bomber airfield which sent its check signals only until noon, and then went off the air.

If a mission was to be flown in the evening, the radio station would renew its checking transmissions in the late afternoon, or at least long before take-off. Research indicated that Graveley took part in every raid. Therefore, an advance warning could be given on the basis of quarterly-hour procedure at Graveley.

In the summer, new possibilities for early warning were explored since it was known that the Allies were fond of changing tactics suddenly. In addition to the continuous search for traffic on medium frequency, an effort was made to obtain a Sigint picture of all active squadrons, and to arrange the information according to the following pattern in order to decide whether night attacks were impending or not:

- Airfield
- Number of aircraft heard
- Number of tuning messages intercepted
- Landing and peculiar messages

However, the evaluation of these tables was performed too superficially, and as a result no valuable intelligence was gleaned from them. For this reason a small, select group of specialists was continually on the lookout for new methods of obtaining early warning. First, they proposed examining all the daytime radio traffic of 8 Pathfinder Group because there were no large-scale missions flown over Germany or the western occupied areas without Pathfinders, which represented the brain of such an attack. If the radio traffic of this group yielded hints of an operation, then the method developed could be applied in the same way to the main body of bombers. The entire Sigint picture of No. 8 Group over a month could be reconstructed relatively quickly, and so the real work of evaluation could be started. The research proceeded on the theory that daytime radio traffic on non-operational days must be noticeably different in certain characteristics from traffic on days when no attacks followed. Thus the radio traffic of all airfields of 8 Group was separated into different periods of the day and subjected to a detailed examination. From this, the following was determined:

On non-operational days, daytime radio traffic between aircraft and their airfields had no special risk. During the forenoon there was mostly identification and tuning traffic, with no special indication of haste by the ground station. During the noon hours there was almost a complete lull in activity – the RAF 'partook generously of their noonday ease'. In the afternoon tuning traffic began again, and occasionally DF traffic was heard. In scrutinising the traffic of the airfield DF sections, special attention was paid to those aircraft performing cross-country flights. Moreover, the W/T intercept companies monitoring Bomber Command reported those Pathfinder aircraft call signs which appeared in the traffic of other groups. After the traffic of the Conversion Unit at Wyton in Cambridgeshire – which was quite voluminous – had been eliminated, there remained a good picture of the Pathfinder activity. The Sigint picture of this unit, on a day immediately preceding a night raid, looked roughly as follows:

In the morning there was lively tuning and recognition traffic, the peak being reached between 1000 and 1130 hours. The small amount of DF traffic appearing during the noonday hours was ascribed to ferry flights to and from the repair shops. At noon came the 'briefing pause', and so very few Pathfinder aircraft were heard. To properly evaluate the noonday radio silence, an exact knowledge of weather conditions over the take-off areas was important. Therefore a weather map was made, and no source of information was ignored in building up the truest picture of the weather over the 8 Group bases. The recall of RAF training units around noon would be an unquestionable indication of an expected deterioration of the weather. Frequently the Sigint picture would definitely indicate a raid, and then the sudden appearance of a bad weather front would cause the mission to be cancelled.

When later the RAF flew daylight missions, there was also included information as to which units had completed their missions. A digest of this information, together with a record of the missions which followed, was kept in a diary so that every radio characteristic could be referred to which seemed important to certain intercept problems. Much effort was in vain, because it emerged that Pathfinders of 5 Group tuned to the zero beat of their frequency long before their radio traffic over the target was heard and that the same whistling tones could be heard from jamming aircraft of 100 Group shortly after they took off from Foulsham in Norfolk. Moreover, the 5 Group operators were changed frequently on non-operational days, while during a mission the same operator remained on the key.

The ever more frequent RAF daylight raids were predicted without difficulty. If, for example, 3 Group was to fly at noon, an alerted group maintained radio silence. Tuning traffic probably originated with the ground personnel rather than with the airborne radio operators. Perhaps it was also sent during repair shop flights over an airfield, but this was not absolutely necessary. The non-appearance of this tuning traffic became one of the most important clues for Sigint in predicting a coming attack. Whatever further traffic was intercepted from the bomber formations on their outward flight could no longer be used tactically. Only if German long-range night fighters pursued the bombers on their return flight did these messages have any tactical value.

Tracking the USAAF

By far the greater part of the effort was consciously directed to producing possibilities for early warning from RAF Bomber Command traffic. All the possibilities uncovered were similarly applied to monitoring 8th USAAF. But no such exertion was needed as that following the RAF. The Americans were much more massive and primitive in their tactics, and can scarcely be said to have practiced restraint in their voluminous W/T and R/T traffic. Long-interval advance warnings of raids by US bomber formations could usually be given as early as 2300 hours on the night before a daylight attack. The first indication of the raid proper was the interception of traffic from weather reconnaissance aircraft. Weather ships sent their reports to their home bases as well as to certain prescribed headquarters. In this way they could be found by DF, then it could be stated definitely into which areas 8th USAAF would fly. Zero beat tuning was heard on the bomber division frequencies in the early morning hours preceding a raid. Next, the take-off of the individual units was monitored. During the assembly, which continued for as long as two hours, depending on the size of the raid, an exact picture of the composition and strength of the formations was obtained from VHF R/T traffic. A certain code word then indicated that the bomber division was setting its course. Research work, as with the RAF, was not necessary – the Americans spoke of what they were doing quite openly.

Chapter 15

Foreign Office Cryptography

Introduction

The story of the genesis, history and operations of the German Foreign Office Cryptanalytic Section (Pers ZS) can be neither complete nor absolutely accurate because of the paucity of data available at the end of the war. Indeed its existence was never definitely established until the Section was captured in April 1945. As such, there was little or no background information to assist TICOM interrogators. Moreover, it was the first major exploitation undertaken by TICOM, and so the interrogators suffered from a general lack of experience. Indeed, the interrogations were not extensive enough because the field covered by Pers ZS was so large – more than fifty countries during a twenty-five year period.

There were few interrogators who could meet the Germans on their own ground. The interrogations, therefore, covered little more than those highlights which the Germans most readily recalled. Cryptanalysis was emphasised, while intelligence was almost completely neglected. There were serious deficiencies in the captured documents, most of which antedated 1942. This chapter, therefore, cannot be seen as a complete statement of the Pers ZS organisation, its cryptanalytic effort or its achievements.

Organisation

The German Foreign Office cryptanalytic activities were concentrated in the cryptanalytic section, Z branch, Personnel Bureau, and was known as Pers ZS. It was engaged on foreign diplomatic codes and ciphers. It did not work on military problems. Z Branch was organised into four sections:

- 'Special' or Cryptanalytic Section, involved in cryptanalysis;
- Cryptographic Section engaged in compiling and distributing codes and ciphers;
- Communications Section handled communications systems including teletype circuits, telephone switchboards and radio links; and
- Administrative Section, responsible for personnel and administration.

History and strength 1919-1937

Codes and cipher work had originally been done in Bureau I (Abteilung I), the normal administrative bureau in a German government department, and was probably called the Political Intelligence Bureau. As late as 1925 cryptanalysis and cryptography were unified under one head. It is not known when it began its cryptanalytic efforts after World War One. It is probably safe to assume that the Foreign Office cryptanalytic efforts were well advanced before the conclusion of the peace treaty. No documentary evidence is available on its strength during 1920-1937, but it is likely to have begun with twenty to thirty people in 1918, increasing to about thirty in 1930.

Expansion 1937-1945

Captured documents show that Pers Z and its four sections comprised 77 personnel on 1 November, 1937 and 72 on 1 July 1938, with 92 on 1 December 1939, and had recruited 45 people between September and December 1939. In 1939, the Cryptographic Section (Pers Z Chi) had ten of its thirteen cryptographers over fifty years old, six over sixty and night work was too much of a strain for them. When the Section was captured its leaders stated that the peak in personnel was in 1945 when 180-200 were employed.

Developments 1943-1945

No major organisational changes were made until December 1943 when Berlin-Dahlem was partially evacuated because of Allied bombing, being split into one large group and two smaller groups. No intercept traffic was received after March 1945, but some cryptanalytic work was continued on back material until they were overrun in April 1945.

Intercept control and traffic analysis

Pers ZS had one small intercept station under its own control, called the Landhaus, at Dahlem, and was used to cover priority links such as Berlin-Ankara and Berlin-Lisbon. Otherwise it was dependent for the bulk of its intercept on OKW/Chi, Goering's Research Bureau and the German Post Office.

Cryptanalysis

General organisation

Pers ZS evacuated Berlin in November 1943, and despite the difficulties this entailed, one cardinal organisational principal was retained: that mathematical cryptanalysis involving the initial solutions of extremely difficult systems, the solution of complex encipherments and additives, and the application of machine techniques of these problems, were kept separate from linguistic cryptanalysis. The latter was roughly defined as including current solution of known additive and enciphering systems, code book reconstruction, translation and publication. The linguistic section consisted of a number of small groups organised along semi-linguistic or semi-geographical lines. The mathematical section had had its own IBM machinery since 1942 and was used principally in solution of difficult additives and superencipherments, and not for bookbuilding purposes. At the end of the war, the installations included twenty punches, ten sorters, two collators, two reproducers, six tabulators, one multiplier and additional special machinery. The most useful device was the 'automaton', a rapid deciphering machine developed for use on US diplomatic cipher. Another machine, a type of comparator, was developed to solve Japanese transposition ciphers by dragging the end of the message through the cipher text.

Summary of cryptanalytic successes

Considering its relatively small staff, Pers ZS the conclusion must be drawn that its cryptanalytic successes were considerable, with work being conducted on about 50 countries. Of these, apparently only three used diplomatic systems completely defied successful cryptanalysis: Russia, Czechoslovakia and Poland after 1942-1943. Pers ZS was also able to read the Swiss Enigma for a short time and to solve the Japanese Red machine. In the solution of foreign diplomatic codes, the agency displayed 'an extraordinary degree of competence'.

With the exception of Russian, substantial segments of the medium grade diplomatic code and cipher systems used by the major powers were read. Britain, the US, France, Italy – where the greatest success was achieved – China and Japan were read. With Turkey, Bulgaria, Belgium, Spain, Switzerland, Portugal and Poland (until 1942), nearly 100 percent success was achieved. In Latin American countries, and the smaller European and Near-Eastern countries, complete success was apparently achievable, insofar as limitations of personnel and relatively trivial message content might warrant. Had there been backing from Foreign Minister Joachim von Ribbentrop, and had there not been crippling jealousies at agency-head levels, there might have been even greater successes.

Below is a list of successes by country:

Argentina: At least three main codes were known, one of which, a five-figure, one-part, 110,000 group system, usually enciphered by the addition or subtraction of a constant, was ready almost without gaps, and 240 messages were decoded in 1942.

Belgium: Pers ZS was familiar with three Belgian codes. The main systems were four-figure, one-part or partially alphabetical codes, containing about 10,000 groups. They were usually enciphered with a daily changing unsystematic bigram substitution table and 373 messages were published in 1942, a small proportion of the total intercepted and broken.

Brazil: Prior to 1943, Pers ZS seems to have read nearly all the major Brazilian diplomatic codes. Three systems in particular seem to have been read almost without gaps: a five-figure, one-part 165,000 group code (Known as Bras B1 by the Germans), a five-letter, partially alphabetic 82,000 group code (Bras B2) and a five-figure, one-part 100,000 group system (Bras Z1). The basic book for Bras B2 was available in photostat form. Traffic totals fell off sharply after the rupture of diplomatic relations in January 1942.

Bulgaria: Bulgaria used two basic five-figure 35-40,000 group code books. Both were one-part codes, repaginated for various links, usually used enciphered. Goering's Research Bureau had provided photocopies of the two books and from 1943 all major Bulgarian links were read.

Chile: Little information about success is known after 1942, but the one-part, two, three and four-letter 42,000 group code known to the Chileans as 'Clave Solar', was read at least until late 1942 and possibly until the end of the war.

China: There is little direct information regarding success against Chinese systems. Two three-letter codes, one military, and the other, an attaché system, were solved. Another three-letter system called 'Uti' was read in 1941-1942.

Ireland: Considerable work was done on the Irish diplomatic links to Berlin. The Irish used the British Government Telegraphic Code (GTC) – called 'B-22' by the Germans – enciphered with substitution alphabets. This code, a five-letter, one-part 84,000 group system, was captured at Bergen in 1940.

France: Success against French diplomatic systems was considerable. A 1941 report stated that seventy-five percent of French diplomatic transmissions were read. *Mexico*: No information is available after 1942, but the principal codes – Pomos – a one-part, five-letter code, and Xepit – a similar system – both enciphered by substitution alphabets, were read through 1942. The Xepit book was compromised in November 1942, although it had been broken prior to compromise.

Near East (excluding Iran and Turkey): Little work was done on systems originating in Afghanistan, Egypt, Iraq or Saudi Arabia. Traffic was usually inconsequential in content, lacking in depth and there was never sufficient people to permit exploitation.

Poland: Relative little progress was made after 1942. Polish codes were unbreakable in practice – there were too many of them – and they required too much work. The principal Polish diplomatic code (called PD-1 by the Germans), an enciphered four-figure, two-part code, was broken in 1940 and read 100 percent until October 1942, when it went out of use.

Portugal: A five-figure, partially alphabetic 50,000 group book (called '302' by the Germans), was read with some success in 1941. Two other five-figure, partially alphabetic 61,500 group books were compromised in December 1942 when a basic book (called '205') was received from OKW/Chi. After then, traffic was read 100 percent.

Rumania: A 1940 report listed seven known diplomatic systems (called R-11 to R17 by the Germans), all five-figure codes, varying from 70-100,00 groups and enciphered by means of ten-place substitution tables. Captured code book reconstructions indicate about a five to ten per cent recovery on book groups.

Russia: Work on Russian diplomatic systems does not seem to have been a Pers ZS commitment. Russian systems had been read until 1927 but there was no success afterwards.

Scandinavia (Denmark, Norway and Sweden): Work was conducted for about three months in 1941, after which responsibility was transferred to OKW/Chi.

Spain: Little work was done on Spanish systems, but in 1941 and 1942, the only years for which reports were available, work was done on '04' (German name), a four-figure, partially alphabetic 10,000 group code book. The book was partially recovered.

Thailand: The main Thai code was a one-part, five-figure 110,000 group English language code, both enciphered and unenciphered, and was read almost without gaps.

Turkey: Work began on Turkish systems after the Montreux Conference in 1934 and most diplomatic traffic was read. Three codes were usually in use, changing monthly. In 1944-1945 the codes were chiefly one-part, with a cyclic additive, and were readily broken.

United Kingdom (and British Empire): Principal success was against medium grade letter codes. The Government Telegraph Code (GTC), used in communication with Canada, Australia and Ireland, and another Government Telegraph Code (called 'B-23' by the Germans), used solely for South African communications, were read. These were five-letter, one-part 84,000 group codes, usually unenciphered. The former was completely compromised at Bergen in 1940. The four-letter, two-part codes (called B-25, B-30 and B-31 by the Germans) had more significant message content and B-25 and B-31 were considered most important by the Germans. The five-figure Interdepartmental Cipher, also compromised at Bergen, was worked on in 1941 and 1942, the bulk of the work being done by Goering's Research Bureau.

United States: Main successes included the Grey Code (called B-3 by the Germans), the Brown Code (B8) and the State Department strip systems. The Grey Code had been in use since June 1918 and the Brown Code since 1938. Both systems were readable, the Brown Code having been compromised in 1941. The Strip System C-1 was partially read in 1941, and the Strip System O-2 was solved early in 1943. The strip systems were not read currently, but only after a delay of months.

Vatican: In 1940 half the traffic could be read but was not a major Pers ZS commitment. Most of the book groups were secured from Goering's Research Bureau.

Yugoslavia: Not much light was shed on Pers ZS work on these systems, but some work was done in 1940-1941.

Liaison with other agencies

Introduction

Liaison with other German cryptographic organisations was bad – Supreme Command of the Armed Forces (OKW/Chi) and Goering's Research Bureau also worked on diplomatic systems and the relations of all three agencies was marked by jealousy rather than co-operation. There was no overall co-ordination of policy for various German cryptographic bureaux. Liaison with the Research Bureau appears to have been extensive and there was frequent collaboration. There is no mention of co-operation with the Army High Command after 1941-1942. The Army, Air and Navy High Commands were mainly involved in military matters.

Collaboration with OKW/Chi at least at lower administrative and technical levels appears to have been the most extensive of all. OKW/Chi was never allowed to know the details of the ciphers used by the Foreign Office. Even towards the end, when there was a further attempt to centralise security under OKW/Chi, the Foreign Office would not come into line. Pers Z preferred to remain independent. In 1944-1945, the picture shows strong Foreign Office intransigence in the attempt by OKW/Chi to be the senior German agency on all matters on security and code and cipher compilation.

Cryptanalytic co-operation

Relations with OKW/Chi in the cryptanalytic field contrasted sharply with that in the cryptographic field. Both organisations considered diplomatic codes and ciphers as a primary commitment, with military attaché systems as the exclusive province of OKW/Chi. Since OKW/Chi was junior in the field to Pers ZS, a greater degree of jealousy and a lesser amount of co-operation might have been expected. However, the cryptanalytic collaboration between both agencies was the most extensive and probably the most successful of all Pers ZS co-operation ventures, although there was much duplication. Parts of OKW/Chi were accommodated with the Foreign Office, for instance, in March 1945 when OKW/Chi was moved to Halle-Nietleben, the equivalent parts of the Foreign Office went with it and these departments were then moved to Eilenburg, ten miles from Zschepplin, in Saxony, the final location of a large part of Pers ZS. A summary of the main countries involving OKW/Chi-Pers ZS co-operation follows:

Japan: *JB-57* was a major Japanese diplomatic code and towards the end of 1941, Pers ZS and OKW/Chi, working independently, solved the first daily keys. With the *Red machine*, Pers ZS worked on even days and OKW/Chi on odd days.

Russia: There was no confirmed example of Pers ZS-OKW/Chi collaboration on Russian systems. In February 1934, there were Reichswehr-Pers ZS discussions on Russian military systems, but later OKW/Chi did not work on Russian diplomatic traffic.

United Kingdom: On the Interdepartmental Cipher (a five-figure system), Pers ZS did not work on this after summer 1942 or early 1943, but OKW/Chi furnished a copy of the captured book and the solved additive sequence to Pers ZS. Code B-30 was a four-figure, two-part code and at the beginning of November 1942 about 750 groups were turned over to OKW/Chi for copying. Code B-31 was another four-figure, two-part code, and in August 1942 Pers ZS turned over about 1,500 solved groups to OKW/Chi. Thereafter a regular exchange of solved groups was carried out between them. B-22 was a five-figure, one-part code, known as the British Government Telegraph Code. It was also used by Ireland for diplomatic transmissions. Pers ZS gave OKW/Chi all the Irish substitution and additive keys on this code.

Italy: Pers ZS considered itself the senior partner in the co-operative effort undertaken on Italian systems. A 1939-1940 reports states that Pers ZS had broken the Italian diplomatic codes after OKW/Chi and the Austrian cryptanalytic organisation had said the work was impossible. Reports implied that Pers ZS considered its collaboration with Goering's Research Bureau more fruitful than that with OKW/Chi, although the OKW/Chi intercept was considered to be superior. At the end of 1940, OKW/Chi and Pers ZS exchanged book groups on four codes, and there was a current exchange of solved encipherment tables. There is little information covering 1941-1945, although there was close collaboration on Italian systems.

United States: A five-letter code B-6A (called A1 by the Americans) was solved in September 1939 and a photocopy was received from OKW/Chi in 1941. There is no direct mention of liaison on the B-7 system, but Pers ZS seemed cognisant of the status of solution at other agencies, including OKW/Chi.

At the end of June 1941, Pers ZS received a copy of B-8 (the Brown Code) from OKW/Chi. In summer 1941, Pers ZS received from OKW/Chi a photocopy of the instructions for the use of SV (Diplomatic Strip System 01) and four series of strips, which deciphered a number of messages, which appears to have been strip device M-138A.

Intelligence

Summary and conclusions

No definite information was available as to the distribution of Pers ZS decodes, their intelligence content or their consideration and reception by higher authorities. The organisation seemed overly preoccupied with cryptanalysis as a science, and apparently did not think in terms of cryptanalysis as a prime source of intelligence. The Pers ZS organisation for intelligence, its evaluation and dissemination seemed to have been weak. From von Ribbentrop down, those interrogated could recall little important information which had been obtained from their work. Either there was little or no importance in the decodes, or the material contained therein was never properly evaluated and fed back by higher authorities. However, an organisation which read the Japanese Red machine and achieved nearly 100 percent success on Italian diplomatic codes must have produced some important intelligence. This may have been the fault of internal organisation – or lack of organisation – for intelligence, or the attitude of the organisation's leaders. In an organisation which worked on the systems of some 50 countries and was invariably short of personnel, it is doubtful whether a separate evaluation group was overly desirable or efficient.

Handling and processing intelligence

No intelligence was extracted from the material produced, except such as was necessary to continue reading the traffic. Since Pers ZS apparently never had sufficient personnel to allow adequate cryptanalysis, it is probable that the group heads never had sufficient time to do a thorough analysis of the solved traffic. Moreover, TICOM interrogators placed little emphasis on intelligence and must share a part of the responsibility for the lack of information. It also seems that pride in careful translation gives the impression that care and precision in all phases of the work took precedence over considerations of urgency. Cryptanalysis, an abstract science and the principal element in Sigint, may have become an end in itself, and that the raison d'être of cryptanalysis – the production of intelligence – may have been obscured by these considerations.

Lack of recognition by higher authorities

This tendency can be magnified if cryptanalysts are not kept constantly aware of the meaning and significance of their products, the importance of key messages, and the action taken by other authorities on the strength of cryptanalytic information. In this important respect Pers ZS seems to have been deficient. If higher authorities did not tell the cryptanalysts that their work was of significant importance, it is not to be wondered that the technicians felt their work ignored and withdrew more and more into their own world of two-part codes and enciphering tables. According to one Pers ZS member, from time to time copies of messages had been returned to them bearing a stamp indicating that they had been seen by Hitler.

Some responsibility for the failure to disseminate internally information concerning successes must be consigned to the Pers ZS leaders. There was little encouragement given to the communication of results inside the organisation by junior members, who were encouraged to mind their own business. Apparently the leaders knew in a general way of their successes, but denied this information to juniors, who most needed the encouragement. In all probability the leaders were just not intelligence-minded. They were cryptanalysts, they thought primarily in terms of cryptanalysis, and intelligence was to them a by-product of their work.

Handling and processing of decodes

The distribution given to decodes is not known. Apparently, von Ribbentrop only read twenty to thirty percent of the material produced, and saw between one and four items a day, or less. It seems that at least five people were involved in determining the distribution of decodes, with the consequent disadvantages of divided responsibility and possible loss of continuity. It is not known where and how the Pers ZS intelligence was integrated into the total intelligence picture, and that there was no central clearing house for intelligence at the top. There is some evidence that, due to the lack of high level co-ordination, the same decode might be passed to a ministry from two or three sources.

Cryptographic Section

Introduction

The cryptographic section was responsible for the compilation, preparation and distribution of codes and ciphers used by the Foreign Office as well as the security of these systems.

Cryptographic work

One individual told TICOM that the Germans were convinced that their systems were cryptographically secured. It is possible that this complacent attitude was responsible for some of the Anglo-American successes against Foreign Office systems. Pers ZS must have been responsible for the Deutsches Satzbuch and the additive system used for its encipherment, all of which were read by Anglo-American cryptanalysts. One of the additive systems was theoretically a one-time pad system, but was insecure because the additive used was predictable.

The cryptographic section seems to have been interested in improvements to the Enigma machine and in February 1942 there were discussions on the construction of a new cipher machine with Willi Korn, chief engineer of the Enigma firm of Heimsoeth and Rincke of Berlin. It was to be called Machine 42 and was in effect an Army plugboard Enigma with three additional rotors inserted in front of the plugboard. The machine never passed the theoretical development stage because of engineering and procurement difficulties. A plugboard Enigma with a printing attachment, bearing the Foreign Office label, was captured, indicating that the military-style Enigma was used for Foreign Office communications. It also used the military-style cipher teleprinters. As far as is known, the cryptographic section did not collaborate with any other German cryptographic agency.

Chapter 16

Goering's Research Bureau (FA)

Summary of history, organisation and operations

The Reichsluftfahrtministeriums/Forschungsamt was Goering's Research Bureau and known as the FA. It was the Nazi Party cryptanalytic agency and was composed of about 2,000 people with final responsibility to Reichsmarshal Hermann Goering. It was independent of the Luftwaffe and was comprised of civilians. The main office was led by Gottfried Schapper and was divided into six main sections (Hauptabteilungen) and fifteen sections (Abteilungen).

In addition there were one branch office and at least four regional offices besides an undetermined number of intercept stations. Main Section IV (about 180 people) was the cryptanalytic branch and handled that portion of the raw material, possibly twenty percent, which was in code or cipher.

The FA was charged with providing reliable diplomatic, economic and political information from monitoring all internal German telephone, telegraph, and wireless communications – including those from within Germany to foreign countries. It also handled foreign commercial and diplomatic wireless communications, foreign press and news broadcasts and speeches of politicians, and the study of newspapers and periodicals. To this end, it operated its own intercept and monitoring service. The FA co-operated with the FA and the Gestapo in censoring all communications in Germany and German occupied territory. The information produced was distributed as finished reports to Goering and Hitler and to top Nazi officials and interested government departments.

Discovery of the FA's existence

The existence of the FA was unknown to the Allies prior to its discovery by TICOM, who learned of its existence while questioning Foreign Office cryptanalytic staff on 28 April 1945 and on 9 May a TICOM team discovered the abandoned quarters of the FA in barracks near Kaufbeuren airfield, 50 miles south-west of Munich.

Founding of the FA

The FA was brought about by Goering himself in 1933. Previous to 1933, when the Nazis came to power, the Foreign Office had established a similar monitoring system for intercepting wireless messages, and the police had monitored telephone conversations etc. But Goering wanted one organisation of his own to handle all phases under one central control. The work of the FA comprised two almost completely separate activities – telephone monitoring and interception and cryptanalysis. Goering used to visit them only once a year because they worked so well on their own.

FA relations with other agencies

Some OKW/Chi personnel were recruited into the FA which created some ill-feeling between the two organisations and relations were always strained. The FA was the last entrant into the cryptanalytic field and it had the reputation of paying its employees 'exceptionally well'. There is no evidence of liaison between OKW/Chi and the FA on cryptanalytic matters although the FA did supply intercepted traffic and was represented on the OKW/Chi committee on cryptographic security.

This lack of co-operation extended to the IBM equipment developed by the OKW/Chi, which was offered to the High Commands of the Army, Navy and Air Force but not to the FA. There was an attempt by the FA to take over OKW/Chi after the disgrace of the Supreme Command of the Armed Forces over the 20 July 1944 bomb plot against Hitler. OKW/Chi was taken over by Reichsführer SS Heinrich Himmler and his RSHA – Reich Security Head Office – following the July bomb plot through Sicherheitsdienst (SD) chief SS Brigadeführer Walter Schellenberg. The best relationship existed with the Foreign Office and there is evidence of technical exchange with the Army, Navy and Air Force Sigint agencies. The Gestapo eventually took over the telephone monitoring of the Abwehr and the FA in the middle of 1944.

The FA as a Nazi Party organisation

The FA was created by the Nazis to provide a counterpart for the various service Sigint agencies and of the Foreign Office, on whose loyalty they could not rely on when the FA was formed in 1933. The SS and the RSHA did not maintain any cryptanalytic bureau of their own. Schellenberg had established relations with the OKW deciphering department in 1942 because he wanted to exploit the experience of the Wehrmacht both in W/T Abwehr as also in the development of German coding methods for his own use. Schellenberg made early contact with General Erich Fellgiebel, German Army chief of signals and his department chief, General Fritz Thiele, both killed following the July bomb plot. Thiele became Fellgiebel's successor and wanted to unite all deciphering services in one hand and put them at the exclusive disposal of the Geheime Meldedienst for systematic interpretation and use.

Apart from the Foreign Office, which possessed an extensive deciphering service, the FA was above all the organisation which had not only a virtual 100 percent telephone monitoring service, but also a very large deciphering department and also monitored normal broadcast services – which was also done by the Foreign Office, Propaganda Ministry and the OKW! The FA also embraced an extensive press and publication interpretation department as well as one of the best archives. In his interrogation, Schellenberg maintained that apart from the obvious reasons of saving personnel and other grounds of economy, the Amt Ausland (Overseas Department – Abwehr) together with the FA deciphering department was really a domain of the Geheime Meldedienst. Schellenberg also saw that there was no need for the telephone monitoring service to be independent, but that it really belonged to Amt IV of the RSHA – the Gestapo. But as early as 1942, Himmler refused to talk to Goering about the request by Schellenberg that he should take over the FA. Schellenberg therefore acted independently. He needed the results both of the FA and the OKW/Chi.

At the beginning of 1943, Schellenberg had come to a working agreement with Prussian Secretary of State Dr Paul Koerner, in charge of FA finances, and by the end of 1944 Koerner was prepared to concede the FA to Schellenberg except for telephone monitoring, which since the middle of 1944 belonged to the Gestapo. The takeover began in February 1945, but because of the situation the move did not take practical shape. The testimony of Schellenberg to Himmler's unwillingness to infringe on Goering's field even in 1942, evidence of collaboration on cryptanalytic matters, coupled with the lack of evidence that the SS possessed a cryptologic unit of its own, and the importance Schellenberg placed on the FA in his plans for a glorified intelligence service after the Party had completed its domination of the OKW/Chi, indicate the real position of the FA within the Nazi organisation.

FA operations April 1933-May 1945

Only a sketchy outline of the FA's operational history can be drawn. It was created in April 1933 and by the end of the year had been assigned the task of monitoring all telephone circuits within the Reich. It is rumoured to have been concerned in the 'blood purge' of 30 June 1934. At the time of the Anschluss (March 1938) the FA telephone monitoring and deciphering activities were in operation. In September 1941 the FA produced a book containing the names of all foreign diplomats in Berlin, their partners in all conversations and summaries of these conversations. The FA continued to work on available diplomatic and commercial material and press broadcasts throughout the war. Operations were hampered by bombing.

On 1 November 1943 and again on 7 July 1944, the Schillerstrasse quarters of the FA were heavily bombed, and after each bombing a part of the FA was evacuated. Either at the beginning of 1944 or 1945, the telephone monitoring service was given to the Gestapo, although documents providing for the closing down of the Breslau outstations reveal that telephone monitoring stations were still controlled by the FA.

Liaison officers responsible for passing FA materials to the other ministries remained in Berlin and a special section for evaluation was set up. A Berlin branch office and the Berlin outstation also continued to function. Five FA members were transferred to the Navy High Command Sigint agency on 16 May 1945 and were arrested on 23 May. They were the departmental heads left in Berlin and it is obvious that a carefully co-ordinated split into both a northern and southern FA section was arranged as had been done for OKW/Chi.

The FA was originally located in Berlin at Charlottenburg 2, Schillerstrasse 116/124. On moving to Breslau it took over the Hartlieb Barracks in Klettendorf. At Kaufbeuren TICOM found the FA located in six blocks of a barracks near the airfield. In the moves from Berlin the number of personnel decreased from the estimated 1,500 to 2,000 employed there. Only about 450 continued to Kaufbeuren and only around 100 were left at Rosenheim.

A special section was created in Berlin to deal with the closing down of Breslau and all members released for duty were to be immediately reported available to the FA.

FA operational organisation

Main Bureau organisation

The following FA operational organisation is intended to represent its structure while in Berlin. At the head was a director responsible for managing all official business, and under him the Main Office at Berlin as well as the liaison offices, regional offices and intercept stations. The main office was composed of six main sections – Hauptabteilung – which were subdivided into fifteens sections, or Abteilung, which in turn were broken down into various sub-sections. It was in the Hauptabteilung and Abteilung that the main FA work was accomplished.

Hauptabteilung

I:Administration
II: Personnel
III: Intercept
IV: Codes and Ciphers
V: Evaluation
VI: Technical

FA intercept stations and regional offices

The FA operational functions were carried out by the intercept stations of five different types. These stations, called Forschungsstellen, were categorised as follows:

A Stations: telephone intercept
B Stations: wireless intercept
C Stations: radio broadcast monitoring
D Stations: teletype and telegraph intercept
F Stations: mail censorship

A stations were scattered throughout Germany and later in the occupied countries. They were equipped with one or two interceptor switchboards which enabled operators to cut in on any conversation at any time. The tapping was done at the main Post Office telephone exchange and piped directly to the station, which was usually located in a private building. Included in the equipment was a wireless recorder which could be brought into use when desired. B stations were usually outside towns at points of good wireless reception, not being faced with the problem of necessary proximity to telephone or cable lines. Radio messages were intercepted by short wave and then relayed in written form to the FA headquarters.

After war started, this type of intercept became increasingly important insofar as foreign information was concerned because of telephonic communication from Germany to other countries. There was only one C station, which performed a pure monitoring service of public broadcasts from other countries. The three D stations were located at Berlin, Vienna and Dortmund, the chief centres of cablegrams leaving Germany. The F stations were organised after war began and were never very extensive in their operations. Censorship offices were operated by the OKW and later by the RSHA. The F stations consisted of small groups attached to these censorship posts. The regional offices were as follows:

Forschungsstelle

A: Breslau with 'D' functions
B: Breslau-Deutsch Lissa
C: Breslau-Deutsch Lissa
A: Litzmannstadt (Lodz)
A: Posen (Posnan)
B: Leba

In addition, Forschungsstelle 'A' Danzig was instructed to move as quickly as possible to Berlin and unite with the Forschungsleitstelle Berlin. A directive for the reorganisation of the FA at Kaufbeuren of 9 March 1945 revealed the existence of four Forschungsleitstellen at Berlin, Hamburg, Munich and Vienna. Breslau covered Eastern Germany and Poland, Munich covered Southern Germany, Vienna covered Austria, Hamburg covered Western Germany (and possibly Denmark) and Berlin covered Central Germany. This monitoring service, particularly telephone monitoring, was probably chiefly involved in liaison with the Abwehr and the RSHA. An order of 14 April 1945 gives evidence of the Copenhagen and Stettin Forschungsstellen.

Evaluation of the FA

FA effectiveness and liaison

The FA was a 'highly effective intelligence-producing agency'. TICOM interrogated General Alfred Jodl, Chief of Armed Forces Operations Staff; Grand Admiral Karl Dönitz, Navy C-in-C; Field Marshal Wilhelm Keitel, Chief of the Armed Forces; Foreign Minister Joachim von Ribbentrop and Reichsmarshal Hermann Goering (see Appendix 2). There was an appreciation by them of the value of Sigint and at times a surprising knowledge of technical details and evaluation of the various agencies. Ribbentrop and Goering gave two different opinions about Hitler's views on Sigint. According to Ribbentrop, 'Hitler had a queer, rather particular view about it – he did not like this type of intelligence very much and said it was unreliable and often misleading. It was better to use one's own common sense.' Goering said, ' Hitler's view of the products of the FA was that they were very reliable – the material had to be presented factually to Hitler with no argument nor appreciation – only with the verbatim conversation or actual text.'

Extent of liaison at operational level

Much of the evidence for FA success was derived from the archives and records of the other organisations – no trace of the official FA archives were found. Liaison with other Sigint agencies shows active and detailed co-operation. A special FA liaison officer was assigned to the OKW but not OKW/Chi. It involved the passing of intelligence – not cryptanalytic matters – but intercepted traffic was also exchanged. As has already been stated, there was early friction between the cryptanalysts of the two organisations. The unwillingness of the OKW/Chi to give up its monitoring is understandable, but because of FA interest in this area, it would seem that the duplication was unnecessary.

Great liaison existed between the FA and the Army High Command Sigint, who were not too well informed on the FA organisation or operation. There was actual division of tasks and sharing of personnel as well as liaison over IBM developments. It was from interrogation of Army Sigint that the most important cryptanalytic achievement of the FA was revealed – that they were able to read Russian teletype traffic, and had reconstructed the machine. It had a very long cycle, being not prime, but the product of several smaller cycles like the Lorenz SZ-42 cipher attachment.

Later, the traffic found by the FA stopped after the Russians altered the system. It was recalled that the cycle of one of the wheels was thirty-seven and the others were believed to vary widely from thirty to eighty. The Russian teletype machine had been analysed in 1943 and the FA recognised that it must have been based on a machine having certain similarities with the SZ-40. According to an Army Sigint interrogation, the Russian machine gave only thirty-two different substitution alphabets, the succession of which became periodic only after an astronomically large number of steps. This succession was given by a system of pin wheels, the peripheries of which were prime to each other and at an estimate lay between thirty and ninety. There was no complicated mutual influence of the pin wheels on each other as with the T-52d.

On liaison with Luftwaffe Sigint, the Air Force was concerned with air traffic, which was no concern of the FA. However, the FA did supply Luftwaffe Sigint with some diplomatic and general intelligence. FA reports did provide much significant information on economic and political matters of use to the Luftwaffe in the West. Reports from foreign broadcasts – as those of the BBC – were particularly important, especially for the period between the invasion and the collapse, when they were often the only source of reliable information on the war situation.

On liaison with the Navy, there was co-operation with the FA and the Army on the British Interdepartmental Cipher. Around three percent of all Navy traffic came from the FA, who supplied them with traffic from commercial links. The liaison between the FA and the Foreign Office PZ is referred to in the previous chapter. TICOM comments, 'The existence of technical cryptanalysis liaison between the FA and the other cryptologic agencies cannot be denied, and the categorical denial that technical liaison existed must be seriously questioned'. Close co-operation with the SS and the Abwehr must be inferred. Only regarding OKW/Chi is there direct evidence that cryptanalytic liaison did not exist, although there was liaison on security matters, an exchange of decodes, interchange of intercepted traffic and a definite agreement that the FA would not work on military traffic.

Final evaluation of the FA

The FA work continued even under the vicissitudes brought on by bombing and moving. Careful arrangements for dissemination of information existed and there is evidence that this exchange functioned at all levels. Cryptanalysis supplied less than twenty percent of the information delivered by the FA, and the other eighty percent was considered so important that special arrangements were made for its continued production at Berlin and finally at Flensburg up to the very end. A shift in emphasis by the FA from telephone monitoring to commercial traffic and press and broadcast material is indicated throughout its existence.

The cryptanalytic element probably remained of constant importance throughout the FA's history, with the press monitoring increasing towards the end of the wear as other sources of readily available information diminished. TICOM states that, 'In the light of all the evidence available the FA must be recognised as a highly successful source of intelligence in the fullest sense of the word. So important was the intelligence produced that careful arrangements were made for furnishing it throughout the final stages of the war.' The relationship between the FA, the Abwehr, Gestapo and regular police in general censorship operations and in counter-measures against agents can only be indicated. The FA appears to have served the Abwehr and the OKW in telephone monitoring in Germany and the occupied territories and served the SS, the RSHA, the regular police and the Radio Defence Corps as a cryptanalytic agency for agent traffic.

Country systems worked on by the FA

The following list details the cryptanalytic phase of FA operations. Only about eighty references to traffic worked were gleaned from available material concerning the FA. Many of these references were vague. The archives and reports of other Sigint agencies – Foreign Office, Navy High Command and the Supreme Command of the Armed Forces revealed considerably more detail as to which systems were worked on by the FA in liaison with other agencies. There is considerable evidence that the FA possessed copies of a surprising number of code books, although in TICOM interrogations there is no indication as to how these items were procured or even a hint that they were in FA possession. The following is a summary of systems worked on by the FA:

United Kingdom

Consular systems: A message from the British Consul at Cairo gave some information and Jodl recalls important information having been gained from this source.

Diplomatic systems: Hitler apparently delayed his discussions with Prime Minister Neville Chamberlain during the 1938 Munich conference for several hours while a message sent to London by the Prime Minister could be decoded. Clear text and a basic book were captured in Norway but the Germans had no success with them cryptographically. Unenciphered low grade systems were read and diplomatic second, third and fourth grade systems were also read.

Interdepartmental Cipher and/or Code: From the middle of 1942 results fell off because of less material, but the Germans continued to decipher a good percentage of the material that came in, but the cipher went out of force in December 1942. Messages consisted 'again and again' of information about U-boat losses and British shipping losses etc. This was in the first months of 1943 up to the summer of that year.

Code B-30: The FA had a list of about fifty recovered groups.

Bank of England Code: A Bank of England code was broken in 1941 (see Intabank system, p168).

United States

Strip system: A strip system was read but not currently, and was finally given up as it took too many people.

Five-Figure system: Plain systems were read and subsequently a five-letter book system enciphered by monoalphabetic and bigram substitution. It was not read currently, but only with back material several months to a year old. The tables changed within the message and this change was shown by an indicator. The successor to this system was not broken because there was no indicator in the middle of the message to show where the tables changed.

State Department system: Messages from Berne were mentioned as examples of Sigint by Jodl and Goering and by cryptanalysts of several agencies. They were sent in the compromised Brown code.

Joint US-UK systems: There was success with unenciphered codes but there was no instance of an important message being sent in a low grade system. US and UK commercial messages were read, some concerning ship movements. These were mainly concerned with individual ships – convoy information was not dealt with by the Evaluation Section.

Russia

The FA claimed in 1943 that it had achieved some success with a teletype machine and had constructed it.

Agent traffic: The Ordnungspolizei (Orpo) requested cryptographic advice on Russian agents systems. The Orpo were given copies of systems captured with agents, and analysis was limited almost entirely to a study of characteristics and recognition signals with a view to advising on the possibility of a 'gegenspiel' – employing the agent after capture or pretending to be the agent. Around 1,500 different keys were used, mostly hand substitution systems, mostly in Russian but many in German. Of these, only four or five were solved without a completely captured key. One achievement was the use of an ordinary book left behind by an agent to solve his traffic.

Belgium
The Belgians used one book with and without substitution encipherment and both were read.

Bulgaria
Bulgarian systems were basically a few five-digit codes with repaginations or relineations. A 1940 report from Pers ZS mentioned that the FA had furnished them with photocopies of two Bulgarian codes.

China
Chinese traffic was worked on at one time, but nothing was read.

Clandestine traffic
Clandestine traffic of detained persons was mostly scattered messages in individualistic systems which were rarely solved.

Czechoslovakia
Skoda Company Commercial Code: One of the major undertakings in the pre-war FA was the code used by Skoda to Iran and Iraq in 1935, concerned almost entirely with bridge-building projects.

Denmark
About fifty percent of the traffic in the old diplomatic code was read until 1940. Nothing was solved thereafter except an occasional message in the old code on some minor commercial matter.

Ethiopia
The FA did some work on an Ethiopian code.

Finland
The FA had at one time cribs for the Finnish Hagelin machine and broke in. It was possible to break this machine if they had 4,000 letters or more of text.

France
Diplomatic ciphers: Goering stated that the ciphers of the French Foreign Office had been obtained. An Associated Press story, based on Goering's

personal copy of his own telephone conversations at the time of the Anschluss, indicated that these ciphers may well have been a very high grade system. The conversations revealed Goering telephoning Hitler that no action by France was to be feared because Britain had refused to back her in display of force. Goering assured Hitler that the information was certain because it was based on information from Brown Reports taken from decoded telegrams of the French Foreign Office.

Code 19: Work was carried out in 1941 on a 10,000 group figure code designated '19'. The first solution was said to have been achieved by the FA using captured tables which were later given to Pers ZS. The FA apparently had success with all French unenciphered books.

Vichy Code: The easiest system of all for the FA to break was the French Vichy code, since Vichy only changed its code about every four weeks. It would be expected that Vichy codes would have been available to the Germans, but it may be that the FA and the Foreign Office did not receive diplomatic codes or ciphers through the German Armistice Commission, which may not have been interested in such liaison.

Germany

Commercial codes were worked on, involving those in the German language affecting traffic of German firms to foreign countries.

Greece

Two Greek plain codes were read.

Hagelin machines

Hagelin messages were never broken because they were not long enough. It was estimated that 5,000 letters would be needed, although one interrogation revealed that Finnish and Swedish systems were read through cribs and that Hagelin could be read on 4,000 letters.

Hungary

The Hungarians used an additive system which changed with every message and was not solved.

Intabank system

In 1944 the code used by Intabank – the International Bank at Basle – was solved. The code used was an old Bank of England code which had been solved in 1941. The pages were shuffled and an encipherment added, but solution was achieved by cribs and common form messages, of which the best was a statement of the daily exchange rates between the various countries. The system used bigram substitution from a table different for each link and changing every three months. The text was divided into segments of three or four groups, and the plaintext bigrams for encipherment were prearranged pairs as 1 and 15, 2 and 14, 6 and 10 etc. Very long depths and near-depths were produced on closely similar number values and this was the entry. The whole solution took about six months, starting with 1942-1943 and working up to 1944. Traffic interception was not systemised and not more than fifty percent of the traffic is believed to have been read.

Ireland

Work was carried out by the FA on enciphered codes with considerable success up to the end of the war. Pers ZS prisoners referred to the Government Telegraph Code, used by Ireland for diplomatic communications, with an encipherment by two substitution alphabets. The FA solved the keys used on the Berlin and Madrid links in 1943 and Pers ZS took over the keys from the FA in 1944.

Italy

There was some success on high grade diplomatic systems.

Japan

There was some success with diplomatic systems. Goering remembered that information was obtained from the Japanese ambassador in Berlin reporting home. There was success until the last phase of the war against a main diplomatic system which employed a code book enciphered by a combination of transposition and Raster – a hand cipher. Another system was broken in 1941-1942 which was thought to be a machine system, although their solution was not mechanical but employed simply paper strips.

Latin America

The FA read all Mexican traffic and that of some smaller countries such as Costa Rica, Paraguay and Venezuela.

Norway

An unenciphered five-letter diplomatic code was read completely up to 1940. Nothing was read after the Norwegian government moved to London.

Poland
Diplomatic code: A diplomatic code was solved in 1940-1941.

Portugal
The Portuguese used a five-digit code plus substitution which was 'very, very simple' to solve.

Spain
Additive system: Spain had a system of additives differing according to traffic link, and each link had ten tables with 100 four-digit groups on each table. The unenciphered indicator was the serial number and came in the second or third place.

Sweden
Consular traffic: There was a four or five-digit non-alphabetic code especially used on the Stockholm-Tokyo link. Almost all the other links went over to machine in 1939, but Tokyo was unable to convert. The machine was Swedish and called 'KRYTAA' – possibly either the KRYHA or Hagelin machine. None of the main consular links to Washington, London or Paris were read.

Swedish-Turkey commercial: This traffic was solved but yielded none of the expected information on shipping possibilities.

Switzerland
Swiss Enigma: Swiss Enigma was broken for a while, but only when it was improperly used. The same internal settings were used for a long time, and after the inner settings changed there was no more solution. At first, the wheels were reconstructed from cribs and because the inner settings remained the same. In 1941 the FA furnished Pers ZS with a partial solution which they completed.
Three-letter code: Tables of a 2,304 group were solved.

Turkey
There was some success with high grade diplomatic systems.

Vatican
A Pers ZS report of 1940 indicated that most of the work on Vatican systems was received from the FA.

Chapter 17

Other Axis Sigint

Italy

Cryptology centred on the Army and Navy

Two organisations – primarily intelligence and not cryptologic bureaux – performed the major cryptologic work for Italy before the surrender in September 1943:

Army Intelligence Service (Servizio Informazioni Militari, SIM)
Navy Intelligence Service (Servizio Informazioni Speciali, SIS)

Each of them had both a cryptographic and a cryptanalytic section. There were also nine small Sigint field units attached to Italian armies. Two ministries had minor cryptologic bureaux – the Ministry of Foreign Affairs, which prepared diplomatic codes and ciphers – and the Ministry of the Interior Inspector General of the Political Police, which scrutinised communist and foreign agent codes and ciphers. The Air Force Intelligence Service had no cryptanalytic section. The Army Intelligence Service had eight sections and came under the General Staff. Three sections were directly concerned with cryptology and only two with military intelligence in the usual sense. The other three were evaluation, administration and secretariat. As such, cryptanalysis and cryptography were major functions of Army intelligence.

Cryptanalytic Section

Only twenty-five cryptanalysts and twenty-five linguists and clerks made up the Army Intelligence Service cryptanalytic section. General Vittorio Gamba was in command from World War One to the Armistice. He experienced difficulty in procuring cryptanalysts after 1918 and the handicap was never overcome. There was also a lack of funds and of IBM equipment. At first IBM machines were used only at the office of the Watson Corporation (Italian IBM) in Rome. Another complication was the poor liaison with the intercept branch. All negotiations had to go through the SIM headquarters. All personnel wore civilian clothes. Generally, the section read only those diplomatic systems which had been in use for a long time. All statistical operations were accomplished by hand and it was not until the last stage of the war that IBM machines were used regularly. By the Armistice, no general success had been achieved in breaking US and British military systems. Exceptions were US military attaché systems involving traffic from Cairo, Basra and Tehran in 1942, Berne, Madrid and Lisbon traffic after November 1942 and the State Department Brown Code, which had been compromised.

Cryptanalytic section had three sub-sections – Diplomatic, Military and Research, and Commercial. Diplomatic sub-section and was subdivided into nine groups: Great Britain, Dominions, USA and Sweden were the responsibility of one group, consisting of two cryptanalysts. Military and Research consisted of five cryptanalysts was divided into military and research units. Research unit was handicapped by its late adoption of IBM methods, and did not have any machines until late in the war. The work was processed at the offices of the Watson Corporation by its employees, who worked under SIM orders. With the acquisition of IBM machines, more ambitious projects were tackled.

Commercial section, with one cryptanalyst, was concerned with Italian commercial codes and ciphers. Its function was to censor Italian commercial traffic and to detect deviations from ordinary commercial code procedures. It was not concerned with foreign commercial codes. The Cryptanalytic Section received its traffic from the Intercept Section's four stationary intercept stations in Italy, and from its seven mobile units located in Italy, possessions and occupied territory. The final evaluation of the section is best made in the words of General Gamba: it was of a 'dilettante nature'.

Army field Sigint groups

These groups combined cryptanalysis and interception. There existed in the Italian Army prior to June 1942 separate cryptanalytic field units and separate intercept units assigned to various Armies by the SIM. However, in June 1942, in Russia, the Italian Eighth Army combined its cryptanalytic unit of ten officers and six NCOs with its intercept company, which had a strength of 300 officers and men. Intercept functions were put under the control of the cryptanalytic unit, where previously each group had been responsible to Eighth Army HQ. The group's intercept unit had twenty-four receivers of which nine were in mobile vans. The main contribution of the cryptanalytic group was intelligence derived from traffic analysis. Cryptanalysis was hampered by inexperience, ignorance of the Russian language and lack of German co-operation. By contrast, intercept personnel were highly efficient and able to identify individual Russian operators and discover changes of frequency, giving an excellent evaluation of the Russian Order of Battle. The Germans appear to have been surprised by the Italian ability to produce this intelligence.

The Italian Eighth Army Group success led to the formation of similar units. SIM ordered the setting up of a similar Group for each field army and were to be patterned after British and American units, with special reference to the experience gained by the Italian Eighth Army, and eight new Groups were set up. A Group cryptanalytic element consisted of from one to fifteen offices plus NCOs who acted as translators and typists. The intercept unit varied in strength from a section to a company and half. However, these Groups never measured up to expectations – but the Sixth Army Group was able to predict the Sicily landing.

Naval intelligence

Naval intelligence was located in Rome and was directly responsible to the General Staff. It was organised into four branches, all of which had the common mission of discovering the enemy's power, organisation, location, activities and future plans. They were set up as follows:

Branch B: Intelligence based on radio intercept
Branch C: Evaluation of intelligence
Branch D: Intelligence based on espionage
Branch E: Counter-intelligence

Branch B was divided into four sub-sections: cryptanalytic, intercept and DF, security and clandestine radio intercept. It directed its operations against the Royal Navy and RAF operational codes. Royal Navy tactical codes and RAF code enciphering tables were considered simple problems, despite the daily changes with the latter. The unit also solved a four-figure Royal Navy code in 1941 and 1942, but this system was not read after the North Africa landings. A four-figure Anglo-American Naval Code was also read.

The Intercept and Direction Finding unit maintained seven principal intercept stations in Italy and its possessions, six of which were linked by teletype to facilitate operations, particularly with respect to direction finding. The maintenance of 150 watches daily, along with the traffic received from German intercept stations located outside the

Mediterranean, produced a daily average of 3,000 messages. This unit also controlled intercept groups which were located on the flagships of all commands. The Security unit had as its mission the cryptanalysis of Italian naval codes, ciphers and call signs. To maintain the inquiry on a purely cryptanalytic level, the sub section was kept in complete ignorance of Italian naval activity. The Clandestine Radio Intercept unit organised and controlled stations for Branch D. Messages were promptly relayed to the Navy Intelligence Service. Branch C evaluated all the intelligence produced by Branches B and D, except those of an immediate operational nature and was organised on the basis of countries or groups of countries. It circulated translations among higher authorities and served as an information section for the other Branches.

Branch D produced intelligence based on espionage, and initially depended on ship captains and informers for information that was of doubtful value. Gradually it built up its own espionage centres in Europe, North Africa and Asia Minor which were highly effective, but attempts at espionage in Allied countries failed. The main mission of these centres was to collect naval information. The secondary mission was to collect political information. Reports were relayed back to the Branch by clandestine stations, for instance aircraft flights were reported by fishing boats in the Mediterranean and Atlantic. Towards the end of the war, the Branch was given the task of sabotage. The Italian Air Force relied on the Navy for cryptanalytic work during the war. The Navy also carried out the intercept function as well, until 1941, when the Air Force set up its own intercept station, but intercepts from this station were sent to the Navy for solution.

Mutual Italian-German distrust

Liaison on military traffic began in 1939 with an emphasis on French traffic. The Italians and the Germans were supposed to collaborate on the recovery of an enciphered code system which had a forty-day period. There was great rivalry and no interchange of information was permitted by either side until the recovery had been completed. Neither side ever expressed willingness for complete co-operation.

In 1942 the Italians learned from the Germans that certain of their ciphers (not named) were insecure, and recommended adopting the Playfair cipher using ten tables. The Italian Army adopted the system for a short time and then dropped it. The Italian cryptanalytic section found the recommended system to be insecure and expressed the fear that the Germans favoured the system because they could read it.

In January 1942, Captain Augusto Bigi, a cryptanalyst, was sent to Berlin to investigate German cryptanalytic procedures, with special emphasis on IBM techniques. As a result of the mission's report to the SIM, it was decided to undertake small scale experiments with IBM machines. With a view to expanding the use of IBM machines – should the experiments prove successful – Captain Bigi was again sent to Berlin in December 1942. However, the Germans did not allow him to re-examine their installations and expressed a preference for sending a technician to consult with the Italians.

Italians gave German liaison officers what purported to be true copies of their weekly summaries, but in fact these were edited and abridged documents which contained nothing which was contrary to the German view of the political and military situation. This was especially true regarding Russia. Another example of mistrust was in relations between the German naval Sigint and the Italian Naval Intelligence Service. Liaison began in 1933 on French systems, but was very slight from 1934 to 1937, at which time opinions were exchanged regarding security of Italian systems. In 1938 the Italians failed to elicit information about Royal Navy operational systems. The Germans did provide information on administrative systems, but did not give any information on operational systems until 1940.

The lack of confidence in Italian cipher security influenced the Germans in their reluctance to provide the Italians with information about Royal Navy Cipher No 3 – for convoys – until 1942. Collaboration on this system continued until the Badoglio revolution in July 1943. After that time, liaison came to a gradual standstill, and all liaison ended with the surrender in September 1943. The prevailing German opinion was that the Italians were temperamentally unsuited to cryptanalysis, and German analysts appear to have been unwilling to initiate any action with the Italians without direct orders from above.

Post-Armistice Italian activity

The military intelligence service terminated its existence as a de jure organisation with the signing of the Armistice. Personnel scattered to the Allies, to Mussolini, to the Germans or went into hiding. The Germans took command of any remaining intelligence functions. The Military

Intelligence Service was succeeded by the Defence Intelligence Service (SID) and its organisation paralleled that of the old Army intelligence service and was a continuation of the previous organisation.

However, the Germans discouraged the development of intercept services. It had only twelve cryptanalysts for a task that had been too great for twice that number. In addition, there was a lack of intercept facilities. The cryptanalytic and intercept activities of the SID were reorganised in June 1944 and were combined into one unit, known as the Intercept Section (IN), which was subdivided into three bureaux:

First Bureau: Consisted of naval personnel and handled tactical air traffic and, to a smaller, degree, naval traffic, Its personnel were incorporated into the Second Bureau in November 1944;

Second Bureau: Worked on diplomatic and military attaché codes and ciphers but was limited to systems already broken.

Third Bureau: Activity was confined to monitoring press reports, particularly Reuters.

Brigadier General Vittorio Gamba, Director of SIM Cryptographic Section, had a very low opinion of Italian Sigint activities. He attributed the poor showing of the Italians to a lack of capable personnel and a lack of sufficient funds. He summed up successes against Britain and the US, 'It is a fact that at the time of the Armistice no results had been attained in breaking the cipher systems of military and diplomatic traffic from England and the United States.' Gamba claimed that photostats of the US State Department's Brown code were available to the Italians and that SIM had solved a British diplomatic five-figure code and an unenciphered two-part, four-letter code.

Hungary

Organised for large-scale activity

The cryptanalytic bureau came directly under the command of the Hungarian General Staff and was organised in ten sections with fifty personnel, averaging four to five persons in each section. Turkey was the key section because of intelligence derived concerning Allied affairs. Russian and French sections were considered the next most important and the main Russian diplomatic system was read until it changed near the end of the war. Between forty and 100 messages were decoded each day and were sent to the RSHA, to the Regent – Admiral Miklós Horthy – the Chief of the General Staff, the Foreign Minister and the Minister-President.

It is believed the Hungarians depended on the Germans for the solution of many systems. The RSHA liaison officer in Hungary stated that the most important cryptanalytic intelligence available to his group came from the Hungarians. The Germans also received a great volume of results from the Hungarians. About ninety Hungarian codebooks were captured, indicating that they had successfully broken codes from Belgium, Bulgaria, Denmark, France, Greece, Italy, Holland, Portugal, Rumania, Croatia, Sweden and the Vatican.

Among Hungarian failures were the codes and ciphers of American military attachés. Although these codes were compromised 100 percent by the Hungarians, they were turned over to the Italian SIM because the Hungarians could not break them, whereas the Italians succeeded. The Luftwaffe, which maintained intercept stations in Hungary, reported that the Hungarian intercept service was worthless and its traffic analysis reports were useless. They described the Hungarians as 'cagey'.

Hungarian-German liaison

Liaison with the Germans began in the 1920s with the predecessor organisation of OKW/Chi, and this liaison was close. For example, wheels for the Hungarian Enigma were wired by Konski and Krueger in Berlin. OKW/Chi was unable to copy the wirings because Hungarian employees of the firm changed the wirings at night so that they would not conform to the records kept of the wiring. The Germans worked on systems requested by the Hungarians, but there was never an exchange of liaison officers, even during the war.

Liaison with other German agencies began at the start of the war when the RSHA and the Luftwaffe Sigint organisation set up offices in Budapest. The Luftwaffe set up a 'weather station' – a cover name – in Budapest in 1938 which carried out interception and cryptanalysis of Rumanian and Yugoslav traffic. Liaison with the Hungarian intercept service was poor and the Hungarians were always considered inferior. Liaison with the RSHA was marked by great respect for Hungarian cryptanalysis ability. In 1944, the RSHA purchased a Turkish code from the Hungarians and examination showed it had originally been broken by OKW/Chi in 1943 and given to the Hungarians! Liaison with the Italians appears to have been very good and Hungary maintained liaison officers in Rome.

Finland

Radio Intelligence Company

Finland's Sigint activities were a function of a Radio Intelligence Company – known as RTK to the Germans – which concerned itself with military, naval and diplomatic traffic. It consisted of cryptanalytic, intercept and evaluation units, was of battalion strength and was based at Sortavala. The cryptanalytic unit was from between twenty and seventy strong. The Germans regarded the Finnish cryptanalysts as being of the highest calibre and an even match for their own analysts. Finnish cryptanalysis was based on Russian traffic, particularly military and naval – secondary consideration went to Polish, Swedish, Rumanian and American traffic. The Finns reconstructed the Russian five-figure code during the Russo-Finnish war and this book was given to the Germans.

The Russians were aware of the Finnish ability and issued instructions which attributed their successes to security violations and did not admit to the possible cryptanalysis of their systems, but did emphasise the traffic analysis and monitoring aspects. Other achievements against the Russians were identification of the additive for a four-figure naval system and solving a five-figure double-substitution and three and four-figure codes, especially Russian Secret Police codes. They also read a US strip system – known to the Germans as A10 – and a Swedish diplomatic system which revealed the fact that the M-94 was readable.

Interception and evaluation

The RTK intercept unit consisted of a fixed station – about 200 men – at company HQ, four other fixed stations and one motorised company. Despite the age and variety of Finnish intercept and direction finding equipment, the Germans considered their intercept work of good quality and depended on them for interception in the Baltic and for long-range DF. However, the Germans considered the evaluation unit, which comprised about twenty people, to be disorganised and attributed its incompetence to the emphasis placed on cryptanalysis.

Finnish-German relations

Liaison existed prior to 1939 and continued until Finland capitulated to Russia. Not only were there direct and large-scale interchange of work on Russian systems, but there was also interchange on such matters as the US strip system, general intercept and direction-finding problems and there was an instance where Finland turned over a translation of a Swedish message which stated that the M-94 was readable. Liaison consisted of courier service, regular meetings and interchanges arranged by the Finnish General Staff.

For such purposes, the Germans maintained headquarters at Tallinn in Estonia and in Finland at Kirkenes, Mikkeli and Sortavala. At the conclusion of the Russo-Finnish war, OKW/Chi invited the Finns to join it, but no word was heard from them after they crossed the Finnish-Swedish border. Liaison with Hungary was also close. The Germans worked on Finnish traffic despite this closeness, and Goering's Research Bureau broke into either the Finnish or Swedish Hagelin messages several times on the basis of cribs.

Bulgaria

In 1944, OKW/Chi trained Bulgarians in cryptanalysis. The Germans had one intercept station in Bulgaria, for the Luftwaffe, at Varna. Given the cover name of Kommando Nordland, it employed twenty-two people in civilian clothes. Five receivers covered Syria, Greece and Mediterranean ferry-flight traffic. No cryptanalysis was done and all enciphered traffic was sent back to OKW/Chi.

Austria

Small but active bureau

The Cipher Bureau appeared to suffer from a shortage of personnel and from the many holidays provided by the Austrian Civil Service. It used cryptanalysis and interception of the diplomatic traffic of Belgium, Bulgaria, Czechoslovakia, France, Greece, Hungary, Italy, Poland, Rumania, Russia, Serbia, Spain, Turkey, UK, USA and Yugoslavia. There is no evidence of cryptanalysis in naval or military traffic. Although the major effort was on codes, there is some evidence of ability at cryptanalysis of the Enigma machine. Indeed, the Austrians were asked by the Dutch for an opinion on Enigma security. The Austrians rated it insecure on the basis of having read German Enigma-enciphered messages. However, it was probably the non-plugboard commercial Enigma, as the incident occurred prior to 1938.

Close liaison with Germany

The closest possible liaison existed between the Austrians and OKW/Chi and its predecessor, the Cipher Bureau of the German War Ministry, a secret held by only the highest officials. There was a constant interchange of traffic and results of cryptanalysis, and this went through the German embassy in Vienna. A cipher system was used for secret messages between the two agencies and social relationships were maintained. Secret assistance was given by the Germans to the Austrian Cipher Bureau in collecting evidence for treason trials. All this took place at a time – 1935-1937 – when the world believed antagonism was apparent in the official Austrian-German relations. With the 1938 Anschluss, four of the outstanding Austrian cryptanalysts joined OKW/Chi. There is some evidence of liaison with the Dutch and Bulgarians on Serbian traffic.

Chapter 18

Technical Developments

Development and Testing

The Army Ordnance, Development and Testing Group, Signal Branch (Wa Prüf 7) was divided into seven sections:

Group I: raw materials and small equipment;
Group II: telephone and telegraph equipment, ciphony;
Group III: radio communications equipment, teleprinter, facsimile and television equipment, ciphony and cipher devices;
Group IV: radio intercept, direction finding and ciphony deciphering equipment;
Group V: permanent communications equipment for permanent installations;
Group VI: chemical and flare signal equipment;
Group VII: radio remote control devices for rockets.

Wa Prüf 7 handled engineering and development of many of the improvements on the Army Enigma. One of these was the variable notch rotor, which was suggested by OKW/Chi. In order to accommodate the new rotor, Wa Prüf 7 suggested that several positions of the on-off switch be omitted and that the keying pressure be changed to 1,000 grams. Signal Branch also developed printing attachments for both the Army and Navy Enigmas. The proposed new machine, SG-39, which was to combine motion features of the Hagelin and Enigma cipher maze, was also engineered by Signal Branch. Another Signal Branch engineering and development problem was the SG-41, a keyboard Hagelin with interlocking motion. The device was suggested by OKW/Chi and had two forms: the standard keyboard and ten-value keyboard for enciphering weather synoptics, and worked on other OKW/Chi ideas such as producing an aluminium cipher grille (Raster), which was abandoned in that form before being placed into use, and the engineering and development of the cipher box and cipher disc. These last two items were developed simultaneously for the RSHA and the Army.

Teleprinter cipher devices and ciphony

Teleprinter cipher attachments and secret teleprinters were worked on by Wa Prüf 7 for the Army. A synchcronising device to be used on teleprinter circuits to permit them to operate uninterruptedly for twenty-four hour periods was also being considered in co-operation with Feuerstein Laboratories. They were also engaged in development of Army ciphony and equipment for the interception and decipherment of Allied ciphony transmissions, which was carried on at Staats, in Saxony-Anhalt, which was in a cave. None of the experiments reached the stage where complete security was believed to have been achieved. Types worked on included frequency inversion – abandoned in 1942 – 'time-delay' and the 'stepping stone', which were frequency scramblers, and noise superimposition devices. For these latter tests, a ciphony link was set up between Athens, Crete and Derna, but failed to produce satisfactory results. Intercept equipment for Russian three and nine-channel transmissions was designed and success was achieved in intercepting the Baudot link between Paris and Moscow. Equipment was also designed to intercept US Baudot traffic. Study of captured French three-channel equipment was carried on, with an attempt to improve quality by introducing frequency modulation, but the design proved faulty.

Radio Defence Corps

Locating Allied agents' transmissions

About 2,500 people were engaged in the Radio Defence Corps (RDC) activities and during the war it had a number of successes:

- It predicted and spotted all attacks on the German 'Colmar bridgehead' on the west bank of the Rhine in January 1945 by traffic analysis of French agent traffic in that locality;
- It located and captured the large Russian Schulze-Boysen spy net;
- It located, intercepted and furnished information for the capture of a net carrying illicit Czech traffic;
- It located, intercepted and occasionally broke up traffic nets of Tito's agents;
- It located an Italian test transmitter said by the Italians to be proof against direction finding;
- It provided men, equipment and information to Luftwaffe night fighters for locating and destroying Allied airborne agent control stations;
- It set up an IBM section for recording and analysis of unknown traffic.

However, the Radio Defence Corps failed as follows:

- It could not maintain effective control over illicit traffic originating in France;
- It could not control the Mihailovitch-Cairo traffic;
- It could not control illicit transmissions in Warsaw;
- It did not maintain effective liaison with the RSHA;
- It had almost no liaison with the Italians.

The Radio Defence Corps was of the opinion that it could have performed more effectively if the Supreme Command had allocated more personnel to it.

Location of US agents' transmissions

The RDC had various opinions about Allied agents. The Americans were 'initially poor' with marked improvement towards the end of the war, while the British were 'generally one of the best' and unbreakable at the end of the war due to new procedures and the general breakdown of the RDC. The French were 'medium quality' but with a tremendous advantage derived from the co-operation of a great portion of the population. The Poles were 'very good' especially regarding mobility of transmitters, while the Russians were 'technically poor' but with a massive organisation that precluded all but superficial German counter-measures. According to the RDC, measures that could have been taken by by agents to make the location and recognition of their transmitters most difficult were:

- Camouflage of agent traffic as authorised traffic of the country in which the agent was operating;
- Camouflage of the agent control station traffic as regular traffic normally issuing from the country of origin;
- Frequent change of frequency and time of transmission;
- Frequent change of position of the transmitter.

Measures that could have made locating of VHF transmitters difficult and ineffectual include:

- Operation of transmitters on six to twelve metres only at locations close to the front;
- Use in each net of two separate frequencies by control station and the agent;
- Elimination of transmissions in clear;

- Use of very low power outputs;
- Instruction of agents in the proper use of equipment so that messages would be copied completely on the first transmission.

RDC not alone in its field

There were other organisations whose work paralleled or interlocked with the RDC. The Abwehr Radio Supervising Office did direction finding for military intelligence purposes and the 3rd Battalion of Air Signals Regiment 352 and its predecessors co-operated in direction finding. The RSHA and the Secret Field Police – SD Kommando and SIPO – normally handled the arrest and interrogation of agents in such a way that the work of the RDC in counter-intelligence was hindered. RDC cryptanalysis was carried out by In 7/VI.

Laboratorium Feuerstein

History

The laboratory was located on a small mountain near Ebermannstadt in Upper Franconia, some 15 miles from Bamberg and was owned and operated by Dr Oskar Vierling. Shortly before the end of the war he was ordered to remove the speech privacy projects to the Bavarian Alps and eventually a small laboratory was fitted up near Lofer in the Berchtesgaden area. He was ordered to destroy all other projects and equipment but concealed much of his best equipment in the bombproof vault, screening it from inspectors by putting up a false wall, and hid a number of parts at various places in the vicinity. When TICOM discovered the site it was being used as a German military hospital.

Dr Vierling and his staff co-operated in restoring the laboratory to working condition and in reassembling dismantled projects. Under TICOM direction the available force of some thirty people rushed work on selected projects and made new drawings to replace those destroyed. During the wartime peak, some 150-200 people were employed at the laboratory. Work under TICOM involved filter design, four separate projects involving high speed transmitters for use by agents, speech scramblers and associated equipment, teleprinter cipher attachments – Lorenz machines were turned over to the laboratory for study – and other various projects.

Meteorological Service Cryptology

History

Located at Glindow, Potsdam, it was known as the Central Weather Service Group and expanded during the war with a second office in Athens. The intercept and other functions were carried out by the Meteorological Intercept Control, known as WENUEB and covered German, German allied and enemy weather reports. An outstanding feature of the organisation was its close co-operation with the Luftwaffe, who had standing orders to pass all weather information to them.

This information was derived primarily from Allied planes in the area. One occasional unusual method was the dropping of parachutists behind Russian lines to obtain weather reports. For transmission of synoptics, the Met Office originally used the international five-figure code with encipherment by means of substitution tables for the initial digraph and the final trigraph of each group. The period for each table was three hours, but this system was dropped because the operators could not distinguish between clear code and the enciphered version, which resulted in security violations. To circumvent this difficulty, the five-figure group was represented as a six-figure group. The final digit of the first trigraph and the initial digit of the second trigraph represented the third digit of the original five-figure group. The six figures were then enciphered in the form of two trigraphs and transmitted as a six-figure group.

The substitution tables for the six-figure traffic were known as Siegfried tables. One of the most common weather reporting systems was the Zenit Code and was used originally in its form, but later its letter groups, and still later its figure groups, were enciphered. It was used by reconnaissance planes to report weather conditions over enemy territory, but had to be discontinued because of Allied air superiority, and a time lag resulted when reports had to be delayed until the reconnaissance planes were again over German territory. As a supplement to the Zenit Code, another code known as the Astra Figures was introduced. Two other systems for enciphering meteorological data were the Barbara Key – known to the Allies since 1939 – but which was not replaced until 1945, and the Raster, introduced in 1944. Besides the use of Enigma, the SG-41 was also used for weather reports, used either with the standard keyboard or as a special model with ten keys. For telephoning secret weather reports, cipher elements were limited to the cover name FASAN, which indicated that the reports were weather, and the Group WIDDER, which preceded two five-element groups which designated the station source. Encipherment of such reports took place only if the reports later went on air.

Russian weather systems

In 1939 and 1940 Germany stopped the circulation of reports and synoptics in clear, prompting similar action by the Russians. However, the Russians exchanged information concerning European Russia until the Germans discovered that they were giving the German information to the Allies. Early Russian encipherment was by the Copenhagen Cipher, with the later addition of additive tables. In 1944 this system was worked on by the German meteorological service and by Regiment 353 using weather personnel. Russian enciphering tables were captured early in the war and presented little difficulty. Prior to the capture the Germans only read two or three days of each three-week period.

The reconstructed and captured tables were used to read messages in Berlin, and then the messages were re-enciphered and sent out by radio, which sometimes resulted in a time lag. It soon became noticeable that the quality and quantity of Russian reports deteriorated and this gave rise to the belief that they knew of the compromise. The quality improved when the Russian front reached Hungary, but the cipher was so simple that front line units read the reports easily.

The other major meteorological missions were concerned with British weather reports and those from the Mediterranean. Although British weather reports could be read occasionally, OKW/Chi was not able to break the system early in the war and the meteorological service had no greater success. The fact that Canada, the US and Asiatic Russia did not encipher weather at the beginning of the war was of inestimable aid to Germany. The Athens group was aided considerably because reports from Egypt and Sudan were not enciphered. Because reports from the Azores continued to be unenciphered for many months after the Allied occupation, was also of great assistance. There was little interest in US reports.

In 1941 and 1942, the Turkish weather systems were easily broken, but later changes made solution impossible. No attempt was made to read Japanese systems.

The German Meteorological Service success may be measured in part by the fact that in winter 1942-1943, it had available almost all of the European and many non-European secret weather reports and synoptics in greater volume than all the data normally available in peacetime. The intercept services were of added value in that they were able to predict the Allied air attacks from southern Italy on Rumania and Hungary by evaluating the turning traffic over the various airfields.

Physical Compromises

Introduction

A very small part of the success of the Axis powers in dealing with foreign cryptographic systems was due to physical compromise of the systems. A few cases are known to be of the 'cloak and dagger' kind, where a document was bought or stolen. But more are cases of simple capture, either in action or after the owner had fled, such as at Dunkirk.

United States systems

US systems known from TICOM sources to have been physically compromised by European Axis powers are:

- State Department A-1 Code, called B-6a by the Germans;
- The Brown Code;
- A consular code called by the Germans 'Z-3' or 'Red';
- A military attaché five-letter code, no designation known, which the Italians received from the Hungarians;
- War Department Confidential Code No. 2, called by the Germans 'Mil I';
- Navy strip cipher which the Germans called 'DUPYH' from the indicator.

Other national systems

OKW/Chi had a Portuguese diplomatic code and a Manchurian codebook. The Italians claimed to have read all Rumanian codes with the help of photostats. TICOM said it knew of two cases of physical compromise in connection with cipher machines such as at Dunkirk and from downed planes. One was a small cipher machine 'of Swedish origin' and the Germans claimed to have read all messages from the Italian theatre enciphered by this machine.

The other was a Croatian Enigma machine which was compromised before it was ever used because a German firm made the machines and reported the wirings promptly to the authorities, and to be doubly sure, the Germans even bought one of the first keys used. At the Italian Armistice, two German officers walked into the Italian cipher office in Athens and began to pack up the material they saw lying about. But some Italian officers came in and began shouting 'rather excitedly'. The Germans discreetly retreated, fetching, however, what booty they had already collected. A breakdown by countries of the systems reported by German and Italian POWs as having been physically compromised is as follows:

France	25 codes and ciphers
UK	9 codes and ciphers
Yugoslavia	4 codes and ciphers
Rumania and Turkey	4 codes each
Russia	2 codes
Belgium, Brazil Bulgaria, Chile, Greece, Manchuria, Mexico, Poland, Portugal, Spain, Uruguay	1 code each.

It is likely that the large number of French physical compromises can be ascribed to the 'voluntary' relinquishment of codes after the Fall of France. A list of physically compromised systems discovered by TICOM is as follows:

France	68 codes and ciphers
Greece	1 code
Italy	1 code
Poland	3 codes
Portugal	1 code
Rumania	2 codes
Yugoslavia	1 code

Chapter 19

Security of Russian Communications

General security

Although the Russians monitored their own military communications for the more outstanding breaches of cryptographic and transmission security, company and second commands were very careless with their radio-telephone transmissions. Code cover names were rarely heard by the Germans, but many private conversations were intercepted as the Russians tended to use radio-telephone facilities as an ordinary telephone. Also, Russian radio operators committed violations in security which greatly facilitated the work of the Germans. Russians habitually engaged in 'operator chat'. Although radio-telephone traffic was low on security, Morse and non-Morse traffic reached a high degree of security later in the war, due to increased training, extra amounts of traffic they had to send and the subsequent efficiency which came from practice. Partisan nets employed good operators and in the winter of 1943 the Germans formed a detachment to trace these nets, but they were unsuccessful as the nets were only operating in short durations.

On Army and Air Force nets, as radio facilities were used without restrictions because of inadequate line communications, traffic intercept and analysis, as a primary source of intelligence to the Germans, reached a high degree of efficiency. Due to inadequate line communications, Air units of the Russian armies were forced to exercise command from Air Army downwards by radio. In nets from division downwards in the Army composition, radio-telephone channels were used for the passing of communications in addition to the use of Morse traffic. In the latter stages of the war, this use of radio-telephone increased.

Radio procedure

During the first days of the war the speed of transmitting operators was very low and at the end of the war the average speed was sixteen to eighteen words a minute, while on some of the more important point-to-point radio sets the average was twenty-five words a minute. The international 'Q' and 'Z' signal groups were used as procedure signals, and some of the Russians appear to have been trained by the British as they used abbreviations such as 'OK', 'PSE', 'FOR', 'FM', 'TKS' etc. A certain amount of amateur radio procedure was also used. In addition, as a separator between call signs, the Russians used both 'de' and 'a' and the letter 'r' was used as a break between numbered groups in cipher text, while a comma was used in clear-text messages. No break sign was used in the higher headquarters nets, the only break-sign indication being a pause after a word or code group had been completed. This aided the Germans to identify traffic from higher headquarters. When Russian nets underwent call sign or frequency changes the German interceptors had little difficulty in identify the nets since a lack of security in turning on radio sets and checking frequencies – tuning – invariably permitted recognition of changes in the nets.

The Russian call sign system was a continuation from a previously known system which the Germans had analysed. The production of call sign books was by the same method used with the older system, but the manner of selection of call signs by encipherment of the radio station basic numbers was new. This latter system was almost identical to that used by the Germans after November 1944 when all their call sign systems were changed. One difference between the two methods was that the Germans enciphered a call sign, which was determined by the enciphered basic radio station number.

The Russians merely used the enciphered basic number for determining directly the page, row and column in the call sign book where the new call sign would be found. Consequently, the German system was 'unbreakable' without, say, captured data, but the Russian system was breakable given sufficient call signs and day-to-day continuity. When the Germans first began studying the Russian system of call signs their purpose was to establish the call sign books or systems from which call signs were taken, the method of selection of the call signs from the book and the various groups of call sign users. The objective was to determine, on the basis of call signs used, the character and composition of any given net, to identify in that net the various formations and to maintain continuity throughout call sign changes.

Success against Russian Air Armies

The main purpose for the existence of the Russian Air Armies in the military command was for the support they could give to ground forces.

German traffic analysts worked hand-in-hand with intercept operators on the Russian traffic. Successes on the Southern Front and information gained from sources other than cryptanalysis were:

- The Russian Air situation;
- Organisation and Order of Battle of Russian Air Armies;
- Strength of Russian units including aircraft types and armament;
- Location and occupation of airfields;
- Movements and concentrations of Russian air-ground units;
- Operational intentions;
- Amount and type of air transport;
- Supply situation;
- Probable targets.

The Germans obtained an accurate picture of the Russian Order of Battle and could often predict the time and location of impending offensives in sufficient time to take advantage of the information. A considerable amount of medium and low-grade traffic was read. Russian cryptanalytic security was based almost entirely on the one-time pad system for high level traffic and the use of a large number of code books and enciphering tables for medium and low-level traffic. The main source of information came from the Russian use of call signs and indicator groups and from stereotyped DF reports. The Russians had a habit of using the surname of officers and pilots for code and cover names, especially in the Air Force, and was considered very valuable by the Germans.

The Russian Air Forces were an integral part of the Army and their operations were confined primarily to the tactical air support of ground operations. During operations, actual command was by the ground forces commanders, with the air commanders acting in an advisory capacity and having sole responsibility for the successful execution of missions. Of some 12,000 Russian aircraft identified by Luftwaffe Sigint, almost 10,000 – or more than eighty per cent – were fighters and fighter-bombers, the remainder were bombers and operated mainly against frontline targets. At the end of the war there were eleven Russian Air Armies operating on the Eastern Front. Point-to-point nets of the Long-Range Bomber Forces (ADD) alone were sufficient to build up an accurate picture of the ADD organisation. When the 18th Russian Army was reorganised, the Germans immediately recognised such steps from traffic on these nets. Traffic intercepted on these point-to-point nets gave considerable information regarding intended operations and offensives. One outstanding success was a proposed attack on Shavli, Lithuania, where a Panzer Army was immobilised due to a lack of fuel. Sigint enabled fighters to attack the Russian planes while JU-52s dropped petrol to the tanks below, enabling them to escape encirclement.

Call signs and frequencies

Three-character call signs were used between the Air Army and its Corps. They were changed once during the day and once at night, when the frequencies also changed. Call signs were based on an arbitrary combination of letters and digits and were selected from a call sign list that changed monthly. Traffic between Corps and Divisions took place with a periodic change of call signs, but on fixed frequencies, which aided interception tasks. Frequencies were in the 2,500-5,000 kcs band – the normal Russian military frequency band. Call sign systems and time of change differed from Corps to Corps and this was an aid in identifying various units. Each radio link had two different frequencies for use during the day and two at night. Night frequencies were in the 3,400-4,500 kcs band and by day between 5,000 and 8,000 kcs. As the seasons of the year advanced, the day frequencies gradually moved up to a maximum of 10,000 kcs.

Air-to-Ground traffic

Assignment of call signs and frequencies used in air-to-ground traffic of the Long-Range Bomber Forces was performed individually by Corps signals officers and did not follow any uniform procedure throughout the entire Air Army. It was therefore simple to identify various individual Corps by their call signs and frequencies. Ground frequency stations generally lay between 2,500-3,000 kcs while that of the aircraft was between 3,000 and 3,700 kcs. Because tuning traffic before take-off was transmitted on a frequency allotted for the purpose, it was immediately recognised. Navigational training of the Long-Range Bomber Force crews was so poor that bearings had to be constantly given by ground crews while the planes were heading for their target. Moreover, the Russians usually flew direct to their target without any feint movements.

Air Service Command traffic

The largest unit of the Air Service Command was the District Air Base Depot (RAB) and for the Naval Air Force the Naval Air Base Depot

(MAB). As a rule, each Air Army had three to five RABs, whose reports contained details on the number of serviceable and unserviceable aircraft in the tactical units. Airfield locations could easily be determined from the contents of traffic between battalions and RABs and from direction finding of the sending stations. Reports on the building of new airfields were of special value to the Germans, since these reports often revealed enemy intentions and permitted the Germans to prepare both defence and offence. Radio traffic involving the movements of airfield battalions could give clues to the direction in which tactical units would later move. Valuable intelligence was also obtained from interception of radio traffic which gave details on fuel supplies, ammunition and other materials. Details of railway movements of supplies were transmitted by the RABs to their subordinate airfield battalions, and contained information on the destination, number of railway cars being used, amount and type of supplies and the scheduled time of arrival. When the trains arrived at their destination a message announcing their arrival was sent to the airfield battalions, enabling them to be bombed soon after they arrived at their destination.

The Russian Air Service Command also reported by radio on the salvaging of German aircraft which gave information about missing crew, and in many cases enabled families to be informed that they were POWs. Reports of interrogations of captured German military personnel were often intercepted and in some cases the Germans conducted court martial proceedings where the information revealed that the POW had revealed secret information. Before an attack, smoke markers were often placed in the frontal area the day before as an orientation point, giving the direction of both air and ground forces, and were lit thirty minutes to an hour before the attack, enabling twenty-four hours warning to be given.

Air Raid Warning Service

Russia's Air Raid Warning Service was regularly monitored and provided information such as reports of German, Russian and US aircraft over Russian territory and their positions. For flights made entirely over Russian territory, the time of departure and airfield destination was included. For flights which crossed into German territory the time of arrival at the front was given. German Sigint was able to warn their pilots that their position was known and recommend a change of course or other evasive action.

Russian naval traffic

The Russian Navy had its own Air Force which provided protection of naval units and their bases, supported naval operations and combated enemy naval forces. The intelligence derived was due primarily to having solved the call sign encipherment table used by naval units, which was foolishly kept in use for more than a year and was completely reconstructed. The information enabled convoys and U-boats to be warned in sufficient time.

Advance warning reports

Advance warning reports and route-tracking was often possible through Flivos – Luftwaffe liaison officers, who consistently transmitted messages which contained the starting time and course of the Russian Air units to which they were assigned. The Germans also had success in locating points of armoured concentration since orders asking for special air support would be sent by the Flivos. The Flivo messages provided an excellent means of making tactical evaluations of immediate value, especially when they contained Russian observations of German strong and weak defensive points. From information gained by the Flivos, Luftwaffe Sigint provided the German High Command with full knowledge of Soviet troop concentrations at Stalingrad, when five Air Divisions moved into the area. From Flivo messages it was discovered that when five Air Divisions were present in any area, it could be expected that the armies of those Divisions would appear in a short time. From the same source they knew of plans for the last drive on Berlin.

When Sigint intercepted operation orders it was easy to track the course flown by Long-Range Bomber Force formations. The Russian Air Defence organisations also frequently transmitted notification of impending missions which gave data regarding the course to be flown over Russian territory. It was also possible to predict bomber raids from intercepting weather reconnaissance reports, which were usually carried out in the target area prior to an attack. It could be predicted if a raid was to take place because it would normally only occur if the ceiling over the target area was at least 3,000 metres and there was no more than six to ten per cent of cloud cover. Route tracking of weather reconnaissance planes was aided because they transmitted messages every five to ten minutes, sometimes even reporting their position, and thus making direction finding unnecessary.

As a result of early warning through 'flash' reports – the interception of Long-Range Bomber Force traffic – defensive preparations could be put in place during the morning preceding a night raid. Radar intercept brought only insignificant results as the Russians made little use of radar equipment.

APPENDIX 1

TICOM Origin and Operations

Origins

TICOM was the cover name for a joint combined Target Intelligence Committee which, formed in October 1944, acted under the authority and on behalf of the Chairman, London Sigint Board, the Chief of Staff ETOUSA – European Theatre of Operations USA – and the European C-in-C US Navy (COMNAVEU). As constituted, the committee's operations were limited to the European theatre of operations. TICOM was purely an Anglo-American organisation to exploit specifically the main German signal intelligence installations and organisations. Four main general considerations were involved:

First, in order to improved Allied code and cipher security it was essential to get data on cryptanalytic successes with British and American systems.

Second, it was essential to capitalise on knowledge of Japanese systems;

Third, it was desirable to exploit the research and planning undertaken by the Germans to improve their own cryptographic security; and

Fourth, it was imperative, after exploitation, to disperse personnel and destroy installations, thus preventing a re-emergence of the German cryptanalytic effort after the war.

Schedule of subjects for investigation

- Complete cryptographic and cryptanalytic data on file at German centres, as well as equipment and operating instructions pertaining to the same.
- Information as to the exchange of technical cryptographic and cryptanalytic knowledge between the Germans and other Axis powers, together with information on the cryptographic and cryptanalytic methods used by the latter so far as is known to the Germans.
- Equipment used for intercept and direction finding purposes; special methods and apparatus for the rapid forwarding of raw material to cryptanalytic centres.

- Methods and procedures employed in traffic analysis.
- Methods and procedures employed in correlating and fusing information from traffic analysis and cryptanalysis.
- Speech secrecy equipment, cryptographic facsimile encipherment, and all non-Morse cryptographic equipment as used both on wire lines and on radio circuits.
- The chemical names as well as the military designations of all secret inks, the formula of the developers, details of the manufacture of micro-photographs, and all details of all methods, film and paper.
- Radio and radar-jamming and anti-jamming equipment and techniques.
- Complete information on the HS-293 and FX-1400 guided missiles, together with complete details of other similar remote control equipment.

Mission and operation

Initial planning was done chiefly at the Government Code and Cypher School in England. Detailed briefs were compiled covering the locations and personnel of the principal German cryptanalytic organisations. All available sources were used, including Ultra. Initial consideration was given to six targets, all located in the Berlin area. Priorities were as follows:

> *Priority 1*: Signal Intelligence Agency of the Supreme Command of the Armed Forces (OKW/Chi), thought to be the principal diplomatic cryptanalytic agency;
>
> *Priority 2*: This was assigned to three agencies – Army Inspectorate 7/VI, the Signal Intelligence Agencies of the Air Force High Command and the Navy High Command;
>
> *Priority 3*: This was assigned to two other targets – The Army High Command Signal Control Station and the German Admiralty Headquarters.

Goering's Research Bureau (FA) and the Foreign Office Cryptanalytic Section (Pers ZS) were either not known or not listed at the time. Neither were the changes in German Army Sigint organisation after October 1944 properly outlined and evaluated. All six priority organisations were designated as Class B targets, that is, large Sigint installations to be exploited by TICOM specialists. The smaller Sigint organisations which had operated with tactical commands (Class A targets) were to be exploited in the same manner as other captured personnel and installations, with TICOM specialists available if required.

Since the Class B targets listed above were located in the Berlin area, eventually to be occupied by the Russians, initial consideration was given to a plan worked out in conjunction with T(arget)-Force Berlin. This plan contemplated a simultaneous seizure and exploitation of the chief Sigint centres through an airborne action, and plans were nearly completed in December 1944, but by February 1945 it was clear that the proposed action was no longer feasible. The rapid Allied advances, the tactical, administrative and diplomatic problems involved, and the fact that most of the chief centres had either decentralised their activities, moved or were preparing to move, were the decisive factors in the decision.

The ultimate action which TICOM took in regard to exploitation was based largely on expediency and the exploitation plan, as revised in March 1945, provided for six UK-US target exploitation teams. In the actual exploitation, team assignments were largely disregarded. Administrative questions and availability of personnel were the principal criteria used for assignments. Teams were despatched to targets as they were overrun, notice being channelled back through the British Intelligence 21 Army Group, through Signal Intelligence Division (SID) ETOUSA, or through General Staff – Intelligence (GSI(a)) SHAEF. All six teams were eventually dispatched to targets.

Only two major German Sigint centres were found reasonably intact and controlling the majority of their assigned personnel. Team No. 6, the first team sent out, left the UK in April 1945, and operated in the Neumünster-Plön-Flensburg area. They succeeded in apprehending and isolating most of the key personnel in the Navy High Command Sigint agency, while Team No. 3 operated in the Halle-Weimar-Leipzig area from the end of April 1945 until 15 May 1945. They succeeded in apprehending and evacuating most of the personnel and some of the documents belonging to the Foreign Office Cryptanalytic Section – Pers ZS. Due to circumstances beyond their control the other teams did not achieve similar successes. Goering's Research Bureau (FA), OKW/Chi, the Army installations and the Air Force High Command Sigint had all been partially dispersed out of Berlin due to the bombing.

In March and April 1945 these agencies had attempted to move south into the Munich-Salzburg area, but as transportation became more chaotic, and as place after place was overrun, most of the organisations appear to have disintegrated. Equipment and records were lost or destroyed and personnel returned to their homes, or simply scattered at the approach of Allied armies. Team No. 1, despatched to the Berchtesgaden area to search for traces of OKW/Chi, turned up the former headquarters of the FA and a handful of its personnel, secured the radio teleprinter communications train which had been attached to Field Marshal Kesselring's headquarters, and located a German unit designed to intercept Russian non-Morse traffic. Team No. 2, sent to the same general area with no specific mission, searched the Innsbruck area, and was eventually despatched to the Pilsen area, where they took charge of and evacuated the key personnel in the Army Sigint Regiment KONA No. 1 attached to Army Group Centre. Team No. 4 left the UK in June 1945 and proceeded to the vicinity of Ebermannstadt, where they exploited the Vierling Laboratory (speech scrambling development) at Unterstein. They also made an unsuccessful search for documents of the OKW/Chi in the Schliersee area. Team No. 5, consisting of two officers only, supervised the diving operations in Schliersee, which recovered many of the cryptanalytic records belonging to the OKW/Chi.

TICOM operation appraisal

In appraising TICOM operations the effort achieved partial success in its principal objective – the exploitation of all the principal German Sigint centres. Through the efforts of Teams No. 3 and No. 6, detailed information was secured on the organisation and success of the Naval and Foreign Office cryptanalytic organisations. OKW/Chi personnel who surrendered at Flensburg or were fished out of POW camps, together with the Schliersee documents, gave a reasonably complete picture of the OKW/Chi organisation and successes. Dr Voegele, chief cryptanalyst of the Air Force Sigint agency was captured in the French area. His information, along with that supplied by senior Luftwaffe Sigint officers and technical personnel at forward units, produced a good picture of the Air Sigint organisation and its cryptanalytic successes. The first definite information on the FA came with the discovery of its former headquarters at Kaufbeuren. A few of its personnel were taken, but its records and machinery were never located. The Army organisations, with the notable exceptions of Nachrichten Aufklärungs Abteilung 11 (NAA 11), in Norway, the Signal Intelligence Regiment No. 1 – Kommandeur der Nachrichten Aufklärung No. 1 (KONA No. 1), and a handful of specialists, seem to have dissolved neatly into POW camps or the German countryside. The TICOM organisation continued to function until 25 November 1945 in order to register and distribute the documents captured.

APPENDIX 2

[This Appendix is numbered TICOM/I-143 on each page and is listed in the National Archives at Kew as HW/40/158. The interrogations related solely to Signals Intelligence.]

Report on the Interrogation of Five Leading Germans at Nuremburg on 27th September, 1945

Attached are the reports of the interrogation of:

- GeneralOberst Jodl
- Grand Admiral Dönitz
- General Field Marshal Keitel
- Herr von Ribbentrop
- Field Marshal Goering

The interrogations were carried out on 27th September, 1945 in Room 164 in the Court-House at Nuremburg by:

- Commander Dudley-Smith RN
- Major Seaman, US Army
- Lt. Commander Manson USNR
- Major Owen, I.C (Interpreter)

Lt. Colonel T S Hinkel, US Army, of the Interrogation Division, Office of US Chief of Counsel (Nürnberg), War Crimes Commission, was also present. The detailed arrangements for the interrogation were made by Colonel John K. Amen, US Army, Chief of the Interrogation Division, Nürnberg.

All the prisoners, with the exception of Ribbentrop, appeared willing to answer to the best of their ability the questions put to them. It was clear to the interrogators that the prisoners found the subject of Signals Intelligence a welcome relief in contrast to that of responsibility for war crimes.

It must be borne in mind that these interrogations required a somewhat different handling from the previous norm of such TICOM procedures, Because of the potential security danger inherent in the forthcoming war guilt trials, when these men will be publicly prosecuted and will speak from the box, it was impossible to exploit them to the full. Many significant 'leads' had thus to be neglected by the interrogators.

The following standard questionnaire was used as general basis for all interrogations:

A. How valuable was Sigint to you? In what years best? Poorest? What countries and types best? To what extent did you control the work programme of the cipher-breaking bureau under your orders? What was the high level channel of responsibility, from the chief cryptanalyst to yourself? Who on your immediate personal staff handled the detail? Selected your reading?

B. Were there any special series of decodes which received a very restricted distribution?

C. Who were the most outstanding cryptanalysts in your bureau?

D. What is your opinion of the other crypto bureau?

E. To what extent did a single co-ordinated overall policy for all crypto bureaux exist?

F. To what extent did you attempt to bring about closer collaboration?

G. What mistakes were made? In retrospect, what changes would you have instituted to rectify these?

H. What do you know of successes in capturing Allied ciphers and cipher machines?

GENERALOBERST ALFRED JODL
(Chief of the Wehrmacht Operations Staff) (11:10am)

Jodl stated that Sigint certainly provided the most important intelligence available to the German Army. One of the most outstanding examples had been very valuable reports on the war situation in North Africa which were sent to Washington in 1942 by an American military official (who signed himself as Consul but who must have been a Staff Officer) in the Cairo or Suez area.

These reports continued for several months during the time of the fighting at Tobruk and at the El Faiza and Halfya Passes. Eventually the key was changed and no further success was obtained. The traffic was taken by a German Army intercept unit stationed in Italy. Another example, but of much less importance, was the telegrams of the American Minister at Berne, which were read by the Forschungsamt. These contained a considerable amount of intelligence regarding agents and similar matters but were difficult to interpret.

As far as military traffic proper was concerned, the most important item was the working out of Order of Battle. This was particularly important in England before D-Day, but was mainly obtained, not from deciphered messages, but by traffic analysis; similarly, Allied military police networks in France were a very profitable source of Order of Battle information. The intelligence was obtained both from messages in clear and from those which had been broken and decoded, in addition to straightforward traffic analysis. Very often messages whose contents in themselves were harmless were of great value.

Signals Intelligence, however, provided very little definite information regarding the invasion before D-Day. They had not much idea where the Schwerpunkt was going to be but thought it would probably be at Cherbourg, with a second attack in the Pas de Calais.

From the military point of view their best effort in the early days of the war had been the exploitation of Russian traffic; W/T discipline had been very bad but was later tightened up to the considerable loss of the Germans. British Army W/T discipline was much better and not much had been given away. To begin with, the American position was similar to the Russian, but greatly improved as the war sent on. The W/T discipline of operational troops was generally good and it was the 'hangers-on' and rear organisations which provided good results.

Not much else was obtained regarding the intentions of the British High Command in North Africa; agents and FFI traffic between England and France etc., had been valuable and a good many conclusions had thence been drawn about our intentions, landings, etc. This information was not obtained by cryptanalytic breaking but by D/F'ing the agent's wireless, rounding-up the man, and capturing his cipher keys. These agents were often 'turned round'.

In answer to the question whether any other long-term Allied intentions were ever given away, he again mentioned agents and Maquis traffic before D-Day, but said that no high level operational traffic was ever obtained.

They were sometimes given a general indication but never knew the exact day. Advance information on the Salerno landings (but not the Sicilian ones) was obtained from shipping movements; nothing about the landings in the south of France came to them in advance from Sigint and it was true that none of the major operations of the English and American forces were known to them beforehand from this source.

Jodl stated that he did not control the work programme of the cryptanalysts and was only concerned with the results produced by the chief of the bureau. He did lay down certain intelligence requirements, but the methods employed, whether agents, crypto, etc., were not his concern. The intelligence produced by the Abwehr was the worst to deal with owing to its ambiguity: they often predicted everything, right and wrong, and reported separately each and every possible development. He thought that the Allies originated a lot of deceptive traffic to mislead the German High Command. When the same report came in from several different agent sources he was always particularly suspicious that it was 'planted' by the British Intelligence Service. Sigint on the other hand was always reliable.

The intelligence offices Foreign Armies East and Foreign Armies West each combined all sources of available intelligence and sent in their summarised reports every two days. These reports reached him through his Ic (Intelligence Staff Officer), who during the last year and a half had been Oberst Krummacher (had been at school in England); this officer consolidated the reports with any other available sources, e.g., those from the Navy, when they had anything of particular interest. The Navy and GAF were inclined to send their reports direct to Hitler, but Jodl had a full composite summary made for him which provided the complete overall picture.

If a very special message came in then he received it straight away without waiting for the 48 hourly report; this did not happen very often however, but even so such reports were often wrong; for example, on one occasion a report was sent direct to Hitler by Himmler to the effect that there had been a landing of strong English forces on the Dalmatian coast. Hitler rang up Jodl and there was general consternation.

It eventually turned out to be a bad report which had come from an agent via Vienna and actually related to a small Commando raid on an island which had already taken place some days before and which had been wiped out immediately. He took steps to prevent such alarmist reports being circulated in future before they had received proper correlation by Ic.

He knew of no special series of decodes which received very restricted distribution; all distribution was the same, i.e., to the General Staffs of the Army, GAF and Navy; only if they were of economic interest did they have additional circulation. He did not know the names of any cryptanalysts, but stated that the Chi Stelle of the Army was to some extent technically under the Abwehr.

Jodl said he was unable to discriminate between the efficiency of the different cryptanalytic bureau, all of them were good and he was very satisfied with the whole output. The Army was probably best but the OKW were very good. He did not receive the products of the Foreign Office bureau (located at Grüneweld) which went straight to the Foreign Minister.

He knew that they broke some political traffic since he heard of it indirectly at military lectures, etc; he remembered references to Greek, Yugoslav and other Baltic States; exiled governments in London communicating with their own countries and often revealing considerable differences of political opinion; the Turkish Ambassador in London; and a certain amount of Polish. He knew of no Dutch or Belgian material.

He knew little about the RLM/Forschungsamt; it was a large office and efficiently organised, but since it was Goering's special affair he only knew about it from conversation and indirect hearsay. There seemed to him to be a great deal of duplication going on. The results were sent to Keitel who passed on to Jodl in a special folder such items as he thought would interest him; Jodl returned these when he had read them.

As regards OKW/Chi, particularly valuable reports came straight to him, but the decodes normally went first to Foreign Armies West and East. Jodl was greatly in favour of the concept of one intelligence office receiving everything, although this in fact was only partly realised. After 1942 however, when the Fuehrer took over command of the Eastern Armies, Jodl had nothing further to do with Foreign Armies East; both offices were always adjacent, at Berlin and at Zossen, and there was close collaboration between the two. The head of Foreign Armies East, Oberstleutnant Scheibe, had been captured by the British at Flensburg.

He knew little of the cryptanalytic side of the GAF; there was a very good Ic organisation who issued consolidated fortnightly reports, well illustrated with sketches and plans. He was doubtful whether a centralised Luftwaffe Chi Stelle existed in the Reich.

Earlier in the interrogation Jodl had stated that Germany had not found out much about the British Navy, whose 'disguise was very good', but when questioned specifically about OKM/4 SKL III, he said that he believed them to be quite efficient; they had had the longest experience in the work and were very good at dealing with matters such as ship movements, but did not go in for the same amount of detail as did the Army.

He knew that when U-boat commanders reported their sinkings, OKM checked up the truth of their reports with 4 SKL III and that in general the two tallied.

No single co-ordinated overall policy for signals intelligence existed. Each bureau worked for itself but probably they discussed their experiences with one another. There was unfortunately a certain amount of duplication in many cases. He himself had succeeded in co-ordinating the intelligence effort between the Wehrmacht and the three services as from 1943, but the Forschungsamt had stayed out.

On the general intelligence evaluation level he had periodic discussion with the chief of the Abwehr. There was no technical cryptanalytic co-ordination.

Jodl thought that Allied ciphers had probably been captured early in 1940, at Dunkirk. No captures had ever been reported specifically to him, but he knew that at the time of the first German clash with an English brigade in Norway, cipher material and keys had been obtained but that the keys were changed straight away. He thought that nothing of particular advantage to the High Command was captured in North Africa, only the systems of lower formations. He could not remember ever hearing of cipher machines being captured.

GRANDADMIRAL KARL DÖNITZ (Commander-in-Chief of the Navy and latterly, Reichschancellor) (11:45am)

Dönitz stated emphatically that Sigint had been very valuable to him. It had been the best source of Naval Intelligence, and indeed, when air recce, etc., were not available, it had often been the only source of operational information. It had been at its best in the summer of 1942 and had greatly deteriorated after then.

In 1942 and earlier years the Allies had kept the same keys in force for a long time, but from some time in 1943 the keys were changed much more frequently; it was essential to possess a certain minimum quantity of messages on any key in order to achieve cryptanalytic success, and these conditions ceased to be obtained; just as his bureau was on the point of getting a break-in, the key would be changed and the work had to start all over again.

In 1942 Signals Intelligence concerning convoy operations in the Atlantic had been of the highest order. At that time Dönitz considered that the Allied procedure of keeping successive convoys on the same routes was very bad; he had been told that Mr Churchill had in the Autumn of 1942 dismissed the operational staffs concerned; he himself had noticed a very marked difference after that time in the organisation of convoy operations. After some time in 1943 the German Naval Signals Intelligence Service had no success at all as far as matter of real strategic importance were concerned, despite very considerable efforts, including the double banking of intercept stations. This situation continued until the end of the war. He was unable to discriminate between successes with British, American and Combined Anglo-American systems.

From a practical point of view, traffic analysis had proved to be of very little use; they had been able to draw certain conclusions from it but these were not hard and fast and were generally unsatisfactory. Direction finding was employed but had not proved itself a very important source of intelligence. He emphasised the difference between the detailed and exact information regarding convoy rendezvous, etc., in 1942 and the vague conclusions from traffic analysis which were subsequently available.

During their period of great success in 1942, he had held the post of Admiral Commanding U-boats, and the control of the work programme of the Cipher Bureau would then have been from OKM in Berlin; when later he became Commander-in-Chief of the Navy, the situation had changed and nothing important was being broken, the technical staff had been increased in size but to no avail; when the experts were no longer successful it was impossible for him as a layman to solve their difficulties; he had naturally become less interested in their activities when nothing important was being read.

While he was BDU he had a 'B-Dienst' [Naval cryptologic department] teleprinter from Berlin to his headquarters on the Biscay coast. Korvettenkapitän Meckel, a member of his personal staff, handled the material for him in 1942. Dönitz knew of no special series of decodes receiving a restricted distribution. He himself did not see the reports of other bureaux such as OKW/Chi.

He considered Korvettenkapitän Teubner to be the most outstanding professional cryptographer of the B-Dienst; this officer had spent all his life on this type of work, he had about 600 people on his staff at OKM in Berlin. They were largely mathematical experts 'who concerned themselves with permutations and combinations'. Dr Tarnow was another first-class cryptanalyst.

Dönitz stated that he had no knowledge whatsoever regarding the crypto bureaux of the other services and departments. He had never heard of OKH/In 7/VI and had no information on the OKL organisation; such matters, he said, were of no interest to him. In answer to the question whether there was a close liaison between the Navy and the Luftwaffe on Sigint matters, he stated that he hoped there had been between the technicians, but that was no concern of his. As for the civil bureaux, he had never tried to find out; they were of no use to him.

When asked what alterations might have been made to better the Naval Sigint Service, he replied that he would not have changed it. Perhaps in 1942 he might have put more people on to the work in order to break in even more quickly; this perhaps might have resulted in their being less put out by the introduction of more frequent changes of Allied keys. In all, about 1,000 men were employed on purely cryptanalytic duties. When, in 1943, no results were being obtained, it was suggested that such a large staff was not justified. He, however, intended to increase the staff and called in Teubner and Meckel to discuss the matter. They explained that such a step would be futile since it was no good playing about unless there were an essential minimum number of messages available on any key.

Dönitz stated that there had been no successes in capturing Allied systems. They would very much have liked to have had them, especially in 1943 when things were getting sticky, but in actual fact although a considerable effort was made, none were ever obtained. He stated that no Allied cipher machines had ever been captured so far as he knew.

This prisoner was not, in any sense, unco-operative, but of all the five interviewed he was the most crisp – that is, he seldom dilated upon a question put to him, as though continually on guard less questions seemingly of a technical nature might in fact be a trap and commit him to discussion of strategic or political subjects. In this guardedness he was the antithesis of Goering and Keitel.

GENERAL FELDMARSCHALL WILHELM KEITEL (Chief of the Wehrmacht) (14:10pm)

Keitel stated that German Signals Intelligence successes had only been intermittent. As far as the Army were concerned their best intelligence had been from this source, even though at times it was only derived from traffic analysis and not from cipher breaking. For example, when keys were changed and breaking was no longer possible for the time and direct intelligence from texts of cipher messages ceased to be available, they were often able to draw useful strategic conclusions from traffic analysis. Russian military traffic had been the easiest to follow and English the most difficult. The Russian wireless discipline on certain parts of the front did however improve as the war went on and especially at times when important operations were pending.

The organisation of cryptanalytic effort was such that the Head of Wehrmacht Signals (WNW) was also in control of the Army organisation, and in addition had a co-ordinating influence over all the bureaux. Chef WNW was General der Nachrichtentruppen Praun, his predecessor had been General Fellgiebel, now dead. The officer who carried out the actual duties of co-ordinator for all three services had been Generalleutnant Thiele, who was succeeded by Generalleutnant Gimborn.

Keitel said that he knew very little about the diplomatic side of the work carried out by OKW/Chi, but that General Praun would know the details. The organisation had a number of fixed intercept stations which had been in existence before the war. They took various fixed services W/T traffic, such as that between the United Kingdom and the Balkans. The OKW/Chi personnel were drawn from all three services, as Praun in addition to his double function of working both for OKW and OKH, was also in close contact with OKM and with the Luftwaffe, and drew personnel from them.

The peak years for Signals Intelligence had been 1941 and 1942; the most outstanding success was, he thought, the obtaining of General Alexander's plans and intentions in North Africa through the reading of the telegrams of the American Liaison Officer (or Mission) attached to General Alexander's staff. He thought that this source had only lasted for two or three weeks. He remembered that traffic between the United States and Turkey had been especially valuable, but he could not remember whether it was American or Turkish traffic; however General Praun would know. He could not recollect any further outstanding examples other than certain unspecified successes with Russian traffic.

He himself had not controlled the work programme of OKW/Chi, or at least he had only done so to a very small extent. He and Jodl formulated general intelligence requirements, but General Thiele (and later Gimborn) had passed more detailed instructions to Praun and Fellgiebel. Thiele had been an outstanding man, he was very efficient and had carried out these duties better than anyone else. OKW/Chi also had various monitored commitments for German service communications, both from the point of view of cipher security and for keeping a check on W/T discipline.

Keitel's Sigint reading matter was selected for him by the Head of the Chi Stelle of OKW who sent him a daily package of reports which contained about half an hour's reading matter. He picked out all the more important ones and marked these with a cross for Jodl to see, Jodl returned them to him in due course. These OKW/Chi reports were all marked 'VN' in red; he did not know the meaning of the initials. VNs had an extremely restricted distribution and a review of their distribution list was made every six months in order to keep it as small as possible.

He did not know what the distribution was, but it certainly included the heads of the services. In addition to the VNs there were various other more general reports based on Signals Intelligence, for instance Abwehr Amt Ausland (Abwehr Intelligence HQ, Berlin) acted as collecting point and evaluation centre for intelligence from all sources and issued routine reports. A marked distinction was always made in Germany between the technical side of intelligence production (e.g., interception and cryptanalysis, operating of agents, etc) and the collation and evaluation of intelligence thereby obtained.

He was unable to name any outstanding cryptanalysts and could not even remember the name of the Head of OKW/Chi. At the time when the shortage of manpower became acute and the authorities were calling for drastic reductions in the number of personnel, he had insisted that this should not apply to the staff of OKW/Chi, as this type of specialists was very hard to replace. Experience had shown that women and girls were particularly good at this work, especially girls who had received University training and had specialised in mathematics.

Keitel knew nothing of Pers ZS, the Foreign Office Bureau, other than that he himself had put a few people at the disposal of Ribbentrop for this purpose at the outbreak of war. The German Foreign Office were extremely secretive and jealous about anything their bureau produced; Ribbentrop always wanted to keep it strictly to himself. If, by any chance, Keitel produced direct to Hitler an OKW/Chi diplomatic decode, and did not pass it via the Foreign Office they became extremely annoyed.

Actually, this only happened very rarely, in general if it was known that a message decoded by OKW/Chi was not also in the hands of the Foreign Office, then a copy of the VN was passed to them. It was only in very exceptional circumstances that Keitel handed anything of a political nature direct to Hitler. At the twice-daily meetings when military affairs were discussed all the important new items were mentioned, Jodl bringing up the military ones, and so on. In actual fact Hitler generally knew of them already through his own personal intelligence liaison officers, and information staff.

Keitel described the RLM/Forschungsamt as the 'third competitor'. He used to receive some of their so-called 'Brown Reports' but was never able to fathom the special and rather mysterious selection which had been made especially for him; it appeared to him to be on an erratic and irrational basis.

Of the three bureaux who worked on diplomatic systems, he thought that OKW/Chi was probably the best, he could not be quite certain since he did not see many of the products of the other two. In peacetime each had had its special field to cover, the Forschungsamt domestic political matters, and the Foreign Office diplomatic affairs; but once the war started they all grabbed at everything and there was a great deal of duplication. Keitel said that before the war he had tried to institute an arrangement to prevent this, but the war had begun before he had achieved anything and action was then almost impossible. Before the war he had endeavoured to arrange that all this type of work should be concentrated in one single office and under one authority.

Both Goering and Ribbentrop were completely against any such suggestion and would not hear of its implementation. Keitel added that in any case he himself would not willingly have given up his own bureau if a proposal had been made to concentrate all cryptanalytic work under the auspices of the Foreign Office. Nevertheless, under war conditions some sort of mutual assistance on technical and practical levels had existed and there was also a limited exchange of intelligence. Keitel said that he had never opposed in any way this exchange and mutual assistance, there was no question of prestige as far as he was concerned.

When questioned about the Chi Stelle of the Luftwaffe he disclaimed any detailed knowledge but said that Praun would know. He thought the organisation was an efficient one as General Martini, an old Army man whom he knew to be good, was in charge. Martini kept in very close contact with Chef WNW. A healthy spirit of competition existed between the three services; there was a full exchange of appropriate intercepted traffic which was effected via Chef WNW who passed the material to OKW/Chi who were the clearing-house. The Foreign Office and Forschungsamt remained outside and independent but otherwise a fair measure of co-operation existed.

The only information Keitel could give on 4 SKL III, the Naval Bureau, was that they were excellent at their job and had a first class staff. The Navy had possessed a very good Signals Intelligence organisation in peacetime and they had the advantage of having a larger number of experienced personnel than did the Army. During the course of the various campaigns of the war the Army had lost in action many of its senior and more valuable signals personnel; this was because the Army had a greater requirement for keep a number of Sigint units well forward. The Luftwaffe enjoyed similar conditions to the Navy in this respect.

As regards the capture of Allied ciphers, Keitel said that a large number of Russian systems had fallen into their hands, a few American ones, and a certain amount of English material in North Africa and Greece during Rommel's campaign in 1942. He thought that the latter must have been forward unit material and unimportant, but he could make no conclusive statement and Praun would know more accurately.

He had heard that cipher machines had been captured but pointed out that a captured machine, as such, was no use at all without the keys. He thought that British cipher machines must undoubtedly have been taken at the time of Dunkirk and probably in Africa and Crete, but could give no details. In any case they never provided any sensational results.

HERR JOACHIM VON RIBBENTROP (Minister of Foreign Affairs) (15:15pm)

Ribbentrop stated that when he took over the Ministry of Foreign Affairs in 1938 he discovered that practically nothing existed in the way of a political intelligence organisation, there were various unsubstantial connections in various countries abroad but they did not amount to much and only about 30 or 40 people were employed on intelligence within the Ministry. Nearly everything was in the hands of the SS and the Wehrmacht; this was unfortunate because everything went direct to Hitler and there was no central clearing house. The Intelligence Section of the SD, which had perhaps handled the bulk of political intelligence, had been successively under the control of Heydrich, Himmler and Kaltenbrunner.

The Foreign Office cryptanalytic bureau Pers ZS was under Herr Selchow who had been engaged in this work during the First World War. Exactly how Pers ZS was organised Ribbentrop did not know, unfortunately he had been preoccupied with a multitude of affairs and had been unable to devote as much time to this side of the work as perhaps he should have done. Selchow, he knew, liaised closely with RLM/Forschungsamt, the organisation which produced the 'Brown Reports'.

He knew that Pers ZS was able to decipher diplomatic traffic continually. They only read the easier English codes and never had any success with high grade ones; he was uncertain whether they had any success with Russian (at first he said they did and later contradicted himself); they sometimes read USA telegrams but this success was only occasional. They exploited the Italian traffic all the time, and Turkish to a very considerable extent; he thought, but was not certain, that the telegrams of some of the South American republics were also decoded. He pointed out that when a cipher was changed it often took quite a long time, three or six or 12 months, before they managed to read the telegrams again.

On being asked how valuable Signals Intelligence was to him and which countries provided the best material he hesitated for a very long time; the value of this intelligence did not amount to very much – Hitler had a queer, rather particular, view about it – he did not like this type of intelligence very much and said it was unreliable and often misleading, it was better to use one's own commonsense. Ribbentrop said that occasionally a really important piece of intelligence was produced, but even when pressed he said he could not recollect a single specific example.

The selection of decodes for his own personal reading was made by Inspektor Schmidt; he only saw between one and four items a day, perhaps it was even less. His instructions to Pers ZS were that they should decipher everything they could; very occasionally a specific request might be made, but for the most part they were only given this general directive – they had to use their own judgement. Some of the decodes were passed to the services; any that were really important to other departments were distributed to them at once; his principal assistant, van Steengracht, or an Under-Secretary of State, determined what distribution should be made outside the Ministry of Foreign Affairs; van Steengracht also drew Ribbentrop's attention to certain items.

He stated that the RLM/Forschungsamt covered precisely the same field as Pers ZS and there was unfortunately almost complete duplication. The Forschungsamt produced their decodes more quickly than the Foreign Office but their texts were far less clear and tended to be inaccurate. Originally work on diplomatic ciphers had been centralised in the Ministry of Foreign Affairs, but the Forschungsamt had taken on a lot of this work for themselves a number of years before Ribbentrop's time. Selchow had maintained a liaison on technical matters with OKW/Chi and probably compared notes with them; there was also some sort of technical exchange between OKW/Chi and the Forschungsamt.

There was, he was sure, no overall co-ordination of policy for the various German cryptanalytic bureaux (he did not know how many there were in all); he was afraid that in this respect the higher policy was not well directed. He himself had had occasional talks with those concerned with a view to preventing all this double work, but nothing had resulted.

He was unable to give an opinion of the efficiency of OKW/Chi; he did not even receive their reports and he only saw between one and three of the 'Brown Report' decodes every day. When asked whether he considered the existence of so many bureaux to be desirable, he stated that it would have been very much more advisable to concentrate the effort under one head, but things had gone awry. In consequence of the existing situation, he himself did not receive certain items which were available and which would have been of value to him.

He said: 'I think it possible that I made an effort once to have intelligence as a whole co-ordinated', but that as the system in force was for everyone to go privately and direct to Hitler, it was scarcely worth trying. He thought it possible that at one time he might have made a certain amount of effort to bring about closer co-operation with the services in this sphere, but was not sure whether in fact he had actually done so. Without interpolation, it is almost impossible to give the flavour of the above interrogation. The prisoner appeared grossly ignorant of the material under discussion; this difficulty was further complicated by a grandiose and world-weary manner superimposed on a natural slyness, and by an anxiety neurosis presumably resulting from his present circumstances. By way of general interest, it should be added that this was the only interrogation carried out in English; but even this advantage failed to redeem the proceedings.

REICHSMARSCHALL HERMANN GOERING
(Commander-in-Chief of the Air Force, Minister for Air, etc) (16:00pm)

Goering said that Signals Intelligence had been of very great value, and particularly so as regards the products of thc RLM/Forschungsamt. He had personally formed the Forschungsamt in 1933; it had never in actual fact been part of the Luftwaffe or of the RLM, but as some sort of camouflage was desirable for an organisation of this nature it had been nominally attached to the German Air Ministry for the purposes of 'cover'. In 1933 he had discovered to his astonishment that no organisation existed within the Reich to deal with cryptanalysis on anything approaching a broad and general basis. In its early days the Forschungsamt had covered all fields of traffic – economic, political, diplomatic, private, military etc.

The work of the Forschungsamt comprised two almost completely separate activities, firstly that of telephone monitoring, and secondly that of interception and cryptanalysis. As regards the first commitment, this had originally been limited to listening to telephone conversations to and from foreign embassies and those of important visiting foreigners – in order to obtain political and economic intelligence. At a later date Hitler laid down that all telephone monitoring was to be Goering's responsibility, as far as he remembered this was at the end of 1933; hitherto internal telephone monitoring had been handled by the police.

Inevitably the Reichspost were also concerned for a while, since their co-operation and assistance were necessary for working out the technical side and for arranging special connections; the Forschungsamt dispensed with as much of this liaison as possible as soon as they found their feet. It was laid down that the Post Office had to obtain a specific permit from the Forschungsamt if for any reason they wished to carry out monitoring themselves; later on, however, the Gestapo intruded themselves into the business and worked independently and without authorisation from Goering, they worked clandestinely for their own purposes; he thought it extremely probable that latterly all his personal telephone conversations had been monitored by them. The fact remained, however, that, by and large, the Forschungsamt had done practically all the telephone monitoring in Germany.

The study of the Transatlantic (London-Washington) scrambled telephone was not a commitment of the Forschungsamt, it was done by the Post Office. He knew nothing of the 'special secret process' employed or how it was broken down. He had heard that a conversation between Mr Churchill and President Roosevelt had been obtained and also important conversations regarding the capitulation of Italy. He did not know whether these conversations passed by wireless or by cable.

When asked what he knew of German successes in tapping submarine cables he stated that, of course, various undersea cables had been tapped; he did not know where, when, or how this had been done, but reiterated that the work had definitely been carried out. He pointed out that one does not actually have to 'tap' a cable in order to get results, it was only necessary to get near to it, but he had no technical knowledge of the subject. He thought that the work had been done by the Reichspost although it was not impossible that the Forschungsamt itself might have been directly concerned.

He was very satisfied with the Forschungsamt, which was a first-class organisation employing the very best cryptanalytic staff and with intercept arrangements for taking all available traffic. He thought that they were able to deal with 32 different languages. The virtue of the organisation lay in the fact that they did not confine themselves to any particular field of intelligence and had no political axe to grind, nor ideology to follow; they were just given the technical requirements to intercept and break traffic, and to disseminate intelligence.

Each intelligence resumé of a particular subject, for example, that of aircraft production in the USA, or the Yalta and Tehran conferences was produced as an accurate factual account with no political bias. Reports such as these, often covering quite considerable periods, were frequently produced.

Goering's main principle had always been to keep the Forschungsamt free from outside influence; Admiral Canaris, the Gestapo, and the Foreign Office had continually tried to interfere but he had managed to head them off. At one time the head of the Forschungsamt had formed the idea that they should also deal with agents' traffic – Goering had found this out in about 1934 and had strictly forbidden any such action; such matters should be the concern of the Secret Service, and in any case the intelligence was generally unreliable.

Goering said that the recipients of the daily bulletins, the 'Brown Sheets' (Braunblätter), always emphasised the quality and reliability of the service. In 1940 and 1941 the selected file of reports which was passed to him daily contained as much as two hours reading. This file included intelligence from both types of Forschungsamt source, he was unable to say what proportion consisted of decodes.

He was unable to give examples of any particular outstanding items of intelligence obtained from decodes; he remembered that the American Minister in Berne was very garrulous and sent extremely long messages. On being asked which countries provided the most valuable intelligence, he said, England, France, Russia, USA, Poland, and so on, it varied with the situation – they read everything – they covered all countries – their achievements were global (SIC); the Far East was no exception – China, the Japanese ambassador in Berlin reporting home, and so on. He pointed out that it often happened that when something particularly important was impending, special cipher keys or a change of the existing keys, were introduced.

The intelligence resulting from decoded telegrams was not always useful, they often consisted of absolute rubbish; the extent to which the members of the Diplomatic Corps spread and retailed fantastic rumours was surprising. He himself had often made arrangements to have rumours planted and within a few days he observed them being passed on and spreading. Another commitment of the Forschungsamt was the interception of the broadcasting services of foreign countries, in order to obtain information from political speeches, propaganda broadcasts, etc. This work was also done by other organisations, but here again the Forschungsamt was by far the best; in fact, they took and exploited everything that was going on the air on every wavelength.

The Forschungsamt did not deal with purely military traffic; the bureaux of the Army, Navy and Air Force were independent but maintained contact with the Forschungsamt through liaison officers; this was necessary, inter alia, because there was an exchange of intercepted traffic and the Forschungsamt had to know what the others were picking up. He stated that in the case of systems which were being worked on by several different bureaux, it sometimes happened that one of the services might get in more quickly than the rest, but that in general the Forschungsamt had by far the greatest ability of the lot. In such cases results were exchanged; there was a spirit of healthy competition.

He did not control the work programme of the cryptanalysts; they had a general directive to take everything and to read everything; further detailed direction was left to the head of the Forschungsamt. If it was a question of needing additional staff they applied to State of Secretary

Koerner, who also dealt with their higher administrative matters. The first head of the Forschungsamt had been Kapitänleutnant Schimpf, he had been succeeded by Prince von Hessen, who had eventually returned to the Luftwaffe; the post had then been taken over by Herr Schapper who had always belonged to the organisation and was probably the best technical man of the whole lot. Goering used to visit them only once every year because the organisation worked so well on its own. The high level of responsibility was from Schapper to Koerner and from him to the Reichsmarschall himself.

Other reports existed which were only sent to Goering and to Hitler; it depended on the subject and the existing circumstances; some of them might be subsequently passed by Hitler to the Minister for Foreign Affairs. Typical examples were the Berlin-Rome telephone conversations between Mussolini and Ciano.

Hitler's view of the products of the Forschungsamt was that they were very reliable (Editor's Note: there is a note in the original document pointing out an 'entirely conflicting statement' on this point made by Ribbentrop); the material had to be presented factually to Hitler with no argument or appreciation, only the verbatim conversation or actual deciphered text. Editors were given very definite orders not to make guesses where there were gaps; if any portion was missing or was not clear, a row of dots had to be inserted and the appreciation, if any, inserted within parentheses.

There was a special courier service with particular despatch boxes of which only Goering, Hitler and Ribbentrop possessed the keys. The couriers had to travel in special motorcars and not in railway trains. All the reports had to be returned, and sometimes there were difficulties because odd single sheets had been extracted and retained. In such cases a reminder was sent out asking for the missing sheet. There were special security regulations to prevent the reports being handed on from person to person.

Goering said that he had no great opinion of the ability of OKW/Chi or of Section Pers ZS of the Foreign Office, the other two bureaux who worked on civil ciphers; the Forschungsamt who always achieved the most rapid and efficient breaking had a very close liaison with Pers ZS to avoid unnecessary duplication. He did not know what the relations with OKW/Chi were, he was much too busy to take much interest in this, the most junior member of the family; he thought they did not concern themselves very much with diplomatic traffic but studied tactical and military problems with which the Forschungsamt did not bother themselves. He only received copies of OKW/Chi decodes now and again.

The cryptanalytic bureau of the Luftwaffe, Chi Stelle Ob.d.L was directly subordinated to him and had been successful; they concentrated on all kinds of direction finding and route tracking, etc., in connection with Allied air raids. The GAF Funkhorch-Regiment-West in France, commanded by Hauptmann Ruckheim who was an exceptional man, had been especially important; this officer passed him situation reports every evening at about 6pm over a direct private line. A good deal of information was derived from the study of R/T and it was possible to recognise the voice of individual pilots. Goering himself had listened once for half an hour and had been astonished at the amount of talking that went on.

When asked what successes were achieved with high grade Allied air ciphers, Goering stated that they had largely concentrated on operational traffic but that strategic traffic was broken. The only example he could give of the latter was of their having learned in advance of the flight of a unit of the United States air force over Germany and thence to Poltava in Russia. The advance intelligence gave them the day but not the precise place where they were going to land in Russia; the Luftwaffe therefore followed them in, on the same night a German bomber force strafed them heavily on the ground at Poltava, causing heavy American losses.

The chain of command from Chi Stelle Ob.d.L was through General Martini. He also had his direct contact with Hauptmann Ruckheim, already mentioned; even in the middle of the night, if operations were on, he could ring up Ruckheim and obtain the very latest information on the position; this enabled Goering to break in personally on the conduct of any operation at any time; for example, when his staff said that the raiders were going for Berlin, he might have more up to date intelligence from Ruckheim and could say: 'No, they are going for Stettin'. His Adjutants – the officers appointed to this post were numerous – received reports from all sources and passed them on to him, wherever he was, by means of a loudspeaker broadcast system.

Goering said he knew nothing about the activities of the cryptanalytic bureau of the Navy, and added the comment that the navies of all countries were rather exclusive. If the Navy ever passed them intelligence it was about three months old; the Navy kept largely to themselves and held things back. Conversely, however, the Luftwaffe kept the Navy currently informed and there was proper liaison on their part. He did not remember ever having received a message of real strategic value from the Navy, although Tirpitz was the first to ask the Air Force for information and help when he was in trouble. On a low level there was better liaison between the two services and tactical information was exchanged. There had been an occasion when they had sunk one of their own destroyers by mistake in consequence of a lack of proper co-operation over signals intelligence.

Collaboration with OKH in 7/VI was better than that with the Navy; he had no opinion as to the ability of the Army bureau, and he never received copies of their decodes as such. There was close liaison between the Ic's of the Army and the Air Force, but he did not think that the actual sources of intelligence came into the matter.

There was, he said, no overall policy whatsoever for co-ordinating the activities of the various cryptanalytic bureaux; with the exception of the Forschungsamt whose work was magnificent and completely global ('Ausgezeichnet! Ganz global!!'), they all had their own specialised tasks and problems; the relevant bureau dealt with its own special kind of traffic, and there was the liaison he had already mentioned. When asked whether he had made any effort to improve liaison between the Navy and the Luftwaffe, he said that sometimes the liaison was very good, for example the Navy had once tipped them off about the position of a Murmansk convoy and the Luftwaffe had wiped it out.

Allied ciphers were regularly captured, he said; ordinary operational keys were being picked up all the time, particularly from crashed aircraft. The ciphers of the French Foreign Office at the Quai d'Orsay had been obtained but he did not know the details. Cipher machines were, of course, also captured, in the same way as the Allies captured German ones, but he had no details, it was not his business.

Goering's use of the phrase 'ganz global' in describing the scope of the Forschungsamt is characteristic of his bombastic and possessive attitude about the organisation. Since it was his brainchild, it was, of course, superb. By contrast with certain others of the interrogations, the expansiveness of this prisoner was such that very little prompting produced copious results.

GLOSSARY

Abwehr OKW military intelligence and counter-espionage section. Taken over by RSHA (q.v.) after 20 July 1944 bomb plot against Hitler and known as Militärisches Amt.

AEG Berlin Allgemeine Elektrische Gesellschaft. Commercial firm which worked on speech encipherment.

AgN/NA (Amtsgruppe Nachrichten/Nachrichten Aufklärung – Department of Signals, Signals Intelligence. Cryptanalytic agency for non-Russian traffic 1943-1944. Successor to Inspektion 7/VI (q.v.).

Ag WNV Amtsgruppe Wehrmacht Nachrichten Verbindung – Armed Forces Signal Communications Group.

Air Force Weather Service (see **Wetterdienst der Luftwaffe**)

Air Signal Regiment (see **LN Regiment**)

Armed Forces Signal Communications Group Ag WNV

Army Communication Branch (see **HNV**)

Army Signal Intelligence Regiment (see **KONA**)

Baudot A 32-character alphabet used in transmitting plain or enciphered teleprinter messages.

Chiffrierstelle, Oberbefehlshaber der Luftwaffe (Chi-Stelle OBdL) Signal Intelligence Agency, Air Force C-in-C.

Close Range Signal Intelligence Company (NAK) Nachrichten Nahaufklärung Kompanie

Close Range Signal Intelligence Platoon (NAZ) Nachrichten Nahaufklärungszug

Combined Services Detailed Interrogation Centre CSDIC

Control Station (High Command) (see LNA)

CSDIC Combined Services Detailed Interrogation Centre

Deutsche Telefon und Kabelwerke Commercial firm engaged on speech encipherment

DF stations (see Wo-Stellen)

Dönitz Grandadmiral Karl Commander-in-Chief of the Navy and latterly, Reichschancellor

ETOUSA European Theatre of Operations, United States Army

FA Forschungsamt – Goering's Research Bureau

FA outstation Forschungsleitstelle

FAK Nachrichten Fernaufklärung Kompanie – Long Range Signal Intelligence Company

FAZ Nachrichten Fernaufklärungszug – Long Range Signal Intelligence Platoon.

Fabrik C Lorenz Aktiengesellschaft The company worked on speech encipherment and developed teleprinter enciphering devices.

Fellgiebel Lt.-Gen. Erich Chief Signal Officer Army and Armed Forces High Commands until executed in 1944.

Fenner Wilhelm Principal Specialist. Chief, Division B, OKW/Chi (cryptanalysis). Worked with Korn (q.v.) on development of Enigma.

Feste 1923-1939. Feste Horchstelle (Fixed Intercept Station); 1939-1945: Feste Nachrichten Aufklärungstelle (Feste) – Stationary Intercept Company.

Feuerstein Laboratory Electronic research laboratory owned and managed by Dr Oskar Vierling.

Fighter Wing Jagdkorps

Firestone Laboratory (see **Feuerstein Laboratory**)

Fixed Intercept Station (see **Feste**)

Fliegerkorps Luftwaffe Wing

Flight Luftwaffe Staffel

Foreign Office Cryptanalytic Section (see **Pers ZS**)

Foreign Office Cryptographic Section (see **Pers Z Chi**)

Foreign Security Service (see **SD**)

Forschungsamt Goering's Research Bureau (FA)

Forschungsleitstelle FA outstation

Fricke Dr Walter Chief, Section IIb of OKW/Chi (development of German systems).

Frowein Lt. R Hans-Joachim Assigned temporarily to Naval High Command Signal Security Agency (OKM/4 SKL/II) in 1944 to make security studies on Enigma. He had no previous experience with this machine but developed a workable solution.

Gamba General Vittorio Commander, Italian cryptanalytic Section.

Geheime Kommandosache (GKdoS) Secret German Military Intelligence (Abwehr)

German War Ministry Reichskriegsministerium

German Weather Bureau (see **Goering's Research Bureau** FA – Forschungsamt

Goering Field Marshal Hermann Commander-in-Chief of the Air Force, Minister for Air, etc)

Heimsoeth und Rinke Manufacturer of Enigma rotors and parts

HLS (Horchleitstelle) Intercept Control Station. Central cryptanalytic and evaluation agency 1933-1941.

HNV Heeres Nachrichten Verbindungsabteilung – Army Communication Branch

Horchleitstelle (see **HLS**)

Hüttenhain Dr Erich OKW/Chi chief cryptanalyst 1937-1945.

Inspektion 7/IV In 7/IV (Army High Command Signal Security Agency)

Inspektion 7/VI In 7/VI (A predecessor of the Army High Command Signal Security Agency – OKH/GdNA).

Intercept Control Station(see **HLS**)

Jagdkorps Luftwaffe Fighter Wing.

Jodl General Alfred Chief of Operations Staff, Armed Forces High Command (OKW/Ia).

Keitel Field Marshal Wilhelm Chief of Armed Forces High Command (Chef OKW).

Kettler Col. Hugo OKW/Chi chief 1943-1945.

KONA Kommandeur der Nachrichtenaufklärung (Army Signal Intelligence Regiment).

Konski und Kruger Manufactured Enigma rotors.

Korn Willi Graduate Engineer. Employed by Enigma manufacturer Heimsoeth und Rinke.

LNA Leitstelle der Nachrichten Aufklärung – Control Station of Signal Intelligence. Army High Command central evaluating agency 1942-1944.

LN Regiment Luftnachrichtenregiment (Air Signal Regiment)

Long Range Signal Intelligence Company (FAK) Nachrichten Fernaufklärung Kompanie.

Long Range Signal Intelligence Platoon (FAZ) Nachrichten Fernaufklärungszug.

Martini Lt.-Gen. Hermann Luftwaffe Chief Signal Officer

Menzer Senior Inspector Fritz Chief, Section IIc, OKW/Chi SIA (q.v.) which dealt with the development and production of special ciphers for government departments, industry and the RSHA (q.v.), developing of deciphering aids for agents.

Meteorological Intercept Control (see **WENUEB**)

Mettig Lt.-Col. Head of In 7/VI (q.v.). Second-in-Command OKW/Chi December 1943-1945. Chief of Division A (cryptography).

Military Intelligence (see **Abwehr**)

NAK Nachrichten Nahaufklärung Kompanie – Close Range Signal Intelligence Company.

NAZ Nachrichten Nahaufklärungszug – Close Range Signal Intelligence Platoon.

NKVD Narodni Kommissariat Vnutrinikh Del (People's Commissariat for Internal Affairs).

Oberkommando des Heeres/Chef des Heeresnachrichtenwesens (OKH/Chef HNW) Army Chief Signal Officer.

Oberkommando des Heeres/General der Nachrichten Aufklärung (OKH/GdNA) Army High Command Signal Intelligence Agency.

Oberkommando des Heeres Inspektion 7/VI (In/7/VI) Army High Command Inspectorate 7/VI.

Oberkommando der Luftwaffe Generalnachrichtenführer II, Gruppe IV (OKL/Gen Nafue II/IV) Group IV, Division II of Chief Air Force Signals Officer.

Oberkommando der Luftwaffe Luftnachrichtenabteilung 350 (OKL/LN Abt 350) Air Force High Command Signal Intelligence Agency.

Oberkommando der Marine 4 Seekriegsleitung III (OKM 4 SKL III) Navy High Command Signal Intelligence Agency.

Oberkommando der Wehrmacht/Chef Amtsgruppe Wehrmachtnachrichtenverbindungen (OKW/Chef Ag WNV) Chief, Armed Forces Signal Communications Group.

Oberkommando der Wehrmacht/Chiffrierabteilung (OKW/Chi) Supreme Command Armed Forces Signal Intelligence Agency.

Oberkommando der Wehrmacht Wehrmachtnachrichtenverbindungen/Funküberwachung III (OKW/WNV/Fu III) Radio Defence Corps

Ordnungspolizei (See **Orpo**)

Orpo (Ordnungspolizei) Regular Police.

Oshima Hiroshi Japanese Ambassador to Germany 1943.

Pers Z Chi Chiffrierdienst des Referats Z in der Personalabteilung des Auswärtigen Amtes (Foreign Office Cryptographic Section).

Pers ZS Sonderdienst des Referats Z in der Personalabteilung des Auswärtigen Amtes (Foreign Office Cryptanalytic Section).

Praun Maj.-Gen. Albert Succeeded General Fellgiebel as Armed Forces Chief Signal Officer, 1944.

Radio Defence Corps (Wehrmacht/Wehrmacht nachrichtenverbindungen/Funküberwachung III (OKW/WNV/Fu III).

Radio Intercept Station (see W-Stelle)

Referat Section.

Referat Vauck (see Vauck)

Reich Security Main Office (see **RSHA**)

Reichskriegsministerium German War Ministry.

Reichsluftfahrtministerium Forschungsamt (see **FA**)

Reichssicherheitshauptamt (see **RSHA**)

Reichswetterdienst German Weather Bureau. Charged with cryptanalysis of enemy meteorological ciphers. Part of Luftwaffe and maintained close liaison with the Luftwaffe C-in-C SIA (Chi-Stelle, OBdL).

Research Bureau (see **FA**)

Ribbentrop Herr Joachim Von Minister of Foreign Affairs

RSHA Reichsicherheitshauptamt: Reich Security MainOffice. Controlled the main security organs of the Reich.

Schellenberg SS Brigadeführer Walter Head Amt VI RSHA which took over the Abwehr in Spring 1944.

SD Ausland Sicherheitsdienst. Nazi Party Foreign Security Service.

Section Referat.

Sicherheitsdienst (see **SD Ausland**)

SHAEF Supreme Headquarters Allied Expeditionary Forces.

SIA Servizio Informazioni Aeronautica – Italian Air Force Intelligence Service.

SID Servizio Informazioni Difesa – Italian Defence Intelligence Service.

Siemens und Halske Commercial firm which worked on speech encipherment.

SIM Servizio Informazioni Militari – Italian Army Intelligence cryptanalytic section.

SIS Servizio Informazioni Speciali – Italian Navy Intelligence cryptanalytic section.

Staffel Luftwaffe Flight.

Süddeutsche Apparate Fabriken Commercial firm which worked on speech encipherment.

Telefonbau und Normalzeit Built Cipher Device 39 test models

Telefunken Commercial firm involved in speech encipherment.

Vauck First Lt. Dr. Member Inspektion 7/VI (q.v.), later Section IV Army High Command SIA (OKH/GdNA) (q.v.). Head of sub-section handling agents' traffic (Referat Vauck).

Verlässlsiche Nachricht (see **VN**)

Vierling Dr Oskar Specialised in communications equipment research. Owner and chief engineer of Feuerstein Laboratory (q.v.).

VN Verlässlsiche Nachricht. 'Reliable Report'. German translation of decoded diplomatic message.

Wa Prüf Waffenprüfung. Army Ordnance, Development and Testing Group, Signal Branch. Developed, engineered and tested Signal Corps equipment. Did some non-Morse interception.

Waffenprüfung 7 (see **Wa Prüf** 7)

WENUEB Wetternachrichtenüberwachung (Meteorological Intercept Control).

W-Stelle Wetterfunkempfangsstelle – Radio Intercept Station.

Wetterdienst der Luftwaffe Air Force Weather Service. Conducted cryptanalysis of enemy meteorological ciphers.

Wing Luftwaffe Fliegerkorps

WNV Wehrmachtnachtrichtenverbindung – Armed Forces Signal Communications.

Wo-Stellen Wetterforschungsstellen – DF stations (the used cover name of weather research stations).

INDEX

If you would like to know more about John Jackson and his books please visit:

www.bletchleyparkresearch.co.uk

43106791R00131

Made in the USA
Charleston, SC
17 June 2015